T0110533

Is it Wrong to Buy Sex?

Is it wrong for a man to buy sex from a woman? In this book, Holly Lawford-Smith argues that it is wrong: commercial sex is quint-essentially hierarchical sex, and it is wrong both to have, and to perpetuate a market in, hierarchical sex. Angie Pepper argues that it isn't wrong: men are permitted to buy sex from those women who freely choose to sell it.

Important but different interests are at stake in these two positions. According to the first, we should prioritize the interest of all women in securing a society that has achieved equality between the sexes, and we should make the changes needed to get there including prohibiting men from buying sex from women. In contrast, the second position prioritizes the protection of individuals' rights to engage in consensual commercial sex exchanges and demands that we strive for gender equality without compromising these rights. The two authors debate the ethical issues involved in the decision to buy sex, arguing passionately for very different conclusions, in a way that is lively, constructive, and sure to leave readers with a lot to think about.

Key Features:

- Focuses on the pressing moral issue of whether we're morally permitted to buy sex.
- Advances two different normative ethical approaches to the issue and develops two competing arguments.
- Demonstrates how philosophical debate on controversial topics can be productive and easy-to-follow.
- Provides a glossary with definitions of key terms that are bolded in the main text.

- Includes section summaries that give an overview of the main arguments and a comprehensive bibliography for further reading.

Holly Lawford-Smith is an Associate Professor in Political Philosophy at the University of Melbourne. She is the author of *Gender-Critical Feminism* (2022) and *Sex Matters: Essays in Gender-Critical Philosophy* (2023).

Angie Pepper is a Senior Lecturer in Philosophy at the University of Roehampton.

Little Debates About Big Questions

About the series:

Philosophy asks questions about the fundamental nature of reality, our place in the world, and what we should do. Some of these questions are perennial: for example, *Do we have free will? What is morality?* Some are much newer: for example, *How far should free speech on campus extend? Are race, sex and gender social constructs?* But all of these are among the big questions in philosophy and they remain controversial.

Each book in the *Little Debates About Big Questions* series features two professors on opposite sides of a big question. Each author presents their own side, and the authors then exchange objections and replies. Short, lively, and accessible, these debates showcase diverse and deep answers. Pedagogical features include standard form arguments, section summaries, bolded key terms and principles, glossaries, and annotated reading lists.

The debate format is an ideal way to learn about controversial topics. Whereas the usual essay or book risks overlooking objections against its own proposition or misrepresenting the opposite side, in a debate each side can make their case at equal length, and then present objections the other side must consider. Debates have a more conversational and fun style too, and we selected particularly talented philosophers—in substance and style—for these kinds of encounters.

Debates can be combative—sometimes even descending into anger and animosity. But debates can also be cooperative. While our authors disagree strongly, they work together to help each other and the reader get clearer on the ideas, arguments, and objections. This is intellectual progress, and a much-needed model for civil and constructive disagreement.

The substance and style of the debates will captivate interested readers new to the questions. But there's enough to interest experts too. The debates will be especially useful for courses in philosophy and related subjects—whether as primary or secondary readings—and a few debates can be combined to make up the reading for an entire course.

We thank the authors for their help in constructing this series. We are honored to showcase their work. They are all preeminent scholars or rising-stars in their fields, and through these debates they share what's been discovered with a wider audience. This is a paradigm for public philosophy, and will impress upon students, scholars, and other interested readers the enduring importance of debating the big questions.

Tyron Goldschmidt, Fellow of the Rutgers Center for Philosophy of Religion, USA
Dustin Crummett, University of Washington, Tacoma, USA

Published Titles:

Is it Wrong to Buy Sex?: A Debate
By Holly Lawford-Smith and Angie Pepper

Should You Choose to Live Forever?: A Debate
by Stephen Cave and John Martin Fischer

What Do We Owe Other Animals?: A Debate
by Anja Jauernig and Bob Fischer

What Makes Life Meaningful?: A Debate
by Thaddeus Metz and Joshua W. Seachris

Do Numbers Exist?: A Debate
by William Lane Craig and Peter van Inwagen

Is Morality Real?: A Debate
By Matt Lutz and Spencer Case

What Is Consciousness?: A Debate
By Amy Kind and Daniel Stoljar

Do We Have a Soul?: A Debate
By Eric T. Olson and Aaron Segal

Can War Be Justified?: A Debate
By Andrew Fiala and Jennifer Kling

Does Tomorrow Exist?: A Debate
By Nikk Effingham and Kristie Miller

Should Wealth Be Redistributed?: A Debate
By Steven McMullen and James R. Otteson

Do We Have Free Will?: A Debate
By Robert Kane and Carolina Sartorio

Is There a God?: A Debate
by Kenneth L. Pearce and Graham Oppy

Is Political Authority an Illusion?: A Debate
By Michael Huemer and Daniel Layman

Selected Forthcoming Titles:

Consequentialism or Virtue Ethics?: A Debate
By Jorge L.A. Garcia and Alastair Norcross

For more information about this series, please visit:
https://www.routledge.com/Little-Debates-about-Big-Questions/
book-series/LDABQ

Is it Wrong to Buy Sex?

A Debate

Holly Lawford-Smith and
Angie Pepper

Routledge
Taylor & Francis Group
NEW YORK AND LONDON

Designed cover image: Yuko Yamada / Getty Images

First published 2024
by Routledge
605 Third Avenue, New York, NY 10158

and by Routledge
4 Park Square, Milton Park, Abingdon, Oxon, OX14 4RN

*Routledge is an imprint of the Taylor & Francis Group, an
informa business*

© 2024 Holly Lawford-Smith and Angie Pepper

The right of Holly Lawford-Smith and Angie Pepper to
be identified as authors of this work has been asserted
in accordance with sections 77 and 78 of the Copyright,
Designs and Patents Act 1988.

All rights reserved. No part of this book may be reprinted
or reproduced or utilised in any form or by any electronic,
mechanical, or other means, now known or hereafter
invented, including photocopying and recording, or in
any information storage or retrieval system, without
permission in writing from the publishers.

Trademark notice: Product or corporate names may be
trademarks or registered trademarks, and are used only for
identification and explanation without intent to infringe.

ISBN: 978-0-367-77077-8 (hbk)
ISBN: 978-0-367-77053-2 (pbk)
ISBN: 978-1-003-16969-7 (ebk)

DOI: 10.4324/9781003169697

Typeset in Sabon LT Std
by codeMantra

Contents

Foreword   xi
MICHELLE MADDEN DEMPSEY

Introduction   1
HOLLY LAWFORD-SMITH AND ANGIE PEPPER

PART I
Opening Statements   **5**

1 It Is Wrong to Buy Sex   7
   HOLLY LAWFORD-SMITH

2 It Is Not Wrong to Buy Sex   64
   ANGIE PEPPER

PART II
First Round of Replies   **117**

3 No Such Thing as a Good Sex Buyer:
   First Reply to Angie Pepper   119
   HOLLY LAWFORD-SMITH

4 Why It's Still Not Wrong to Buy Sex:
   First Reply to Holly Lawford-Smith   135
   ANGIE PEPPER

PART III
Second Round of Replies   161

5   What Women Owe to Each Other: Second
    Reply to Angie Pepper   163
    HOLLY LAWFORD-SMITH

6   Finding Common Ground: Second Reply to
    Holly Lawford-Smith   178
    ANGIE PEPPER

    Further Reading   199
    Glossary   203
    Bibliography   210
    Index   223

Foreword

Michelle Madden Dempsey

Dear Reader,

Welcome. You might be reading this book for any number of reasons. Perhaps your reasons are personal: you are wondering if it is wrong for *you* to buy sex, or wondering how you should advise a friend who is considering (or currently) buying sex. Perhaps your reasons are social or political: is buying sex a problem that calls for social or political solutions—maybe even legal ones? Should you support organizations that oppose buying sex—perhaps even those that support criminal prohibition of sex buying? Perhaps your reasons are philosophical: you want to think more clearly about the myriad vexing issues that arise in asking whether it is wrong to buy sex, and better understand how those conflicting considerations inform disagreements regarding this controversial topic.

No matter your reasons for reading this book, you are in for a treat. The debate between Holly Lawford-Smith and Angie Pepper is an engaging and important contribution to both the philosophical literature and public debate regarding commercial sex.[1] It not only facilitates a clearer understanding of the issues, it reveals the deeper philosophical commitments that ground the authors' disagreements.

I will not attempt to summarize the debate between Holly and Angie in full. They do a tremendous job of setting out their own arguments—closely engaging with one another's rebuttals—and ultimately clarifying the nature and grounds of their remaining disagreements. Furthermore, while I am honoured by their careful engagement with my own work on this issue, I will not use this

---

1 Following the authors' lead, I will refer to the authors as 'Holly' and 'Angie', respectively, and respectfully.

opportunity to offer a reply. Instead, in this foreword, I hope to give the reader a sense of their differing methodological commitments, explore how far apart their positions actually are, and offer my thoughts on how empirical evidence regarding commercial sex might inform this debate and, importantly, how this debate might promote better empirical studies regarding commercial sex.

On Methodology

Holly and Angie take themselves to be approaching the question of this book from distinct methodological camps, and I think they are right about that. As Angie observes in her closing section, 'Throughout the discussion Holly has assumed a position that might be described as a radical feminist view, and I have taken up a position that might be described as a liberal feminist view (194). I also think she is right that 'using these labels is not without complications' (ibid.). But I would go further still and argue that these philosophical methods themselves are not without complications.

One complication Angie faces as a result of her particular brand of liberal individualism is that it commits her to making claims such as our 'bodies are our own and not shared with anyone else'—which is a statement that is not true for anyone who has been born (and thus shared their bodies with their mother, at least until the cord was cut); it is not true for pregnant people, who share their bodies at least for a time with their foetuses/babies; it is not true for nursing people, who share the milk produced in their body, nor for the person who latches onto their breast to feed; it is not true for conjoined twins; and it is arguably in tension with the experiences of people whose bodily orifices are penetrated during sexual intercourse (West 2000). Moreover, as Angie acknowledges, her commitment to liberal individualism has normative implications that *always* prioritize the interests of individuals over the interests of a common good, which (I would argue) tends to obscure the ways in which we are all radically interconnected and interdependent on one another and thus blinds us to the sense in which autonomy is a matter of being *in relation to one another*, rather than being *separate* from one another (Nedelsky 2012).

Another complication of Angie's particular form of liberalism is that it leads her to embrace Ronald Dworkin's strong 'trumping' account of rights, according to which good consequences can never override a person's rights unless the consequences cross some very high threshold, such as killing one person to save a million

(138).[2] This account is a complication for Angie's broader frame-work, given that she adopts Joseph Raz's interest theory of rights as a foundational matter (74), and Raz rejects this strong 'trumping' account of rights (Raz 1978). For Raz, rights are not trumps: they are simply potential grounds of duties. Duties are categorical protected reasons: they apply to you irrespective of personal goals and plans, and they give you both a reason to do what they would have you do, and they exclude some reasons you may have to do otherwise. So, for example, my promise to meet a friend for breakfast gives her a right to my attendance and gives me a duty to attend. I cannot escape the duty simply by changing my mind—and when the time comes, my duty gives me a reason to go, and it excludes reasons I have not to go (say, that I'm exhausted and could use the extra rest). Rights are important insofar as they ground duties, and duties shape our rational horizons in important ways—but, as Dworkin himself acknowledged in responding to Raz's critique, rights do not, as Angie claims, trump '*any* good consequences that might be secured by' by overriding the right (138).[3]

Holly's radical feminist methodology is also not without its complications. First, it causes her to bite off more than she needs to chew to convince her readers that buying sex is wrong. While Holly offers eight arguments against buying sex, her main argument (the first one and the one she spends the most time defending) is grounded in an ambitious foundational premise: she argues that *all* 'sex as we know it' (what she calls 'hierarchical sex') is wrong.[4] From this, it follows that buying sex is wrong. Still, one must wonder whether her foundational premise risks alienating readers whose experience of sex as *they* know it does not align with Holly's understanding of hierarchical sex.[5]

---

2 Even if one concedes Angie's strong trumping account of rights, the considerations that Holly points to in her argument seem easily capable of doing the job. As Holly explains, the stakes on her side of the argument are about as high as they can get: the goal is to end male dominance, which has created a world in which women do not have full personhood, so that we might create 'a future in which women are full persons' (63).

3 Dworkin conceded that a right need only override 'a *marginal* case of collective justification' (Dworkin 1978: 366). See also (Yowell 2007).

4 Further, Holly argues that all 'sex as we know it' should be subject to a 'sex reset', wherein there will be 'no interpersonal sexual interactions' for an unspecified length of time (38).

5 Of course, it may be that Holly is not concerned to convince her readers – which would reflect a view regarding the role morality of philosophers with which I am broadly sympathetic (Dempsey 2012: 77). This view—which John Gardner called

Second, while there is much to admire in her consistent commitment to radical feminism, this method, too, can have its blind spots. The central tenets of radical feminism, at least in the account of Catharine MacKinnon, whose work Holly makes liberal use of, include the claims that sex/gender is fundamentally a matter of hierarchy rather than difference, and that sexuality is foundational to male dominance as both a *cause and consequence* of women's subordination. While I am inclined to agree with these tenets, I worry that they may sometimes obscure important considerations that weigh against using legal sanctions to prohibit buying sex. In the introduction, the authors acknowledge an important limitation to their arguments, insofar as they do 'not interrogate the ways that intersectional identities may (or may not) impact on the ethics of commercial sexual exchange' (3). This limitation is even more worrying when it comes to the criminalization of buying sex. Given what we know about the myriad ways in which criminal law is used to create and maintain racialized subordination, an *intersectional* radical feminist method might better illuminate important arguments against criminalization. Thus, while I have previously argued that there is a case to be made for criminalizing sex buying, one that is consistent with both radical feminist and liberal methodologies, it is crucial—no matter which method one employs—to acknowledge the risks that come with criminalization, especially as they relate to the perpetuation of systemic racism (Dempsey 2010: 1774, n142).

I just claimed to have offered an argument about buying sex that is consistent with both radical feminist and liberal commitments—so, clearly, I do not view Holly and Angie's methodological commitments as irreconcilable. No matter whether my previous argument about buying sex was successful on its merits, it did, I believe, successfully marry the central tenets of radical feminism and liberalism. It did so by rejecting liberal neutrality and embracing what might be called an *intersectional radical feminist pluralist perfectionist liberalism.* That's a mouthful, but the basic idea is to reject versions of liberalism that are 'based on individual rights and...agnosticism

---

a 'bureaucratic conception' of the philosopher's role—holds that 'in their academic work, they should aim at true premises, valid arguments, clear thinking, attention to details, avoidance of banality, and so forth, without regard to the consequences of their work, if any, for the development of public policy' (Gardner 2007: 54).

toward what people do with these rights' (Yuracko 2003: 86), in favour of a liberalism that embraces the idea 'that there is an objective good for human beings and that this good lies in flourishing' (Khader 2011: 18). This methodology makes it possible to recognize the ways in which 'adaptive preferences' shape our understanding of our interests, such that we might genuinely believe we have interests that ground rights and duties, where in fact, those purported interests are not consistent with what Serene Khader calls our 'deep preferences'—the preferences that would be retained 'under conditions conducive to flourishing that a person recognizes as such' (Khader 2011: 51). Insofar as it is pluralist, this methodology also makes room for acknowledging that there is 'a wide range of acceptable life patterns, projects, and beliefs, all of which are compatible with human flourishing' (Yuracko 2003: 5).

As applied to the debate between Holly and Angie, a methodology grounded in pluralist perfectionist liberalism may go some way toward bridging the gap between them, allowing recognition of two important truths: (1) 'that women's sexual preferences, desires, and fantasies are a reflection of patriarchal values,' a point which Angie freely acknowledges 'is not without persuasive force' (148); and (2) if one is attempting to convince readers who may resist the truth of this first point (especially those 'women who find their sexual relations with men to be liberating, empowering, and generally positive' (ibid.), these preferences should not be evaluated solely in terms of what women owe to each other' in the advancement of women's liberation—as Holly might be inclined to do (163–169)—but in terms of whether these preferences and the patterns of life in which they are grounded are compatible with human flourishing.

How Far Apart Are Their Conclusions, Really?

At one level, the disagreements between Holly and Angie are stark. Recall, Holly argues that not only is buying sex wrong, but all 'sex as we know it' is wrong. Angie argues that while buying sex can be disvaluable, it is not always *wrong*, at least under certain conditions. Once we examine those conditions, however, the distance between them diminishes significantly. So, let us examine Angie's conditions: there are two sets, one that applies to sellers, the other to buyers.

The central condition for sex-sellers is that they must give *valid* consent to sell sex.[6] Without valid consent from the seller, buying sex is wrong. The criteria for valid consent, as she explains, are three-fold:

1   Valid consent requires the *capacity* to consent, which excludes cases involving children, people with severe cognitive impairments, and those who are under the influence of alcohol or drugs. Given the widespread use of alcohol and drugs as a numbing/coping strategy by sex-sellers (Sallmann 2010), this requirement narrows the scope of non-wrongful commercial sex considerably.

2   Valid consent requires *freely given* consent, which excludes not only cases involving force, but cases in which the sex-seller's 'agency is severely limited because of the terrible options available to them' (78).[7]

3   Valid consent requires *informed* consent. Angie characterizes this criterion thinly, as merely a requirement that the sex-seller understand 'who is putting what where, so to speak' (79). Yet, the requirement of informed consent is arguably thicker than that. For example, when 'loverboy' pimps deceive women into believing they are in a romantic relationship and then manipulate them into selling sex, the deception regarding the

6   A note on terminology. Both Holly and Angie use the phrase 'sex workers' throughout. While I am happy to use that language in referring to people who self-identify as such, I do not use it as a general way of referring to people who provide sex for money. The phrase presupposes a degree of choice and empowerment that is often absent, and I have been informed by many survivors, with whom I am allied and work with at the Villanova Law Institute to Address Commercial Sexual Exploitation, that use of the terms is offensive and harmful. In previous writings, I have used the phrase, 'prostituted-persons', which comes with its own problems. While it is not a perfect compromise, I hope my use of the term 'sex-seller' does not prejudge the circumstances of any particular case. (For example, someone may be trafficked into selling sex, they may be freely choosing to do so from an adequate range of valuable options, or the case may fall somewhere in between.)

7   I have captured the idea of someone with only 'terrible options available' with a similar, albeit more flowery and Aristotelian, phrase: that one is lacking an 'adequate range of valuable options'. Still, the gist of the idea is the same. Angie interprets my phrase to require that people are only freely choosing to sell sex if they 'have the luxury of a wide range of valuable employment options' (111)—but that misinterprets my point. We can argue about what constitutes an 'adequate range' of options and whether there is much distance between a set of 'valuable options' and a set of minimally 'not terrible' options – but my phrase hardly commits me to an implausible or unattainable ideal in which everyone has the 'luxury' of a 'wide range' of valuable options.

true nature of their relationship presumably compromises the women's consent, despite the women understanding the physical mechanics of sex (for a recent example drawn from evidence in the Andrew Tate case, see Tahsin and Shea 2023).

Note that on Angie's account, all three criteria are required: if the sex-seller lacks capacity to consent, then buying sex is wrong; if their consent is not freely given, then buying sex is wrong; if their consent is not informed, then buying sex is wrong. Given these criteria, *how much sex buying that actually occurs in the real world is wrong?* We will revisit this question in the final section, but for now, let us turn to Angie's conditions as they apply to sex-buyers.

Angie's central condition for sex-buyers is that they must be *responsible sex buyers* (98–100). If a sex-buyer is not acting responsibly, then buying sex is wrong. The criteria for responsible sex buying are seven-fold:

1   Sex buyers must 'always make sure' that the seller's consent is valid according to the criteria set out above. Angie seems to interpret this requirement as a matter of epistemic effort. Buyers must make 'a determined effort to ensure that [sellers] are competent to give consent and that their consent is informed and freely given, which requires checking for signs of intoxication, mental impairment, and abusive pimping or other kinds of coercion' (101). Presumably, if the buyer gets it wrong despite making a 'determined effort' to discern the truth, then buying sex is wrong by virtue of the fact that there is no valid consent from the seller. Whereas, if the seller does validly consent, but the buyer fails to 'always make sure' this is the case, then buying sex is wrong by virtue of the buyer's irresponsibility.

2   Sex buyers must always respect the seller's right to withdraw consent.

3   Sex buyers must not be under the influence of alcohol or drugs.

4   Prior to engaging in the sexual act(s), sex buyers must 'explicitly *negotiate, contract,* and *pay*' for the specific sex act(s) (149).

5   Sex buyers must always practice safe sex (e.g., wear condoms).

6   Sex buyers must undertake regular sexual health screenings so that 'are not... exposing [sellers] to unnecessary risks'[8] (100).

---

8 I assume Angie means something close to 'unreasonable risks' rather than 'unnecessary risks' – for, while she argues that buying sex is not always wrong, she never

7   Sex buyers 'must report cases of suspected trafficking, sexual exploitation, and abusive pimping to the relevant law enforcement authorities or charities' (101).

As with the criteria that apply to sex-sellers, all seven of these criteria are required on Angie's account. It is always wrong to buy sex without first making sure that the seller is validly consenting throughout the encounter. It is always wrong to buy sex while under the influence. It is always wrong to buy sex without first clearly negotiating the details and paying up front. It is always wrong to buy 'bare back' sex, even if you pay extra. It is always wrong to buy sex without having a health screening to ensure you are disease-free. It is always wrong to buy sex without being committed to placing yourself in personal danger by reporting trafficking and abusive pimping.

Pause for a moment to combine the two sets of conditions set out above and ask yourself: according to these criteria, how much sex buying that *actually occurs in the real world* is wrong? Is there *any* sex buying that satisfies each and every one of these criteria? Who knows? There may be unicorn cases out there. But I confess to sharing Holly's suspicion as to just 'how large the pool of remaining sex buying is' (125). I suspect the number of actual cases in which each and every one of these criteria is satisfied is tiny, especially when compared to the universe of commercial sex generally.

How Much Sex Buying *that Actually Occurs in the Real World* is Wrong?

As Holly and Angie acknowledge, their 'moral evaluation of sex buyers does depend, to some degree, on how commercial sex actually takes place in the world and the effects it has' (196). And rightly so. This book is not concerned with whether buying sex might be wrong in some parallel universe—or whether buying sex might *not* be wrong, but only in *theory*. It is concerned, ultimately, with whether sex buying *as it actually occurs in the real world* is wrong.

---

defends the claim that it is *necessary*. Thus, any risks it poses are unnecessary risks – but Angie presumably views some of these risks as reasonable and some as unreasonable.

Holly's view is absolute: sex buying is always wrong. This conclusion follows from her foundational premises that hierarchical sex is wrong, and that bought sex is hierarchical sex. Angie's view is that it is *possible* to buy sex in the real world while satisfying the conditions for a non-wrongful exchange. Whether any *actual* cases of buying sex meet these conditions is a point on which Angie and I would likely disagree. But again, who knows? There might be unicorn cases. The more important issue, however, is whether buying sex is *typically* wrong. If buying sex *is* typically wrong, then we should ask whether the value of the unicorn cases (in which it is *not* wrong) justifies maintaining the commercial sex industry. If buying sex typically *is* wrong, and the value of the unicorn cases is small, then we should side with Holly and seek to abolish the commercial sex industry.[9]

Of course, figuring out whether buying sex is typically wrong—or, conversely, whether Angie's cases are not unicorns but are instead quite common—requires empirical evidence. More specifically, it requires what we might call *thickly normative empirical evidence.* Such evidence consists of empirical facts (facts that are observable to the senses) that enable us to draw conclusions regarding thickly normative concepts, such as consent, competence, voluntariness, flourishing, subordination, harm, etc.

For example, to answer the question of whether prostitution is typically consensual, one must seek both (1) an adequate philosophical account of consent, its normative force, and the conditions under which it bears such force, and (2) empirical evidence regarding when those conditions obtain in commercial sex. As Alan Wertheimer has correctly observed, the criteria for what constitutes morally transformative consent must involve *both* empirical evidence and moral evaluation (Wertheimer 2010: 196).

As Angie observes in her closing, through writing this book, she and Holly have come to have a better appreciation of the fact that

---

9 To anticipate an objection from Angie: this point is not just about weighing consequences. The existence of the commercial sex industry results in widespread rights violations, ranging from those whose rights are violated by virtue of the fact that they do not validly consent to selling sex, to those whose rights to full personhood are violated by male dominance. So, my point can easily be translated into rights discourse: if the rights violations that result from maintaining commercial sex trump the rights violations that would result from abolishing commercial sex, then we should abolish commercial sex.

'social scientists, lawyers, and medical professionals who investigate sex work are often partisan: they typically have a preconceived view about the ethics of commercial sex, which means that their enquiries are often underpinned and motivated by a normative and political agenda' (196). I agree. The 'competing camps' mentality that informs empirical research regarding commercial sex undermines its usefulness in figuring out how much real-world sex buying is wrong (Dempsey 2017).

But all is not lost. To improve the quality of empirical evidence on this issue, we need to do at least two things. First, we need improved empirical methods that enlarge sample sizes and thus better justify generalizing empirical claims. This is no easy task, especially in light of the fact that so many sex sellers die young due to violence, addiction, and stress-related illness. Far too often, and tragically, the people who were best positioned to reflect on their experience of selling sex and provide valuable empirical insights are no longer with us. Moreover, there is the difficulty of recruiting potential subjects for empirical research, institutional gatekeeping that throws up barriers to such research (Bosworth et al. 2011), reluctance of subjects to participate in studies, and human subject research protections (which are properly aimed at protecting vulnerable subjects, but which do make such research more difficult). Second, we need an improved philosophical understanding of the concepts that inform empirical research—especially the thick normative concepts which inform the debate over commercial sex. Thankfully, this book goes a long way toward addressing the second concern. Holly and Angie are to be commended for clarifying the philosophical issues at stake and the concepts upon which they rely, thereby laying the groundwork for more illuminating empirical research in the future.

Bibliography

Bosworth, Mary, Carolyn Hoyle, and Michelle Madden Dempsey. 2011. 'Researching Trafficked Women: On Institutional Resistance and the Limits to Feminist Reflexivity', *Qualitative Inquiry* 17(9):769–779.

Dempsey, Michelle Madden. 2010. 'Sex Trafficking and Criminalization: In Defense of Feminist Abolitionism' *University of Pennsylvania Law Review* 158: 1729–1778.

Dempsey, Michelle Madden. 2012. 'How to Argue About Prostitution', *Criminal Law and Philosophy* 6(1): 65–80.

Dempsey, Michelle Madden. 2017. 'What Counts as Trafficking for Sexual Exploitation? How Legal Methods Can Improve Empirical Research', *Journal of Human Trafficking* 3(1): 61–80.

Dworkin, Ronald. 1978. *Taking Rights Seriously*, 2nd edition (Cambridge, MA: Harvard University Press).

Gardner, J. 2007. 'Interview', in M. E. J. Nielsen (ed.) *Legal Philosophy: 5 Questions* (Copenhagen: Automatic Press/VIP).

Khader, Serene J. 2011. *Adaptive Preferences and Women's Empowerment* (Oxford: Oxford University Press).

Nedelsky, Jennifer. 2012. *Law's Relations: A Relational Theory of Self, Autonomy, and Law* (Oxford: Oxford University Press).

Raz, Joseph. 1978. 'Professor Dworkin's Theory of Rights', *Political Studies* 26(1): 123–137.

Sallmann, Jolanda. 2010. '"Going Hand-in-Hand": Connections Between Women's Prostitution and Substance Use', *Journal of Social Work Practice in the Addictions* 10(2): 115–138.

Tahsin, Jamie and Shea, Matt. 2023. 'Andrew Tate: Chats in "War Room" Suggest Dozens of Women Groomed', 31 August, www.bbc.com/news/world-europe-66604827.

Wertheimer, Alan. 2010. 'Consent to Sexual Relations', in F. G. Miller and A. Wertheimer (eds) *The Ethics of Consent*, pp. 195–219 (New York: Oxford University Press).

West, Robin. 2000. 'The Difference in Women's Hedonic Lives: A Phenomenological Critique of Feminist Legal Theory', *Wisconsin Women's Law Journal* 15: 149–215.

Yowell, Paul. 2007. 'Critical Examination of Dworkin's Theory of Rights', *American Journal of Jurisprudence* 52: 93–137.

Yuracko, Kimberley. 2003. *Perfectionism and Contemporary Feminist Values* (Bloomington, IN: Indiana University Press).

Introduction

Holly Lawford-Smith and Angie Pepper

Sex is a commodity; something you can buy and sell. There is much diversity in commercial sexual exchanges. Sexual services are sold and delivered in various settings, including (but by no means limited to) strip clubs, brothels, outdoors, massage parlours, on the telephone, online, in recording studios, hotels, at sex parties, and in clients' or sex workers' homes. Similarly, there is a dizzying array of sexual services available. You can pay for an exotic dance, an erotic massage, a pornographic film, a webcam performance, penetrative sex, oral sex, telephone sex, multiple-partner sex, bondage, role-play, and so on. Again, this is not an exhaustive list, but it serves to illustrate the range and variety of what's on sale. Indeed, whatever your sexual preferences and desires, there is likely someone out there who would be willing to satisfy them for a price.

Well-worn stereotypes of sex buyers as lonely old men, sexually inadequate men, perverted men, and dangerous sexual male predators obscure the facts on the ground: men who buy sex come from all walks of life and increasing numbers of sex buyers are not men. One reason for the diversification in sex buyers, as well as a proliferation in sexual services and sex work markets, is the rise of the internet and other technologies (see, for example, Barwulor et al. 2021; Cunningham and Kendall 2011; Jones 2020; and Sanders et al. 2018). Increasing numbers of sexual services are provided online, and sex workers use the internet to manage and market their businesses, as well as screen clients. This expansion has made the purchase and provision of sexual services more accessible than ever before which may help to explain why there has been a rise in the number and kind of people who pay for sex.

With all this in mind, the ethics of buying sex should not be regarded as a niche moral issue. More and more people are exposed

DOI: 10.4324/9781003169697-1

to the option of buying sex in various forms and so it is important to ask whether we do anything morally wrong if we buy sex. In answering this urgent moral question, we have come to defend opposing positions. In brief, Holly defends the view that it is always wrong for men to buy sex from women in our current social circumstances (her discussion is limited to these interactions, which we agree are the bulk of the existing interactions). Angie, on the other hand, argues that men (or anyone else) need not do anything morally wrong if they buy sex from women (or anyone else) in our current social circumstances.

Importantly, we approach the question of whether we're permitted to buy sex from very different perspectives. As the conversation unfolds, we develop two contrasting **normative ethical frameworks** for thinking about the question we face. Specifically, Holly endorses a hybrid approach that exposes the wrongness of buying sex by appealing to insights from across the big three moral theories: **consequentialism, deontology,** and **virtue theory.** By comparison, Angie's position is straightforwardly deontological: the rightness and wrongness of our choices are determined by whether we have succeeded or failed in satisfying our moral duties. Accordingly, Angie shows that since we are under no duty to refrain from buying sex from consenting adults, we don't do anything wrong when we buy sex from them.

This is an important feature of the book, and it serves as a needed intervention in the political and philosophical debate on this topic. Not only do we provide two different ways of thinking about the question, but by laying bare the normative underpinnings of our respective positions, we reveal something important about the foundations of disagreement (and agreement) in the ethics of buying and selling sex. We show that what has sometimes been regarded as a disagreement over the facts—e.g., exactly how harmful sex work is to sex workers, how much sex work involves trafficked individuals, how many sex workers enjoy their work, and so on—is really a disagreement over which **normative ethical framework** we ought to be committed to. Moreover, we each offer some reasons to think that our preferred approach is superior and give the reader the resources to decide for themselves what position they want to adopt.

There are several things worth mentioning about the debate as it proceeds in this book. First, we are interested in the moral question: is it **morally wrong** to buy sex? This is distinct from the legal question: should it be illegal to buy sex? Whether something is moral does not determine that it should be legal and vice versa. For example, you do something wrong by breaking a promise to attend your friend's birthday party, but it would be an overreach of state power if there were a law making your actions illegal. Similarly, there have been lots of things that have been legal in the past (e.g., slavery, racial segregation, rape within marriage), which are morally wrong. Though we touch on legal issues at various points in our debate, we are primarily concerned with whether you can buy sex without doing anything morally wrong. This makes our debate novel in its orientation. While lots has been written on the question of whether selling and buying sex should be legal, there has been little focus on the morality of buying sex. Irrespective of the legal situation, it is crucial that we consider whether buying sex is morally problematic because the options to buy are both abundant and, for an increasing number of people, attractive.

Second, as you may have noticed, we're interested in the here and now. We're not talking about the possibility of buying sex in a truly fair and just society—some society that does not yet (and may never) exist. This sets our debate apart from philosophical work that discusses the ethics of selling and buying sex in ideal circumstances. Instead, we're interested in whether we're morally allowed to buy sex in the messy and imperfect societies in which we find ourselves. These are societies dealing with legacies of historical injustice and oppression, in which there are multiple and overlapping social hierarchies. Accordingly, the opposing views developed in this book offer practical guidance on how you should act today and though we disagree deeply over what morality demands, there is much that we agree morality rules out.

Third, we acknowledge that our debate is limited because it does not interrogate the ways that intersectional identities may (or may not) impact the ethics of commercial sexual exchange. The central lens through which we approach the ethics of buying sex is sex/gender, which means that we have focused on whether men can buy sex from women. The main reason for this is that currently most sex buyers are men, and most sex sellers are women. Moreover, no society in the world secures social justice for women and so the gendered dynamics of commercial sex cannot be overlooked. However, that does not mean that our arguments do not speak to the fact that people have overlapping identities and experiences. For Holly, any man irrespective of other facets of his identity (e.g., race, disability, class, religion) does something wrong if he buys sex from a woman. For Angie, any man irrespective of other facets of his identity may be morally permitted to buy sex from a woman. Moreover, for Angie, *any* person may be morally permitted to buy sex from *any* other person(s) irrespective of their sex, gender, race, class, disability, religion, and so on.

Finally, the argument of this book is limited insofar as it focuses primarily on the ethics of prostitution and (in Holly's case) pornography. That said, we take a pretty wide-ranging understanding of prostitution: sexual interaction involving bodily contact between two persons (or more), performed as part of a market exchange. This does not mean that we don't mention other kinds of sexual services, or that our arguments have no implications for a wider variety of sexual services. Importantly, Angie's view is a defence of any sexual service that one might care to dream of. By contrast, Holly's argument is more tightly focused on prostitution and pornography, but her argument leaves the door open for a more nuanced and fine-grained analysis of other kinds of sexual services.

The debate before you is the result of a good faith attempt to understand one another's point of view, to respond to one another's objections, and to articulate as best we can the opposing perspectives in this debate. We are sure (and we hope) that you will find much to agree and disagree with. And we invite you to dismantle, reconstruct, and build upon the arguments we have presented here as you reason your way through the thorny moral issues in the ethics of buying sex.

Part I

Opening Statements

Chapter 1

It Is Wrong to Buy Sex

Holly Lawford-Smith

Only if somebody has a dream, and a voice to describe that
dream, does what looked like nature begin to look like culture,
what looked like fate begin to look like a moral abomination.

(Rorty 1991, p. 3)

1 Introduction

Suppose you're a young heterosexual man, envious of all the sex
you mistakenly believe other men are having, yet somehow unable
to move a date from the bar to the bedroom. (A survey of people
in the UK and the US found that men estimated other men to be
having about three times as much sex as they actually are—see
Duffy 2018.) Although you'd never considered it before, a social
encounter with several escorts at a colleague's bucks night sets you
to wondering whether it's okay for you to *buy* sex. What would you
need to know, to settle that question for yourself morally? In this
book, we're interested in more than merely what the law permits
you to do. We're interested in all the moral arguments that there
are, both for and against the permissibility of buying sex, and how
they stack up when it comes to this young man's question. What I
will argue for in this book is that it's *wrong to buy sex*. I'm exclusively interested in men buying sex from women, which is most of
the sex that is bought. So what I'm really arguing for is that it's not
okay *for men* to buy sex *from women*. I won't have much to say
about whether it's okay for women to buy sex from men; my main
reservation about sex-buying in that direction is that it might create
interest in and demand for markets in sex more generally, and thus
pull in the other direction from eliminating markets in sexual access
to women.

DOI: 10.4324/9781003169697-3

I do not argue on intrinsic grounds that there's something about sex that makes it the kind of thing that should never be bought or sold. I do not think that sex is sacred, or pure, or should only be had in the context of a loving, committed relationship. I agree with many people today that sex can be fun, and can be enjoyed casually, and can be had for a variety of reasons, not all of which are to do with whether the sex itself is desired for its prospects of physical pleasure and (in some cases) closeness and intimacy with another person. I am not committed to the view that there is *no possible society* where sex could permissibly be something bought and sold (although the conditions under which this happened would need to be very different). Rather, I argue from looking at the commercial sex industry as it currently is (both prostitution and pornography); and looking at sexual intercourse as it currently is (for many, if not most, people); against the background of sex inequality as it currently is (moral, social, legal, and economic inequality between men and women). I argue that *given those things*, it is impermissible to buy sex.

We're asking in this book about whether it's permissible to buy sex *now*, but some of my arguments require us to think further ahead. Fully comprehending the injustice of women's situation depends on imagining how things might be different, and better. I'll be particularly interested in a future world in which much more progress has been made toward women's liberation, and what we might need to change about our world in order to end up there. Several of my arguments for the impermissibility of buying sex depend on this future: I say that future is the one we should want, and we won't get it if we leave the sex industry in place.

I'll divide this opening statement into three sections. The first section is descriptive: what is it that men who buy sex are buying, and why are they buying it? This takes us beyond prostitution, and into the adjacent areas of pornography and 'ordinary' sex—sex as we currently understand and conceive it. The second section is evaluative: what would a world without social hierarchy based on (biological) sex look like, and what needs to change about our world in order to get us there? The third section is normative (a question in practical morality): given what men are buying and why they're buying it, and given what a world without sex hierarchy would look like and how we might get to it, what do the men who now buy sex do wrong? *Why* is it wrong for them to buy sex?

2   Prostitution, Pornography, Sex

2.1   A Note on Terminology

So far I have been talking in terms of 'commercial' sex as a way to demarcate the difference between sex that is paid for and sex that isn't. It will be useful to be able to distinguish the two more clearly, but 'ordinary sex', for example, normalizes something that I want to bring into question. A term of art is needed. For lack of a better alternative, I'll follow the discussion of contract pregnancy, which uses 'commercial surrogacy' for exchanges within the market, and 'altruistic surrogacy' for exchanges outside the market. In commercial surrogacy, surrogates are paid for their labour; in altruistic surrogacy there are no payments (including payments in goods or resources rather than money); one gifts one's reproductive labour, usually to someone inside one's social network, a family member or friend. Similarly, then, I'll use 'commercial sex' to refer to exchanges of sex within the market, covering most pornography and all prostitution; and '**altruistic sex**' to refer to exchanges outside the market, covering both the casual sex and the sex as part of dating, relationships, and marriages, that people choose to have (and in some cases are forced to have). The term 'altruistic sex' is not perfect either, given that it will apply to some deeply abusive non-commercial sex; but it *is* apt in the sense that it captures a lot of the unpleasurable sex that women have out of duty or because they are simply resigned to the normalcy of this being what sex is (see also Greer 2018).

The parallel between surrogacy and sex is interesting, for it is easier to draw a bright line between commercial surrogacy and altruistic surrogacy than between commercial sex and altruistic sex. We draw the line for surrogacy just by looking at whether the surrogate had a pre-existing relationship with the biological parents or they are strangers to her. But it will be less straightforward to draw a bright line between commercial and altruistic sex, given that sex has developed culturally as part of an institution—marriage—that had the economic dependence of women on men at its heart (see e.g. Radin 1987, p. 1923 and references in her fn. 260; and Sanders 2008, p. 205). For a very long time, a woman's chances in life depending on her entering into a marriage, and sex was just a part of marriage that she was expected to accept whether she wanted it or not (not least because it was necessary to child-bearing, which was also expected). As Andrea Dworkin put it:

> Women have been chattels to men as wives, as prostitutes, as sexual and reproductive servants. Being owned and being fucked are or have been virtually synonymous experiences in the lives of women. He owns you; he fucks you. The fucking conveys the quality of the ownership: he owns you inside out. The fucking conveys the passion of his dominance: it requires access to every hidden inch. ... He can possess her as an individual—be her lord and master—and thus be expressing a private right of ownership (the private right issuing from his gender); or he can possess her by fucking her impersonally and thus be expressing a collective right of ownership without masquerade or manners. Most women are not distinct, private individuals to most men; and so the fuck tends toward the class assertion of dominance.
>
> (Dworkin 1987, p. 83)

Even today and outside of marriage, it is not uncommon to find arrangements where extravagant gifts flow from an older, wealthier man to his younger, less wealthy, lover. Commercial elements seem to be woven into 'altruistic sex' in a way that they are not in the case of altruistic surrogacy.

In my view, there's no talking about the sex industry without talking about sex—which is why I talk about both in my contributions to this book. The sex industry has cultural meaning that contributes to our understanding of sex, and it also enacts the cultural meaning that sex already had (for example, male sexual entitlement in the private realm has translated into male sexual access in the commercial realm). Once private, sex is now public: both the idea of it and the fact of it are used to entertain people and to sell products. We are told that it is one of the 'secrets of long living people' (Tickell 2003). Some men get it for free, others have to pay for it (and some go without—and some of *those* are furious about it, see discussion in Bates 2020). Still, sex as it takes place inside the sex industry is ethically complicated in different ways to sex as it takes place outside of it. Thus even though we need to talk about both, we still need to treat them separately. Let's start with commercial sex.

2.2   Commercial Sex

Not all prostitution is pornography, for not all of it is filmed and shared. But most pornography involves prostitution. (The exceptions are porn that is a representation of human sex without being human sex itself, e.g. animations; and amateur porn, sex that people have and choose to film and upload—although note that a lot of commercial porn is now *presented as though* it was amateur, to meet a demand for 'new' girls.) I will talk about both under the heading of 'commercial sex'.

2.2.1   Prostitution

Here's the legal scholar and feminist Margaret Baldwin, talking about prostitution:

> what most needs hearing on the subject of prostitution. I mean the carnage: the scale of it, the dailiness of it, the seeming inevitability of it; the torture, the rapes, the murders, the beatings, the despair, the hollowing out of the personality, the near extinguishment of hope commonly suffered by women in prostitution.
>
> (Baldwin 1992, p. 49)

For those whose idea of prostitution is formed by popular culture representations like *Secret Diary of A Call Girl* (a British television series based on the memoirs of Brooke Magnanti, pseudonym 'Belle de Jour', in which a glamorous high-end sex worker has her pick of clients and is portrayed more in the vein of a care worker), or *Pretty Woman* (a movie portraying a very wealthy man falling in love with a gorgeous and charismatic street prostitute), Baldwin's description may seem hyperbolic. But it is not: while it might not describe the experiences of *every* woman working in prostitution, it describes the experiences of a great many.

Take women trafficked into sexual slavery, for example. In her landmark book *Female Sexual Slavery* (1979), the American sociologist Kathleen Barry wrote about the global prostitution industry, using the methods of interview, investigation, and research in order to attempt to circumvent the fact that 'little information was readily available' (Barry 1979, pp. 3–13, at p. 6; for a much earlier discussion, see Goldman [1910], 2002). She talked to someone who had attended an auction of girls for sexual slavery in Zanzibar in 1970 (ibid., pp. 53–58). She discussed reports made by INTER-POL since 1965 showing an awareness of the existence of international trafficking of women for sexual slavery, and yet which were withheld from the public (ibid., pp. 58–62). She presented evidence of trafficking happening from Europe to the Near East and Sub-Saharan Africa; from South America to Puerto Rico, the European Mediterranean countries, or the Middle East; from France to Luxembourg and Germany; from Europe to the Ivory Coast and Senegal; from Thailand and the Philippines to other countries; from Arab countries to Lebanon and Kuwait (ibid., pp. 59–60). Because of its illegality, Barry notes, 'There is no way to estimate the incidence of sex slavery. Full and accurate statistics are impossible to calculate' (ibid., p. 60). She reports that between 1971 and 1974, there were investigations in the United States into '165 federal cases of involuntary servitude and slavery' (there was no data for cases at the level of the state) (ibid., p. 66). She reports on trafficking to serve men in the military (ibid., pp. 70–76); and trafficking to serve businessmen, for example from Japan into South Korea or from Thailand into Germany (ibid., pp. 76–80).

To give just two examples of what these women's lives were like, in one case of military prostitution in Corsica, procurers had supplied women who were then 'forced to receive 60 to 80 Legionnaires a day' (ibid., p. 70). A man who had been a Legionnaire and spent 15 years in Corsica told the press when the procurers were convicted that 'he was astonished that military officials were not also accused in this case', because the mobile brothels 'were set up by military leaders who worked with rings to supply the girls' (ibid., p. 71). In a prostitution house in the North African area of Paris, 'six or seven girls each serve 80 to 120 customers a night. On holidays their quota might go up to 150' (ibid., p. 4). In a new introduction to the book written five years after its publication, Barry says that what she had exposed was 'only the tip of the iceberg', and that changes over time were a matter of magnitude only: 'the descriptions of women's experiences of female sexual slavery now today are not essentially different than when this work was originally published (ibid., p. xii).

Are things any better today? Data from 155 countries gathered in 2006 for the United Nations' 'Global Report on Trafficking in Persons' showed that 79% of trafficking was for sexual exploitation, and 79% of the victims were female (66% were women, and 13% were girls). The prostitution industry is estimated to involve between 40–42 million people, and estimates of the proportion of these people who have been trafficked are between 14% at the low end and 60–90% at the high end (Schulze et al. 2014; UNODC 2009; and see discussion in Lawford-Smith 2022a, p. 80). Trafficking, then, is not a marginal problem when it comes to prostitution.

Still, trafficking is just one aspect of prostitution, and one that some pro-prostitution campaigners work hard to separate out from the sex work that does not involve it (whether across state lines within a country, or between countries) (see discussion in Jeffreys 2009, p. 9; cf. Mac and Smith 2018, ch. 3). But it is not as though merely making sure that a sex worker hasn't been trafficked is sufficient to remove any moral complexity from buying sex. A study from Baltimore, Maryland between 2016–2017 found that 61% of female sex workers 'screened positive for PTSD [posttraumatic stress disorder] symptoms', and that these sex workers had 'extensive histories of sexual and physical violence', with 81.8% having experienced some sexual and physical violence in their lifetimes, 15.5% having experienced childhood or adult sexual revictimization, and 37.7% having experienced childhood or adult physical revictimization (Park et al. 2021, p. 10384). The researchers found that 'The levels of PTSD observed among our sample were comparable with that reported among treatment-seeking war veterans' (ibid.).

A recent meta-analysis of 55 studies on female sex workers found the overall prevalence of suicide ideation to be 27%, suicide attempt to be 20%, depression to be 44%, and PTSD to be 29% (Millan-Alanis et al. 2021, p. 867). The cohort size for suicide attempt was 6,166 (ibid., p. 869), which means there was evidence of 1,233 women having attempted suicide in this cohort. The cohort size for depression was 17,581, which means there was evidence of 7,735 women living with depression in this cohort (in self-reports the figure was as high as 48%, and in rater-administered reports it was lower, at 28%, so that is a range of 4,922–8,438 women living with depression) (ibid., p. 869). The prevalence of PTSD was found to be higher among exclusively street-based sex workers (ibid., p. 870). The cohort size for PTSD was 3,042, which means 882 women from this cohort having PTSD. Again this varied between self-report and rater-administered, between 24% for the latter and 32% for the former (which is a range of 730–973 women living with PTSD) (ibid., p. 869). The researchers sum things up this way: 'FSW [female sex workers] are an extremely vulnerable group susceptible to intense psychological stress derived from multiple health, social, economic, and legal barriers where the exposure to different types of violence during their lifetime also plays a key role in the psychopathology of mental health disorders.' They go on, 'when comparing them to other similarly vulnerable populations, especially considering trauma-exposed populations, proportions of depression and PTSD are still higher among the FSW [female sex workers]' (ibid., pp. 872–873).

These are the women who men are buying the use of when they buy sex. Of course, men are also involved in the prostitution industry in other ways than as consumers, for example as traffickers, as pimps, as brothel and strip club owners. But we're particularly interested in this book in the men who buy sex. How many men is that? It is hard to know for sure. One UK study from 2005 showed an increase in the number of men buying sex over time, from 5.6% of 6,000 men aged between 16–44 in 1990, to 8.8% of 4,672 men in the same age bracket in 2000 (Ward et al. 2005; discussed in Sanders 2008, pp. 38–39).

Teela Sanders conducted interviews with men who buy sex in an attempt to understand their reasons for doing so. Previous research undertaken in Scotland had revealed 'five key motivations: the capacity to purchase specific sexual acts; access to a wide variety of women; the ability to contact women with certain characteristics; limited, temporary relationships; and the thrill of the activity' (McKeganey and Barnard 1996; discussed in Sanders 2008, p. 39). A literature review presented a further list of reasons 'why men buy sex: physical unattractiveness, social unattractiveness/psychological maladjustment, psychopathology (poor sexual development), manifestation of cultural gendered role expectations, avoidance of gender role responsibilities and buying sex as an exercise of power for disempowered men' (Atchison et al. 1998; discussed in Sanders 2008, p. 40). Sanders expanded these lists with a range of 'push' and 'pull' factors, where push factors are 'elements of men's lives that are lacking' (Sanders 2008, p. 40), and pull factors are 'aspects of the sex industry that are attractive and are promoted as 'entertainment' (ibid., p. 40). The key push factors she identified were emotional needs, being at a particular stage in one's life, being in / having had unsatisfactory sexual relationships, and not being at ease with 'conventional dating etiquette' (ibid.). The pull factors include the attractive way that sexual services are marketed ('designer brothels and gentlemen's clubs'—ibid., p. 45), the thrill and appeal of the deviant/illicit, and the ability to access a fantasy and take time out from 'reality' (ibid., p. 46).

Sanders's push factors make it seem perfectly understandable that a man would seek out a prostitute, but they leave an important question unanswered. When *women* have specific emotional needs, are at a particular life stage, have unsatisfactory sexual relationships (which, as we shall soon see, is often), and/or are not at ease with conventional dating etiquette, they generally do *not* turn to male prostitutes. There are unstated background assumptions to Sanders's explanations, about male sexuality and the role of sex in male well-being, which we may prefer to contest. Her pull factors provide us with a segue to pornography, which is arguably the main forum through which male sexual fantasy is constructed and disseminated today.

2.2.2 Pornography

When I talk about pornography here, I am talking about sex with women, or representations of sex with women. This includes lesbian sex (which is almost always produced *for* men) and cartoon/animated sex. I'm not talking about gay male pornography, although as with the small corner of prostitution involving male sex workers, that kind of pornography may end up being a casualty of the social interventions on pornography I will defend later—for example if disapproval of 'porn' stretches to *all* porn rather than targeting the porn that requires the mistreatment of women for its creation and acts as propaganda for women's sexual subordination, which is *most* porn. Kathleen Barry wrote powerfully of the way that pornography had become intertwined with ordinary sex:

> Since the mid-1970s with the massive proliferation of pornography, the graphic depiction of what men require of whores, prostitution has been brought into the daily lives of millions of American women. Pornographic movies, magazines, video tapes and paraphernalia are no longer the province of combat zones and prostitution areas of the city. They have found their way into homes through the sexual expectations some men make of their wives, daughters, girlfriends and lovers.
>
> (Barry 1979, pp. xi–xii)

Ariel Levy in her 2007 introduction to Andrea Dworkin's *Intercourse* called pornography 'a source of inspiration for all of popular culture' (Dworkin 1987, p. xx). Teela Sanders says something adjacent, pointing to the role of capitalism in enlarging the influence of pornography: 'Consumer capitalism encourages, cajoles and enflames male desire by actively constructing sexual fantasies, commodifying women's bodies and normalizing commercial sex' (Sanders 2008, p. 201).

Pornography is (usually) prostitution, *plus*. The women being paid to have sex on camera may have been trafficked, be subject to coercive control by partners or pimps, and/or be extremely vulnerable in the ways just outlined for prostitution. But she may also be a woman who is not a sex worker, who has been filmed without her knowledge or without her consent (for example in revenge porn or in spycam/voyeur porn). And she may be none of those things: she may be a woman who finds the idea of other people watching her have sex exciting, she may be an amateur who wants to break into the commercial pornography market and so produces free content in the hope of being able to do that. She may run an *OnlyFans* account and have full control over the content she chooses to produce and share. Some women speak very positively about their experiences in pornography (see e.g. the interview with porn actress 'Luna' for the YouTube channel Soft White Underbelly at www.youtube.com/watch?v=dxxxEShMvag), while other women tell harrowing stories of abuse (see e.g. Lovelace 1980).

That's commercial sex. What about altruistic sex?

2.3   Altruistic Sex

Let's start with what sex is like at the moment. For a start, there is an 'orgasm gap', which means that men are much more likely to *always orgasm when they have sex* than women are. Data from YouGov (UK) gathered in September 2021 and published in February 2022 found that among British women, only 30% said they orgasm every time they have sex (either once or multiple times); 27% said they orgasm most times they have sex, 15% said they orgasm sometimes, 10% said they orgasm rarely, and 7% said they never orgasm (with the remaining 10% saying they don't know or would prefer not to say—Nolsoe and Smith 2022). Compare this to British men, 61% of whom say they orgasm every time they have sex (either once or multiple times); 23% of whom say they orgasm most times they have sex; and only 10% give answers in the range of sometimes, rarely, or never orgasming during sex (the remaining 5% say they don't know or would prefer not to say) (ibid.). Revealingly, many of the male *partners* of heterosexual women appear ignorant of the gap: 42% claim that their partner orgasms every time they have sex, and 22% claim that she has multiple orgasms (while the truth is that 19% orgasm every time and 11% have multiple orgasms) (ibid.). The YouGov survey authors write: 'The data also reveals that some straight men seem oblivious to their partner's lack of ultimate pleasure—or are disinterested'. (They may be non-culpably ignorant, however, if their partners are *faking* orgasms.)

There is more to ending bad sex than merely closing the orgasm gap. But I take the gap to be a clue that there is better and worse sex—at least along one dimension of value—in the world at the moment. Let's start with the worse, which will help to illuminate further dimensions of (dis)value, working from Andrea Dworkin's retelling of the sexual life of Sophie Tolstoy, the wife of Leo Tolstoy. In some sense this is arbitrary: throughout history there are quite literally billions of women with billions of similar stories. But it is noteworthy because of the enduring cultural significance of the individuals involved, and the fact that both parties recorded their perspectives in a way that made them accessible to future people.

Dworkin shifts between Leo Tolstoy's work *The Kreuzer Sonata*, which she takes as autobiographical, and Sophie Tolstoy's diaries, to piece together the story of their long and unhappy marriage (Dworkin 1987, Ch. 1; see also discussion in Pinkham 2014). (Dworkin's own equally unhappy and more brutal experience is recounted in her semi-autobiographical novel *Mercy*, published in 1990). Leo and Sophie married when he was 34 and she was 18. They had thirteen children, and Sophie raised, fed, and educated all of these children. Sophie wrote in her diary 'no one will ever know that he never gave his wife a rest and never—in all these thirty-two years—gave his child a drink of water or spent five minutes by his bedside to give me a chance to rest a little, to sleep, or to go out for a walk, or even just recover from all my labours' (Dworkin 1987, p. 6; quoting S. Tolstoy 1929, p. 126). This was on top of transcribing his books and diaries; managing his estate, money, and copyrights; publishing his books; and negotiating with the state censors over their publication (Dworkin 1987, pp. 6–7). Most important for us, and clearly related to their large number of children, is that Leo fucked Sophie whenever he liked—despite aspiring to chastity (ibid., p. 7). Sophie wrote in her diaries of Leo's 'terrible coldness', his total indifference to her *after* intercourse, which would continue up until the point that he wanted intercourse again. Sophie wrote that physical love to her meant 'something very much akin to suffering' (Dworkin 1987, p. 7; quoting S. Tolstoy 1929, p. 37). He fucked her right up until he was 81 years old, a year before his death, meaning that Sophie endured 47 years of mostly unwanted sex, of sexual *instrumentalization* of the most callous kind (Dworkin 1987, p. 8).

Leo sees women in general as 'something to be desired', 'something to have'. She is an object, a body, a symbol (ibid.). Dworkin thinks that Leo understood how destructive to women sexual instrumentalization is. He wrote in *The Kreuzer Sonata* that women's enslavement depends on men seeing them as a tool of enjoyment, so that even if they allow woman's education and liberation, 'there she is, still the same humiliated and depraved slave, and the man still a depraved slave-owner' (Dworkin 1987, p. 12, quoting L. Tolstoy). Women internalize their own oppression and so come to regard themselves in this way too. But there is a great reversal in who is understood to have power in this situation. Men reduce women to objects of sexual use, but because men then *desire* women, they see women as having power over them. They project onto women that women are sexual temptresses, while women are in fact just going about their lives. Even those women who exploit the opportunities that this set of circumstances make available are only acting out a view of women created by men, in men's interest. Men first make women into sexual objects, and then hate women for 'controlling' them through desire (Dworkin 1987, p. 18).

Dworkin thought that the end of male dominance would mean the end of sex as we know it. *A lot* would have to change about sex as we know it and about the relations between the sexes for intercourse not to be deeply morally compromised. Indeed, she thought that *Leo Tolstoy himself* thought that we needed 'the end of intercourse'. 'The radical social change demanded by Tolstoy in this story … is a measured repudiation of **gynocide**: in order not to kill women, he said, we must stop fucking them' (ibid., p. 10)—although arguably Tolstoy was more interested in what fucking women did to men's spirituality than he was in women not being killed *per se*.

The extreme of Tolstoy's thought shows up in the murder of sex workers (in which case she is not just a tool of enjoyment but a *disposable* tool); in rape; and in the ongoing failure of the legal system to prosecute rape. In the UK, 110 sex workers were murdered while engaging in sex work between 1990–2016 (Platt and

Sanders 2017). The majority of these sex workers were street-based, although since 2011 the proportions have been shifting so that more indoor sex workers than street workers have been murdered (ibid.). The good news is that since 2006, all of the murderers have been prosecuted (although as Platt and Sanders note, 'there should be no perpetrators to sentence'). Another study from Colorado between 1967 and 1999 found that 'active prostitutes were almost 18 times more likely to be murdered than women of a similar age and race during the study interval' (Potterat et al. 2004, p. 782).

The Australian Institute for Health and Welfare estimated in 2020 that 1 in 6 women in Australia—*which today is 1.8 million women*—'have experienced at least 1 sexual assault since the age of 15'. They say that rates of victimization (this time for both sexes) went up more than 30% between 2010–2018, but that 'it is unclear whether this reflects an increased incidence of sexual assault, an increased propensity to report sexual assault to police or increased reporting of historical crimes' (AIHW 2020). For lifetime sexual assault, which is childhood sexual abuse and/or sexual abuse since the age of 15, the Australian Bureau of Statistics put it as 2.2 million women, increasing between 2012–2016 for women, but not men (ABS 2021). At the same time as the prevalence of sexual assault is high and may be increasing, the prosecution of sexual assault is low. In Australia, of 26,334 cases of sexual assault reported to the police in 2018, 5,031 were finalized without legal action, 16,574 investigations were not finalized, and 4,731 cases were finalized with legal action begun. In the two years of 2018–2019, 10,132 sexual assault cases went to court. Of those, the defendant was acquitted in 899 cases, 1,647 cases were withdrawn by the prosecution, 3,045 cases transferred courts, and 4,438 (fewer than half) resulted in a guilty verdict. Sexual assault cases in Australia are 'the second-most likely type of offence to be finalised without proceedings being initiated against an offender (19.1%) and have one of the highest rates of cases not being finalised at 30 days compared with other crimes against the person, such as assault or murder' (Evershed 2021, following the reporting in Precel et al. 2019 and Ting et al. 2020). The punishments attached to the guilty verdicts were that 225 were fined, 284 were given community service, and 2,062 were sent to jail (ibid.). Let me repeat, that *for being found guilty of sexual assault, 509 men were given a fine or community service only.*

All of these facts contribute to social messaging about women and about sex: that women are for fucking and then discarding; that if she is *for* fucking then she cannot really have been wronged when she *is* fucked, even when she resists; that if she isn't really wronged, then it can't really be right to punish *him* for what he did. In Catharine MacKinnon's words: 'the law assumes that, because the rapist did not perceive that the woman did not want him, she was not violated. She had sex. Sex itself cannot be an injury. Women have sex every day. Sex makes a woman a woman. Sex is what women are for' (MacKinnon 1989, p. 181).

Let's consider a more mundane type of case than Sophie Tolstoy's, which from many conversations with women over the years I take to be rather common. In this type of case, the male sexual partner shows some interest in and concern for the female sexual partner's pleasure. At least starting to give her some kind of pleasure will be part of how things begin. In some cases this is merely instrumental: he is warming her up so that he can fuck her, and when she is warm (wet) he will proceed in doing what is pleasurable to him, and her arousal will remain unsatiated. Or he does it so he can feel like a successful man, or feel like he is a 'feminist'—it is still ultimately *for him*.

On the Australian version of the television series *Married at First Sight*, the premiere of which in 2021 had nearly a million viewers, one of the 'wives' was asked about the quality of the sex with her 'husband' (the marriages are not real), and said, 'So I really like … Jason always like, when we have sex, he will always make me come as well. And I feel like that's super important' (video clip embedded in Jary 2021). The reactions from the judges and other couples, and the fact that this comment made news headlines, suggest that this is unusual sex.

In other cases, his efforts are intended to be *for her*, and sometimes he is successful in bringing her to orgasm (as we have seen from the orgasm gap, though, he is probably less successful, more frequently, than he thinks). Still, whether her pleasure comes before the penetrative sex or after it, the penetrative sex is the *main act*. The YouGov survey mentioned above reports that 'close to three quarters of straight women (72%) and bisexual women (75%) say they are on the receiving end of vaginal penetration every or most times they have sex, compared to one in three lesbian women (36%)' (Nolsoe and Smith 2022—the data for bisexual women are similar to the data for straight women, which is probably explained by the fact that most partnered bisexual women have opposite-sex partners; see e.g. Pew Research Center 2019). But 70–90% of women don't orgasm from penetrative sex alone (Thompson 2016). The YouGov survey reports 'very little difference in orgasm frequency among those who receive vaginal penetration (16–18%), but far more likelihood of orgasming every time among those who always indulge in clitoral stimulation (58%) than those who don't (35%)' (Nolsoe and Smith 2022). So if he is not providing clitoral stimulation, or she is not providing that for herself, then she will be unlikely to orgasm. The main act ends when he orgasms, and he may choose to drag it out for a very long time (and why wouldn't he, if it feels good?).

If we could record the amount of time in any heterosexual sexual interaction spent exclusively on the man's pleasure as opposed to exclusively on the woman's pleasure (eliminating as neutral any part of the interaction that is genuinely mutually pleasurable in physical terms), my guess is that ordinary heterosexual sex would be heavily skewed toward exclusive male pleasure. By 'genuinely mutually pleasurable', I mean to include time spent giving pleasure that the giver experiences as enjoyable, arousing, exciting, etc., but to exclude time spent giving pleasure (including being used for the other's pleasure, which may be better described as having pleasure taken from you) that the giver experiences as tedious, dissociative, painful (while not also pleasurable, or where that is not specifically desired), 'a job to be done', etc. For men who watch a lot of pornography, the inequality of pleasure in sex may be particularly hard to see, because pornography depicts the woman *enjoying* whatever the man does to her. As MacKinnon puts it: 'Pornography's world of equality is a harmonious and balanced place. Men and women are perfectly complementary and perfectly bipolar. Women's desire to be fucked by men is equal to men's desire to fuck women. All the ways men love to take and violate women, women love to be taken and violated. The women who most love this are most men's equals, the most liberated' (MacKinnon 1985, p. 17; quoted in McGlynn 2016).

Let's call this type of sex 'altruistic sex', in recognition of the fact that it is sex in which women are mostly giving something to men. Of course this is mostly anecdotal rather than scientific, and readers may disagree with me about the likely frequency of this type of sex. (Remember, though, that we are trying to keep in mind *all* of the sex that is happening *everywhere* in the world at this rough time. Many countries are more sexist and less sexually liberated than the liberal democracies that have made substantial advancements in women's equality, so things are likely to be substantially worse there.) Regardless of its frequency, is this mundane type of case a description of altruistic sex being bad for women, or only of altruistic sex being unequal in one respect? Is everything that is unequal thereby bad? That claim seems too strong: a lesbian relationship in which one woman is capable of multiple orgasm and the other woman is not may be unequal in the sense I have described, and yet morally uncomplicated.

But we're not talking about inequality stemming from the mere idiosyncrasies of individuals. The fact that in one specific couple, the woman orgasms more frequently and experiences more sexual pleasure in their sexual interactions in general, because the man experienced childhood sexual abuse which has lasting impacts on his ability to experience sexual pleasure, is not a political issue (although child abuse more generally is a political issue). But the fact that in another specific couple, the woman orgasms rarely and experiences little sexual pleasure in her and her husband's interactions, because their sexual interactions centre around his pleasure, and they centre around his pleasure *because of* what society has taught him about what he is entitled to and what women are for, *is* a political issue, impacting on women as a class. We're talking about patterned differences between women and men in relation to the quantity of sexual pleasure that occurs within sex, because of the types of activities that *constitute* sex as we know it. For the man, (almost) the entire interaction is physically pleasurable. (If he gives her pleasure, and experiences it as 'a job to be done', then it will be *almost all,* and if he doesn't bother to give her pleasure, or he gives her pleasure and experiences it as enjoyable etc., then it will be *all.* Note that it being physically pleasurable is compatible with it being other things psychologically: some men may experience sex as fraught, stressful, disappointing, etc.). For the woman, (almost) the entire interaction may not be pleasurable. Yet women are likely to be reluctant to describe this kind of sex as bad. This is just what sex *is*, at the moment, and from every source we are told sex is good, fun, natural, healthy, enlivening. It would seem awfully 'sex-negative' to admit that most of the sex one has had or is having with a current partner is bad. A 'good woman' today is supposed to be 'sex-positive'. A woman who claims sex itself is bad (rather than only, there is some bad sex) may seem crazy. (MacKinnon's and Dworkin's critiques of sex were met with ridicule, contempt, and incredulity. See documentation in MacKinnon 1995, p. 143–144, fns. 2 and 3, and discussion in the box below.) But from the perspective of a society that has achieved good sex (on which more in Section 3.3 below), this description is more likely to be accepted.

This view of sex as crucial to women's oppression was a more central part of the conversation radical feminists were having during the second wave than the conversation contemporary feminists are having now (see e.g. Koedt 1968; Firestone 1968; Millett [1970] 2000; Atkinson 1970; Atkinson 1974; Leeds Revolutionary Feminist Group 1981). (One recent book that at least asked some critical questions about sex, although mostly did not answer them, is Srinivasan 2021.) Here's Andrea Dworkin, for example, commenting on Kate Millett's (1970) book *Sexual Politics*:

> In 1970 Kate Millett published *Sexual Politics*. In that book she proved to many of us, who would have staked our lives on denying it, that sexual relations—the literature depicting those relations, the psychology posturing to explain those relations, the economic systems that fix the necessities of those relations, the religious systems that seek to control those relations—are political. She showed us that everything that happens to a woman in her life, everything that touches or moulds her, is political. Women who are feminists, that is women who grasped her analysis and saw that it explained much of their real existence in their real lives, have tried to understand, struggle against, and transform the political system called patriarchy, which exploits our labour, predetermines the ownership of our bodies, and diminishes our selfhood from the day we are born. This struggle has no dimension to it which is abstract, it has touched us in every part of our lives. But nowhere has it touched us more vividly or painfully than in that part of our human lives which we call love and sex.
>
> (Dworkin [1974] 2019)

Dworkin goes on in the essay—titled 'Renouncing Sexual "Equality"'—to argue that women having the goal of equality *within* sex as we know it ('correspondence in quantity, degree, value, rank, ability') is utterly insufficient to women's liberation ('others of us do not see equality as a proper, or sufficient, or moral, or honourable final goal'). Equality without justice or freedom, she said, simply means *sameness with the oppressor,* and that is not a feminist goal. Sex as we know it—'altruistic sex', as I have been calling it, which points to the very selflessness women display in permitting it, although both those words, 'altruism' and 'selflessness', have positive connotations that I think are inappropriate given that what they actually point to is women acquiescing in their own oppression—has to change.

An Aside: 'All Sex Is Rape'

What I said in this section amounts to the claim that most, and perhaps even all, heterosexual sex in our current conditions is morally compromised. Two feminist theorists who made similar claims in the 1980s were Catharine MacKinnon and Andrea Dworkin. They were glossed by their critics as claiming that 'all sex is rape'. MacKinnon vehemently repudiates this characterization of her position. In a 1995 article she meticulously catalogued the sources of this characterization of her own work, which include articles in *Playboy* and *Atlantic* (MacKinnon 1995, p. 143, fn. 2), and Dworkin's, which included articles in *Evening Standard*, *Washington Post*, and *Time* (ibid., pp. 143–144, fn. 3). MacKinnon calls these characterizations 'political libel' (ibid., p. 144) and a 'lie' (p. 143; p. 143, fn. 2). She thinks this reaction, from both the political left and the political right, 'reveals the common nerve struck by questioning the presumptive equality of men and women in sex' (ibid., p. 144). She notes that one author even gave this characterization of her work in a law journal, which was later corrected (ibid., p. 143, fn. 2).

If you look at the 1995 paper, you will see that the documentation of this characterization of MacKinnon's and Dworkin's work by MacKinnon is extensive; the relevant footnotes cover the bulk of two pages of the article. The fact that the note documenting characterizations of her own work ends with her noting that a correction was published, and the note documenting characterizations of Dworkin's work ends with her noting that the research department for *Time* magazine were 'unable to point to a single example that substantiated' their claim (ibid., p. 144, fn. 3), leave the strong impression that it is *absolutely not* either MacKinnon's nor Dworkin's view that all sex is rape. MacKinnon writes 'It is, of course, difficult to provide citations to pages on which something is not said', but directs readers interested in 'Discussions of sexuality in the context of an analysis of gender inequality' in her work to chapter 9, 'Rape: On Coercion and Consent', in her 1989 book (ibid., p. 143, fn. 2).

This vehement repudiation is somewhat puzzling. In Chapter 7, 'Sexuality', in the same book, MacKinnon criticizes feminists who mark rape off as distinct from sex, 'conceiving rape as violence, not sex' (MacKinnon 1989, p. 134). If a man rapes a woman, and that's a matter of violence rather than a matter of sex, we end up stuck facing the question: why didn't he just hit her? (ibid.). She says that instead, 'violence is sex when it is practiced as sex' (ibid.). And she goes on, 'To say rape is violence not sex preserves the "sex is good" norm by simply distinguishing forced sex as "not sex," whether it means sex to the perpetrator or even, later, to the victim, who has difficulty experiencing sex without reexperiencing the rape' (ibid., p. 135). Later she says that the force men use against women can be invisible because of the way that pornography constructs the idea that 'women really want what men want from women', which *makes rape sex*' (ibid., p. 141, my emphasis). She says:

> Compare victims' reports of rape with women's reports of sex. They look a lot alike. Compare victims' reports of rape with what pornography says is sex. They look a lot alike. In this light, the major distinction between intercourse (normal) and rape (abnormal) is that the normal happens so often that one cannot get anyone to see anything wrong with it.
> (MacKinnon 1989, p. 146, notes omitted)

MacKinnon is explicit about the distinction between rape and sex: 'Rape and intercourse are not authoritatively separated by any difference between the physical acts or amount of force involved but only legally, by a standard that centers on the man's interpretation of the encounter' (ibid., p. 150).

But this is a man who has been watching pornography, and in a legal system with a 'passive', 'acquiescent' standard for consent (ibid.). This means there is a difference, but it's not a difference that feminists should care about. For what do feminists care of what a man's perspective on their mistreatment happens to be? (There's a sophisticated presentation of this difference in perspective in the 2022 Netflix series *Anatomy of a Scandal*, exploring the ways that female passivity and acquiescence can come together with male privilege and entitlement in order to create a sexual interaction in which the parties have very different views about what happened: 'it was spontaneous', 'my sense of it was that the encounter fell short of her romantic expectations'; vs. 'he assaulted me', 'he called her a "prick-tease" ... he raped her'—see episode 6.)

It is worth quoting MacKinnon in full on the point that women's sexuality exists in a context of terror, a context which surely undermines consent:

> Given the effects of learning sexuality through force or pressure or imposition; given the constant roulette of sexual violence; given the daily sexualization of every aspect of a woman's presence—for a woman to be sexualized means constant humiliation or threat of it, being invisible as a human being and center stage as a sex object, low pay, and being a target for assault or being assaulted. Given that this is the situation of all women, that one never knows for sure that one is not next on the list of victims until the moment one dies (and then, who knows?) it does not seem exaggerated to say that women are sexual, meaning that women exist, in a context of terror.
>
> (MacKinnon 1995, p. 151)

If women's consent to sex is undermined by the fact that she exists in a context of terror; if the distinction between sex and rape is only the man's perspective on it; if it is wrong to mark off violence as 'not sex'; then what, exactly, is the point of insisting that it is *false* that 'all sex is rape'?

Perhaps this was a political (i.e. strategic) denial rather than an academic one, for perhaps neither Dworkin nor MacKinnon foresaw their ideas being shared so widely, and perhaps they knew that the general public *does* mark off violence as 'not sex', so that to claim 'all sex is rape' cannot be understood except in a way that makes it clearly false. For obviously, not all sex *involves physical violence,* in the sense of the sex being forced, and the sex involving battery of the woman. Perhaps it was too difficult to try to communicate, to the general public, that the *conditions* under which women appear to 'choose' sex are conditions which compromise her choice.

MacKinnon asks, for example, 'On the fear side, if a woman has ever been beaten in a relationship, even if "only once," what does that do to her everyday interactions, or her sexual interactions, with that man? With other men?' (ibid., p. 150).

Feminists do not think that what decides rape is a man's interpretation of the encounter, and nor do we think that rape must involve physical brutality. If certain conditions can nullify consent, and sex without consent is rape, then all the feminist needs to do to establish that 'all sex is rape' is to establish that those conditions obtain for all sex. If consent is the wrong standard, then her task may be even easier. The claim that 'all sex is rape' (which really means, all *heterosexual* sex is rape, and perhaps also the homosexual sex that imitates it) is back on the table for serious feminist consideration.

3   A Future without Sex Hierarchy

How might society might be transformed, so that there is no social hierarchy of male over female? And do commercial and altruistic/hierarchical sex need to change in order to bring that society about?

3.1   Sex and Sex Hierarchy

From this point on, we need a way to distinguish, when talking about altruistic sex, what women submit to, as opposed to what men subject women to. I personally wouldn't mind just using 'sex' without qualification, given that this *is* sex as we know it, but I suspect that this would be confusing when it comes to the question of change. If 'sex' just is a social practice that is morally compromised, then feminists should be *sex abolitionists*, whereas if 'sex' covers all the possibilities for sexual interaction, including in a feminist future, then feminists need only target specific forms of sex. So I'll now introduce the term '**hierarchical sex**' as the corollary of 'altruistic sex': men have, or subject women to, hierarchical sex; women have, or give, altruistic sex.

What *exactly* is it that's bad about women having altruistic sex, men having hierarchical sex (which is just a more precise way of saying, what is bad about men and women having sex as we know it)? I have mentioned inequality of pleasure, instrumentalization, and lack of negative freedom—although not under that name. Most of the time spent in heterosexual sex is spent on the man's pleasure, not the woman's. But the unequal distribution of pleasure is just one way in which sex as we know it is bad. MacKinnon makes this point: 'As if pleasure and how to get it, rather than dominance and how to end it, is the "overall" issue sexuality presents feminism' (MacKinnon 1989, p. 135). Heterosexual sex is instrumentalizing: the man treats the woman's body, the woman herself, as an instrument to achieving his pleasure. As one porn actor memorably put it, 'I used to say it's like borrowing somebody's body to masturbate with' (Wagoner 2012, quoted in Lawford-Smith 2022a, p. 230, fn. 32). We may permissibly instrumentalize a person so long as we *also* treat them as an 'end in themselves', but Tolstoy quite clearly did not treat Sophie as an end in herself; many men do not treat the women they have sex with as ends in themselves, which is to say, as persons who are *for themselves*. We might also argue that sexual instrumentalization is permissible when it is mutual and reciprocal, but again it was not in the Tolstoys' case; it is not in the case of much of the sex that is currently had. Leo sexually instrumentalized Sophie, and not the other way around. Andrea Dworkin's first husband sexually instrumentalized Dworkin, and not the other way around (Dworkin 1991).

Finally, women in heterosexual partnerships often lack *freedom from* sex. This is a violation of their negative freedom, their right to be free from violations of their bodily integrity. Leo fucked Sophie whenever he liked. Given that the law did not recognize rape within marriage until recently, and still does not in some countries, many men now and throughout history are likely to have acted—*be acting*—as Leo did, or as Dworkin's first husband did, and with impunity. (How this plays out in the case of arranged marriages with young girls is told vividly in Neel Mukherjee's 2014 novel *The Lives of Others*.) The failure to adequately prosecute rape, even in progressive countries, contributes to this violation of negative freedom. This is domination in the **republican** sense of the term: men having the ability to *arbitrarily inflict* sex on women, most likely without any consequence. (MacKinnon also talks about 'dominance' in relation to sex, but she means something different by it: something like the fact that men occupy the superior position in the socially constructed hierarchy that is, on her view, both sex and gender.)

SUMMARY

Sex as we know it is bad along at least three dimensions of (dis)value: it contains an unequal distribution of pleasure; it is instrumentalizing (and the fact that it contains an unequal distribution of pleasure is a clue to its being instrumentalizing); and it violates negative freedom, i.e. it is dominating in the republican sense.

3.2   The Sex Industry, Sex, and Sex Hierarchy

Women's oppression has had, and still has, her sexual availability to men—whether to one man or to many men—as a core component. I do not think it is the whole story of her oppression, but it is a substantial part of it (cf. MacKinnon 1989). The sexual exploitation of women is a thousands of years old part of human history. Feminist historians have suggested that when hunter-gatherer tribes first began to roam and conquer, they would kill the men and enslave the women, assimilating the women into the conquering tribe through rape and impregnation (Gerda Lerner described women as submitting for the sake of their children—Lerner 1986, p. 47). Later, an 'exchange in women' was driven by the need for labour sparked by the agricultural revolution, which women could supply by reproducing (creating new workers) (ibid., p. 52). Throughout history, up until fairly recently in some progressive countries, and still ongoing in less progressive countries today, women have been sexual resources for men. Sexual access to a woman was considered by men a benefit of marriage. There was no crime of rape within marriage.

There is still a social practice, in some parts of the world (and in some subcultures within progressive countries), of child brides, of bride prices, of female genital mutilation, of honour killings related to rape, of acid attacks (which are usually connected to sexual or romantic rejection). There is still trafficking in women across international and state borders for the purposes of sexual slavery. There are still millions, if not billions, of women who are economically dependent on their husbands, who are not in a position to deny him when he demands sex, or to leave him and deny it permanently. There are still husbands who beat and rape their wives, and some who also beat and rape their daughters (more recently, there was a sharp increase in domestic violence as a result of stay-at-home orders during the COVID-19 pandemic, see discussion in Lawford-Smith 2022b, section 2.1).

Where men's stereotypes about women used to divide women into the 'Madonnas' and the 'whores' (and in some cases still do, see e.g. Bareket et al. 2018), pornography has now largely succeeded in reconciling the two—a good woman should also be a whore (Barry 1979, and see discussion in Section 2.2.2 above). That he can pay to fuck a woman is just an extension of the idea that a woman is for fucking by him. If he cannot get it for free then he must be able to buy it; that he could simply not have it is inconceivable. That we can watch men who have been paid to do it fucking women who have been paid to allow it is just an extension of the idea that this is an ordinary thing men do to women, that it is ordinary to do it and ordinary to watch it being done. It is ordinary that she is a sexual object, to be manipulated at will; it is ordinary that she will pretend to like everything that is being done to her, as painful and as degrading as it may be. That men will not know it is pretending. When man apprehends woman as a tool of enjoyment, he may struggle to recognize her full humanity—that she is *for herself,* not *for use by him.*

As Margaret Baldwin put it, 'feminism's … primary goal [has been] to be *understood* as deserving of a respected human life, whatever "human" comes to mean once women are considered instances of the species' (Baldwin 1992, p. 56). Or in Richard Rorty, talking about MacKinnon: 'Mackinnon's central point, as I read her, is that 'a woman' is not yet the name of a way of being human—not yet the name of a moral identity, but, at most, the name of a disability' (Rorty 1991, p. 4).

About prostitution, Debra Satz made the argument that because of background facts about sex inequality, the existence of a market in women's sexual labour is wrongful (Satz 2010, ch. 4). Prostitution is wrongful *because* 'the sale of women's sexual labour reinforces broad patterns of sex inequality' ibid., (p. 135). (Satz is noncommittal, however, on which policy response is best in light of that wrongfulness: she does not commit to **asymmetric criminalization**). She says that prostitution causes harm to third parties, namely 'the class of women' (ibid., p. 136). Satz thinks prostitution positions women as inferior, because it is a practice in which the women involved *are* servants to male desire (ibid., p. 147). The messaging of prostitution is not just about women who do sex work, it is about all women (although she notes that this is an empirical claim and should be tested empirically—ibid., pp. 147–148).

Satz thinks that 'the most plausible account of prostitution's wrongness turns on its relationship to the pervasive social inequality between men and women' (ibid., p. 136). Although her focus in the chapter is prostitution and not pornography, she comments that the relationship exists for both: 'I believe that it is a plausible hypothesis that prostitution, along with related practices such as pornography, makes an important contribution to women's inferior social status' (ibid., p. 146); and 'Prostitution, like pornography, is not easily separated from the larger surrounding culture that marginalizes, stereotypes, and stigmatizes women' (ibid., p. 148). She does not talk about altruistic sex, because her focus in the book is on markets (the book is called *Why Some Things Should Not Be For Sale*). But there is no reason why the same argument couldn't be made, albeit with different implications for what we should do about it.

But for prostitution and pornography, altruistic/hierarchical sex might get better on its own, but with them in the mix, I think there is little chance of that. (Pornography plays a bigger role than prostitution, simply because it is more widely accessed; but the widespread knowledge that prostitution exists, and is often supported in at least some forms by the state, contributes to sexist hierarchy even in men who do not themselves buy sex, merely because they could and they know that they could and that other men do). Interestingly, this gives even 'sex-positive' feminists a reason to be critical of commercial sex, because commercial sex provides an obstacle to the improvement of sex.

SUMMARY

Hierarchical sex is a crucial component of sex hierarchy (the hierarchy of the sexes) more generally. Prostitution and pornography both make a significant contribution to keeping sex hierarchy in place. It is unlikely that women's liberation can be achieved without a substantial change to both commercial sex and to altruistic/hierarchical sex.

3.3 The Sex Equality Utopia

What does sex look like in a world where there is sex equality? That would be a world where men see women as full human persons. Women are not *for men*: not for men to fuck; not to bear men's children; not for men to gaze upon and find beautiful; not to provide men with personal service, sexual service, and ego service, as wives, girlfriends, mistresses (Frye 1983, pp. 9–10). That doesn't mean there are no sexual or romantic relationships between men and women, but it does mean that when there are, they are not marked by inequality in the way they tend to be now. We have already considered sexual inequality, but we haven't talked about the fact that women still tend to take a greater share of the domestic burdens of housework and childcare (see e.g. ONS 2016), or that women spend considerably more time and money on beauty services and clothing, or that advertising in many countries presents women as beautiful and sexual in order to sell products to both women and men. In a world where we have achieved sex equality, a woman can be just as unattractive, badly dressed, and out of shape as a man without that compromising how seriously she is taken at work (consider Mary Beard's comments on being 58 and looking it on television—Day 2013). A lesbian will not be thought of as just a person who hasn't met the right man yet. A girl who asserts herself will not be considered 'bossy', a woman who is supremely confident in her abilities will not be considered as someone who does not 'know her place'. There will be no violent retaliation when a woman rejects a man's sexual or romantic advances, for men will be used to sexual and romantic rejection and will not see it as the denial of something that they are entitled to. Women will have economic independence, so that they are never stuck with men who control them, whether violent pimps or violent partners.

It is unimaginable that in a world where we have achieved sex equality, there is yet still a widespread social practice of watching, for entertainment, men fuck women in dominating, degrading, painful, unequal ways. It is unimaginable that there are women available for men to pay for the sexual use of. Most of the social problems that channelled women into sex work will have resolved as **sex hierarchy** was eliminated, and so there will be few (if any) women interested in doing sex work, as well as few (if any) men interested in paying for sex. (Although, interestingly, the more that it is the case that women have better options and so wouldn't choose sex work, the more that it is the case that a man might possibly buy sex ethically, for the risk of the interaction decreases substantially—see further discussion in Section 4.) And it is unimaginable that men have such unequal sex with women, for women simply would not tolerate it.

Is this just a utopia, one that a feminist novelist more talented than me could fill in the details of, and yet which is not accessible to us from the world we're in? Or are there interventions we could make on our social world, to make it the case that one day, we are in the world without sex hierarchy? Below, I suggest two interventions that might take us there, first a legal intervention against commercial sex, and second a social movement against altruistic/hierarchical sex.

3.4   Legal Intervention: Abolition/Reset for Commercial Sex

Above I said that in a world where we have achieved sex equality, it is unimaginable that there are women available for men to pay for the sexual use of. One legal intervention against prostitution that is well-worked out and has been implemented by some countries is asymmetric criminalization, or the 'Nordic Model'. This intervention criminalizes the buyers of sex, but not the sellers (see further discussion, and references, in Lawford-Smith 2022a, ch. 4). Because there has been considerable discussion of the interventions we might make on prostitution, that will not be my focus here. I'll focus, instead, on pornography. I think we should *abolish* prostitution (with asymmetric criminalization), and *reset* pornography.

Before we begin, a clarification. Earlier I said that not all prostitution is pornography, but almost all pornography is prostitution. That gives us a wider category, prostitution, and a mostly overlapping sub-category, pornography. I have been talking about prostitution and pornography under the heading 'commercial sex'. But this is not entirely accurate. *Most* pornography is commercial sex, the difference between prostitution and pornography being only whether the sex is bought for one man to have, or for one man to have *and* many men to watch. But not *all* pornography is commercial sex: some is amateur and uploaded to free websites. We can resolve this in one of two ways. The first is to say that these amateur contributions are still part of the commercial sex industry even though they are not paid. We could think of them like we think of unpaid internships and volunteering in other industries. The second is to deny that these contributions are in fact part of the commercial sex industry, and to put them into the category of 'culture'—imitation of an industry, influence of an industry through popular culture. But this seems to me less desirable, given that amateur pornography is likely to function as a gateway into commercial pornography, for both its sex workers and its consumers. So when I talk about the commercial sex industry I will mean to refer to all the major corporations and small businesses as well as all the amateurs producing pornography for others' consumption.

With that resolved, the main claim I want to defend now is that when it comes to pornography, things have *gone too far*, and that due to the specific features of this industry and its relationship to its consumers, the intervention we should make is to *reset*, which means going back to basics, and allowing the process to repeat but with a clearer sense of where the line for 'too far' is for next time around. Because both prostitution and pornography exist in the public sphere, as industries, it is appropriate to use the tools of law and policy, if needed, to intervene on them. (It is inappropriate, with a few exceptions, to use those tools to intervene on altruistic/hierarchical sex, which happens in the private sphere—the sphere we generally consider to be not the state's business.)

Let me make this general case for this kind of intervention in terms of something other than pornography, so we can see whether it has independent plausibility in at least some cases, and then we can think more about whether it's the right intervention for pornography specifically. This example will share a crucial feature with pornography, which is the way that the dynamics of capitalism push things toward ever greater extremes. That example is the consumption of food.

Let's start by considering very modest diets that don't involve much variety or novelty. Poorer families living in rural parts of Nigeria eat a lot of *fufu*, which is pounded yam (a kind of sweet potato). Poorer families living in rural parts of China eat a lot of rice, or rice porridge. These are plain, filling, foods. They do not set our tastebuds singing and delight our senses; there is not much of an aesthetic to the food. There are not many different ways to present a bowl of rice or mashed sweet potato. The same might be true for wealthier people in times of conflict or natural disaster—food rationing during the Second World War, for example, significantly reduced the range of foods available for consumption. People got by. But people are generally happier when there is salt, when there is not just grinding repetition.

Is something lost in these cases, relative to counterfactuals (whether historical or only hypothetical) where there is more

variety and more novelty? Perhaps; it depends on how heavily pleasure features in your conception of the good. Food—more precisely,
eating—can be a pleasurable experience. I say 'can be' because it
can be a lot of other things instead, like boring, unpleasant, stressful, anxiety-inducing, and more. Consider eating a very large but
undressed salad; eating coriander when you have the genetic condition that makes it taste like soap; eating when you have an eating disorder; eating something messy when you are in sophisticated
company. But if you have the money and the leisure time to enjoy
varied, novel, and/or high-quality food, and then you lose the
option to do that, you may have lost something that contributes to
your living a good life. Perhaps one pleasure can be replaced with
another, so this could be more than fully compensated by listening
to wonderful music, but perhaps different ways of getting pleasure
are distinctive, or provide a higher quality of pleasure relative to
specific people's tastes. I will assume that even if pleasure features
in our conception of the good life, it is to some extent multiply
realizable; but that some pleasures take work (e.g. fully appreciat-
ing classical music) and once that work has been done, it isn't easy
to simply exchange one form of pleasure for another. Moving from
being an epicure (a 'foodie') to being a music-lover isn't simple if
you don't know anything about music.

Now suppose, *contra fact*, that food was roughly the same for
everyone everywhere, and then slowly became more elaborate in
terms of variety, novelty, and quality. Suppose at first it was just
boiled potatoes, and then it was boiled potatoes with butter and
salt and pepper, and then it was mashed potatoes with cream as
a side to a steak that is nice enough but perhaps a bit bland and a
bit tough, and then it was dauphinoise potatoes with fresh thyme
alongside a perfectly seared wagyu beef ribeye steak, and so on,
and so on. People's tastes in food develop and they become more
discerning and more demanding; this demand pushes chefs, restau-
rateurs, and producers, to more creativity. And suppose (although
it shouldn't take much imagination, because it is in fact the case)
that as part of this increasing elaborateness, ethical issues began to
emerge. Animals being raised for meat and dairy products are not
treated well or are kept in miserable conditions; crops that could
be grown sustainably on a slower timeline are instead being grown
unsustainably in a way that is bad for the land; workers are being
exploited; excesses of carbon are being emitted in the transporta-
tion of products so that exotic items from faraway countries can
be consumed; there is cutthroat rivalry between businesses that is

damaging to the business-owners' and workers' mental health; certain ingredients are being stolen or appropriated from indigenous peoples' protected lands without adequate consultation or remuneration; and so on. And this is where we find ourselves, in a situation where we have developed an elaborate food culture, and where that culture is fun, and interesting, and sophisticated, and gives a lot of people pleasure and enjoyment, and yet which also involves a lot of harm to a number of different stakeholders. What's our move?

One obvious approach is regulation—rather than moving to 'abolish the food industry' we could try to introduce laws and policies that would ensure the many injustices involved in the food industry would be eliminated, or at least very much reduced. And indeed, this is what we have actually done about food, for example in moving from caged chickens to free-range chickens in the production of eggs, or putting tariffs on international imports that have the function of incentivizing buying local. We think it's possible to reduce or eliminate injustice *without* making a direct intervention on the extravagance of food culture itself. But it's clear that there are some sorts of harms that we would want to eliminate even if that came at the cost of a reduction in the variety, novelty, and/or quality of food. If indigenous communities refused permission for certain ingredients grown in protected areas to be used then we might just concede doing without those ingredients. If there was no ethical way to produce particular products, such as foie gras—goose liver pâté, ordinarily produced by force-feeding geese (although cf. Baker 2015)—we might accept not having foie gras anymore.

My worry about regulation in the case of pornography is that it cannot stem the tide *given* the constant demand for novelty, which ratchets up the extremity of what is done to pornography's sex workers (see e.g. detail in Dines 2010; and discussion in Lawford-Smith 2022a, ch. 4). When people want to eat eggs, there is nothing about the eggs themselves that dictates whether they are produced by caged chickens or free-range chickens, chickens fed on unsustainable feed or on organic grain. So we can regulate the egg industry without changing the end product, which is eggs. The same is not true for pornography. We can regulate *who* can do sex work (e.g. certification of age), what needs to be in place for them to do so (e.g. mental health checks, vulnerability checks), and we can ban specific acts (e.g. acts that would count as assault or torture outside of a sexual context). But that would soon hit a ceiling in terms of novelty and variety. If men treat women, or categories of women like 'Latino women' or 'big beautiful women', as interchangeable, then it will not satisfy the desire for novelty for the pornography to simply feature the same things being done to a different individual woman. If the demand for novelty is strong enough, which I think we have ample evidence that it is (see e.g. Wilson 2014), then pornography will eventually begin to violate those regulations, because it would be profitable for it to do so even with the risk of legal sanction. So there is no way to keep producing pornography, given current tastes and desires (and addictions), while regulating away the relevant harms of the industry both to the women selling sex within it, and to all women because of its existence.

Aside from merely regulating specific aspects of the pornography industry, the obvious question for this proposal is why we should *reset*, going all the way back to zero (or back to basics), rather than to find where the line is that eliminates or sufficiently reduces harm and then scale back to exactly that. The answer, again, is demand: that the specific way pornography works, in terms of novelty and addiction, is likely to drive the industry well past that line regardless of regulation. If enough money can be made, porn creators will simply accept the risk of legal sanction as the cost of doing business; and there will be a thriving black market where it is even harder to protect those involved from harm. Once we reset, there is less harm to the women working in the sex industry, but there is no qualitative difference in the pleasure available to men: from a baseline of modesty, a flash of ankle is thrilling. The cost of course is to the highly addicted men who have already had their preferences ratcheted way up, who will then have lost a source of pleasure. Feminists might find it hard to sympathize with this man, but philosophers can take seriously the abstract issue of taking something away from people that is pleasurable to them (in the most literal sense).

The loss of pleasure to the porn addict of porn being abolished for some period of time seems to be different in important respects to the loss of pleasure to the music lover or the epicure were music or food to be abolished. There is cultivation of taste, and there is a lot of learning, involved in coming to have a sophisticated appreciation of music and food. Some have made a distinction between 'higher order' and 'lower order' pleasures, where things like the mastery of a difficult musical instrument like the piano would count as a higher order pleasure and watching reality television would count as a lower order pleasure. On this taxonomy, watching porn is certainly a lower order pleasure. (Merely wanting to see something *new* is not the same thing as having cultivated a taste for something that not everyone appreciates, or having achieved mastery of/in something difficult.) Others have objected that such a taxonomy is elitist, that there aren't better and worse pleasures, there are just people with different tastes and preferences, doing what brings pleasure to them. If we agreed with this, then porn would be in with everything else, and the question would be only whether we could justify removing a form of pleasure, which would be to reduce the option sets of those previously engaging with it. If watching porn were *only* bad for the man watching it, then we'd be in the ballpark of discussions about banning cigarettes, or junk food. But because it's also bad for the sex workers used in its creation, we're in the ballpark of discussions about banning contract pregnancy, or sweatshops. Yes, some people get pleasure out of the products of those industries—the baby, the cheap sneakers—but the pleasure is not sufficient to justify the harm, especially when there are other pleasures available to take their place.

One disanalogy between food and sex (commercial and otherwise) in making the case for a 'reset' is that without food we will eventually die (and quickly: with water, within two months; without, within two weeks), whereas without sex we would not, and indeed are unlikely to experience negative health impacts of any kind. Food is a basic need, sex is not (despite a large amount of propaganda claiming that it is). So when we 'reset' with food, we can't go all the way to zero and see how long that lasts, rather we can only go back to basics, things that are cheap, nutritious, and easy to produce, not to mention easy on the environment. We could get rid of cafés and restaurants, close supermarkets, and have simple ingredients available at farmer's markets and small corner stores stocking local, sustainable produce. People adapt—after a while, the simple approach to food, which is after all currently many people's actual approach to food, will seem perfectly normal. With sex we *can* go all the way to zero, which is no altruistic/hierarchical sex, no prostitution, and no pornography (which need not mean no sexual pleasure at all—only no interpersonal sexual interactions).

Another disanalogy is that food is an inanimate good, which may or may not have had human involvement at various points in its lifecycle, from the growth of raw ingredients, through refinement/production/creation, to the end consumer. But the selling of sex cannot be separated from the woman who sells it; despite the attempts to conceive of body and mind separately and frame her as selling 'sex' (product) or 'sexual services' (service), she is selling the use of *herself,* for she is selling the use of her body, and her body *is* herself (Ekman 2013). What is sold is quintessentially animate.

A 'reset' is abolitionist only in the short- to medium-term. Men need to stop being allowed to buy sex without consequence *today,* and we will not shift the relations between the sexes and achieve women's liberation until there has been a reconceptualization of women—particularly, what women are *for,* of sex, and of male sexual entitlement. That is likely to take a long time to fully achieve, so that means we are unlikely to be in a position to reintroduce prostitution in any form for a long time. (What counts as a 'long time'? Let's say a hundred years.) If men are to stop *buying* hierarchical sex, and *having* hierarchical sex, then the propaganda *for* that kind of sex needs to stop, too. (Not to mention that if they cannot buy it, then it follows that it cannot be bought and filmed.) In resetting pornography, we eliminate much of the harm of the current industry. Perhaps there is more latitude for starting again sooner with pornography, given that there are possibilities for producing pornography that do not involve prostitution (in particular, animations and amateur pornography). But we would have to keep an eye on the role that the 'new' pornography plays in cultural messaging about sex, and the relations between the sexes. If we can expect the same content to develop, with the same sexist ideals, then we would be better off abolishing both for the medium term, and perhaps that would end up meaning abolishing them permanently. For once men come to see women as fully human, the social practices of pornography and prostitution may appear as morally repugnant as slavery appears to us today.

SUMMARY

In summary, we can think of pornography as *telling men how to treat women,* and prostitution and non-commercial sex as *where they enact that treatment.* Pornography is not the cause: there was prostitution and hierarchical sex long before there was film, or even print. But there are feedback loops between pornography now and sex now. If we knock out pornography we knock out the major source of propaganda for hierarchical sex, and if we knock out prostitution we knock out men's unconditional sexual access to women. To prevent harm to women and advance social equality, it is permissible to use law and policy as tools to knock out both.

3.5   Social Intervention: (Altruistic/Hierarchical) Sex Strike

The idea of a 'sex strike' goes back at least to *Lysistrata*, written by Aristophanes and thought to be first performed in 411 BCE (adapted more recently as Spike Lee's *Chi-Raq*, 2015). But the sex strike in *Lysistrata* was a collective action undertaken by women in order to end the Peloponnesian War, using sex as a means of controlling men. In this sense it upholds, rather than challenges, the sexual status quo. The 'reset' I am proposing is a kind of sex strike, but it does not use sex as a means of control, rather it seeks to *eliminate* altruistic/hierarchical sex (sex as we know it) as a means to better sex. It is less like workers striking until they get better pay, and more like a consumer boycott of sweatshop sneakers in order to bring about the supply of locally made, high-quality, sustainably produced sneakers.

The 'ratcheting up' dynamics and the way they lead inevitably to the extreme (mis)treatment of women are specific to pornography, so what justifies the 'reset' when it comes to altruistic/hierarchical sex? With altruistic sex, it is a way to create a firm break with sex as we know it and sex as it could be. We stop doing *that*, and at some point we start doing *this other thing* instead. A break, rather than a continuation, also helps to reduce the role of sex in our **conception of the good**. By not having it, we all learn that we are perfectly fine without it. Nothing bad happens. A man's interactions with women are no longer tinted by the thought that he might be able to fuck her. He no longer shows an interest in her that she mistakes for something else, and is deceived by: the male teacher's interest in the female student is because he wants to teach her; the male boss's interest in his female employee is because he wants to make the best use of her talents. For those who think this is infeasible, it's easy to show they are wrong: there are many examples of men, both historically and today, who have chosen celibacy as a matter of pursuing their faith, or for other reasons. And the sex reset isn't even *real* or *permanent* celibacy. There can still be sexual pleasure, just self-administered; and there can still be sex, just not for a while (and with a transformation in meaning).

A reset for sex requires a reset for prostitution (which is achieved by the stronger intervention of abolition). If a man should not *have* hierarchical sex, because of how it positions women (both literally and figuratively), then it doesn't matter whether he pays for it or gets it for free. Paying for it is likely to be worse from the perspective of changing the social meaning of sex, because in a commercial interaction there is absolutely no reason for him to consider her perspective, her comfort, or her pleasure. It reinforces for him that sex is something that he gets to do *to* a woman (even if some of the things he likes to do or is at least willing to do during non-commercial sex are intended to be enjoyable for her).

So we have three things. We have sex as we know it. We have the representation of sex, made cartoonish in a reflection of who is making it and what they imagine their audience want. And we have the sale of sex, where what is bought is somewhere in between sex as we know it and sex as it is propagandized to be. That is, we have sex, prostitution, and pornography. To the extent that pornography is functioning as sex education, we have feedback loops between the three: boys and men start to act out, in sex as we know it, what they see in pornography; and pornography becomes even more cartoonish in its attempt to create a fantasy that is distinct from men's realities (a fantasy which is aspirational, which will sell products).

When things are a certain way, it can be hard to imagine them as very different. That's part of why science-fiction and fantasy, as genres of books, film, and television, are so intriguing: we get a glimpse into a world that is very different from ours, and yet that usually has *us* in it, in some form. Let us try to imagine things as very different when it comes to sex. This creates a comparison by which we can judge our current circumstances, rather than simply accept them as the air we breathe.

First of all, there could be *no sex*. For one example, we could be part of a society that considers it disgusting for individuals to have sexual contact with each other. Sexual *pleasure*, in the sense that our bodies are capable of experiencing arousal and orgasm, could be an entirely private matter, something that individuals did for themselves when the mood struck them. That wouldn't be as often as it is now, because external stimuli—billboards, magazines, television shows, and more—would be de-sexualized. In such a society, there might just be the humans that exist, until the last one dies; because without sex, there is no procreation. Alternatively, this society may have separated sex from procreation, for example pairing sperm and egg in the lab and growing babies in synthetic wombs (as proposed in Firestone 1970). Thinking about a society like this helps to reveal the *primacy* of sex in our current conceptions of the good, and to show that this primacy may be *contingent* rather than necessary. We could have very different attitudes to sex and sexual pleasure, our visual and auditory environment could be organized very differently to reduce what is effectively propaganda *for* sex as we know it, and our conceptions of the good might treat other things as valuable, fulfilling, necessary, rather than sex (such a society is imagined in Charlotte Perkins Gilman's women-only utopia *Herland*—Gilman [1915] 1979).

Second of all, there might be some sexual contact between individuals, but not remotely 'to the current script', which is largely heterosexual and almost entirely male-centred. Instead of penis-in-vagina intercourse that is driven by what the man wants to be doing (or thinks he should want to be doing, because he has gorged himself on that script by watching excesses of mainstream pornography), sexual contact could be a matter of highly specific acts tailored to what feels most pleasurable to each individual. This may not sound as radical as it actually is: there are many women who do not experience pleasure from penetrative sex, so this may mean *no penetrative sex, ever* for those women (as mentioned already, between 70% and 90% of women cannot achieve orgasm through penetration alone—Thompson 2016). 'Sex' may come to mean simply giving and receiving pleasure—what we now think of as 'mere' foreplay, or 'mere' fooling around. Dworkin defends this view:

> I suggest to you that transformation of the male sexual model under which we now all labour and love begins where there is a congruence, not a separation, a congruence of feeling and erotic interest. That it begins in what we do know about female sexuality as distinct from male. Clitoral touch and sensitivity. Multiple orgasms. Erotic sensitivity all over the body, which needn't and shouldn't be localised or contained genitally. In tenderness, in self-respect, and in absolute mutual respect. For men, I suspect this transformation begins in the place they most dread, that is, in a limp penis. I think that men will have to give up their precious erections, and begin to make love as women do together. I am saying that men will have to renounce their phallocentric personalities, and the privileges and powers given to them at birth as a consequence of their anatomy. That they will have to excise everything in them that they now value as distinctively male. No reform or matching of orgasms will accomplish this.

(Dworkin [1974] 2019)

Mutual masturbation, and oral sex, may come to have primacy in what is meant by 'sex'. Even in the case where women do enjoy penetrative sex, things might be very different to how they are now. What she enjoys *some of* at a specific stage in the process of receiving pleasure might not be remotely sufficient to what he would want for his own pleasure, and would expect to be permitted according to current sexual scripts. (In one of the alternative worlds imagined in Joanna Russ's *The Female Man*, a human male is bred from chimpanzee genes and hybridized with technology to create a kind of sexual house pet. There is penetrative sex, and it is mutual/reciprocal, but it is exactly as necessary to give both parties pleasure, and it is entirely controlled by the woman—see esp. Russ [1975] 2010, pp. 189–193.)

Thirdly, although necessarily a part of the second scenario just described, there might be vast differences in confidence, sexual literacy, and passivity, as compared with sex as we know it. If people know what feels pleasurable to them then they will be in a good position to communicate that to sexual partners. If women are confident, then they will be *able* to tell their sexual partners what they want, able to stop things they don't like, and direct things that aren't quite right to be better. The comedian Pete Davidson captures this difference in sexual confidence and communication nicely in his 2020 Netflix stand-up special:

> Girls should tell guys how to make them come. ... I know you don't want to hurt the guy's feelings but, it won't, it doesn't. We could be mid-fuck, and you could be like 'I hate this', and we'll be like 'oh, how's this? Good?' Okay, forgotten, didn't even happen. You should just tell the guy. I guess guy stuff is very self-explanatory ... But yeah, you should just tell the guy. Like I said, guy stuff is very self-explanatory, but if someone ever pulled my pants down and just started like punching my dick, I wouldn't be like 'Ah fuck! I hope she figures it out! Ow, ow, ow, ow, ow, ow ... there's more ...' I would be like, 'Who sent you? What is this? Is this an assassination attempt?'
>
> (Davidson 2020)

If women are not socialized into passivity, or are able to break themselves out of it, then they won't have sex out of politeness, they won't go along with things that don't feel good, and they won't pretend. Their list of reasons for having sex, other than for pleasure or closeness, will dramatically reduce.

In these imaginings, there is *less sex*, the *meaning of 'sex' has changed* (no longer centring penetration), and *women are in control* of the sex that they have. Sex is not something that is *done to them for the benefit of a man*, not something that they endure or passively accept, but something that they actively desire and direct (or simply do not have). The social meaning of sex has changed. Arguably it could not have changed in these ways without a great deal of change outside of sex, first in the relations between the sexes (for we are imagining women who *know* they are not 'for' sex with men, women who are confident and in control), and second in the social institutions relating to sex—the hyper-sexualization of everything exacerbated by the dynamics of capitalism, and the sex industry, which facilitates male sexual entitlement by allowing him to buy what he cannot gain access to 'for free', and which functions as propaganda for sex as we know it and for sexist hierarchy.

I said earlier that it is appropriate to use the tools of law and policy to intervene on prostitution and pornography, but that it is inappropriate, with a few exceptions, to use those tools to intervene on altruistic/hierarchical sex. Let me say a little more about those exceptions, before talking about some other ways to try to bring about a reset for altruistic sex. It is a characteristic of moral and political philosophy—one which might seem peculiar to outsiders—that we do not spill much ink on wrongs that are completely obvious. That is, we do not often bother to write papers saying, for example, that well-known repressive governments should stop violating their citizens' human rights. Of course they should: the fact that we do not write about it doesn't mean we do not think it. Rather, we don't write about it because it is *morally uncomplicated*; there are no difficult philosophical issues to be worked out. This is relevant to thinking about legal changes globally that could advance justice in sex, and (so) between the sexes. All countries should have laws that take rape and other forms of sexual assault seriously, and all of those countries' legal systems should properly police and prosecute those crimes. No country's law should permit rape within marriage, or marriage to underage girls (which will facilitate child sexual abuse). Both domestic law and international law should take sex trafficking seriously, and should take violence against sex workers seriously, whether it's perpetrated by johns, pimps, traffickers, or other third parties. All of this is obvious to all but the most committed misogynist—the challenges are not in what *should* be the case morally, but in how to make it the case. The challenges are institutional and political, not moral and theoretical. This is why I won't dwell on the legal changes that it *would* be justified to make when it comes to sex, even though sex is private, and usually thought to be the domain of morality rather than law. There are legal changes that should be made, and perhaps one day they will be. But in the meantime, we can think about other ways to effect change.

The familiar answers are: through education; through representation; through social movements (Satz also mentions consciousness-raising—see Satz 2010, p. 150). It is not that these are the tools for intervening on sex, and law and policy are the tools for intervening on prostitution and pornography, and the two sets of tools are entirely exclusive. As we have already seen, law and policy should be used in some limited areas to intervene on sex; it is also true that all of the other tools may be used to create a push for legal interventions on prostitution and pornography. When it comes to law, the state might take the lead, but when it does not, the citizenry must push for the legal reforms they want.

Although the details need to be worked out, it is more or less straightforward to see how the social interventions would go. Programmes to educate people about sexual ethics are already running in some countries (although they tend to focus on the concept of consent, that she *really is willing to let him do this to her*, rather than the concepts of reciprocity and equality). Children can be taught—without any sexualized content—about respecting other people's boundaries, about checking in, about clear communication, and about saying 'no' when they feel uncomfortable or don't want something. Adolescents can be talked to more directly about sex and sexual ethics.

A social movement against sex as we know it would have men commit, and signal their commitment, to not using prostitutes. It would have people commit, and signal their commitment, to not watching pornography, and to not having altruistic/hierarchical sex. (The latter is likely to mean, to not having *sex*, at least in the short-term.) It would make sex, and the role of sex in the relations between the sexes, an important social issue that is debated in open forums. Some might think that a social movement against sex—at least without mobilizing religious values likely to be harmful to women in other ways—is infeasible, but in fact it is already happening in some places. A survey in 2013 by the Japan Family Planning Association found that 45% of women in the age bracket 16–24 'were not interested in or despised sexual contact', and that more than 25% of men also felt that way (Haworth 2013). This is in a country where 'there has long been a pragmatic separation of love and sex ... Japan [is] a country mostly free of religious morals' (ibid.). This 'celibacy syndrome' is part of a wider move away from relationships and especially marriage, which Japanese women see as likely to take them away from work that they love (in 2013, roughly 70% of Japanese women left their jobs after having their first child—Wingfield-Hayes 2013) and as subjecting them to 'a relentless tide of domestic burdens' (Rich 2019). Some retain casual sex or 'short-term trysts', but others are 'opting out altogether and replacing love and sex with other urban pastimes' (Haworth 2013). This is not a social movement against sex *per se*, but rather a social move against what love and marriage mean for a woman in Japan. Still, it would not be so surprising if this withdrawal causes a reconfiguration of the relations between the sexes, so that when men and women do come back together, the nature of sex has changed.

Representation is the most complicated. When we talk about lesbian, gay, and bisexual (LGB) representation, for example, we normally mean that we want to see it in culture: we want to see LGB characters in films, in television, as experts on the news, in positions of authority. We want to see the variety of human populations *in* prominent areas of life, rather than seeing only, for example, wealthy white men. But representation of sex as it could be is more complicated, because most representations of sex *are* pornography, and that is something I am arguing against—at least most of it, in its current form. One template for better sex is lesbian sex, which is already mutual pleasure-giving and pleasure-receiving; but representation of lesbian sexuality has been subverted to the point that 'lesbian' is now more familiar as a porn category (for men), and as an 'identity' (for men), than as a sexual orientation of women's. Still, it would be possible for film, television, literature, etc. to represent sex differently, not as it is now but in the more reciprocal and equal form that we have talked about already. It would certainly be possible for those cultural forms to stop sexualizing women, to stop imposing a '**male gaze**' onto viewers and readers.

Other writers have worried about representation as a tool for liberation. Oliver Reeson writes in the *Sydney Review of Books* about the memoir of a nonbinary trans author:

> I don't believe in representation as a means for trans liberation in the same way ... I think it should be approached extremely

cautiously, because of its relationship to capitalism and com-
modification. It's like the cultural concerns of the 90s and early
00s around the dangerous influences of popular culture—that
young minds were being moulded around unrealistic beauty
standards, or the glamorisation of violence, for instance—gave
way almost immediately in the 2010s to demands that everyone
should have the opportunity to see themselves reflected in popular culture. ... We dropped the conversation about the dangers
of letting ourselves be moulded in the image of popular culture
in the first place, and instead started conversations about the
most ethical way to do it.

(Reeson 2022)

Reeson does not deny that representation can be effective ('cultural
representation disseminated awareness very efficiently'—ibid.), but
expresses reservations about popular culture as the vehicle for liberation. The same point can be made for sex; we've ended up where
we have partly *because of* the mainstreaming of pornography into
popular culture, and rather than want to change the precise form of
that representation, we might want to move away from that representation altogether. Amia Srinivasan makes a similar point, when
she says:

The argument that what young people need is better and more
diverse representations of sex is, with the rise of internet porn,
heard increasingly often. Beyond the difficulties of delivering
such a thing, there is a more principled reservation. The demand
for better representation leaves in place the logic of the screen,
according to which sex must be mediated; and the imagination
is limited to imitation, riffing on what it has already absorbed.
Perhaps, today, the logic of the screen is inescapable. If that is
so, then 'better representation' is indeed the best we can hope
for. But something is lost here. While filmed sex seemingly opens
up a world of sexual possibility, all too often it shuts down the
sexual imagination, making it weak, dependent, lazy, codified.
The sexual imagination is transformed into a mimesis-machine,
incapable of generating its own novelty.

(Srinivasan 2021, p. 70)

Srinivasan herself resists the idea that law or education could be
a solution to bring about better sex. She thinks this would need

'negative education', not 'more speech or more images' but rather the stopping of the onslaught of both. She writes that this kind of negative education 'wouldn't assert its authority to tell the truth about sex, but rather remind young people that the authority on what sex is, and could become, lies with them. Sex can, if they choose, remain as generations before them have chosen: violent, selfish and unequal. Or sex can—if they choose—be something more joyful, more equal, freer' (ibid., pp. 71).

For these reasons, we might be better off minimizing the role of representation, or focusing on **negative-representation** (*not* sexual objectification of women, *not* heterosexual sex with the usual dominance/submission dynamics), and focusing more on the elements of education and social movement instead.

All this being said, it is a familiar thought that some social practices can produce outcomes that are unjust or undesirable without our necessarily thinking that an individual who contributes to their production is doing something morally wrong. Someone could grant me my diagnosis of what is unjust in commercial and altruistic/hierarchical sex, and grant me my picture of the future where this injustice has been eliminated, and yet still disagree with me that the individual man who frequents brothels is acting immorally. So the next question is, what is the *individual man* who buys sex doing wrong? (And we could ask the same questions about the individual man who watches pornography, and has hierarchical sex with women.)

SUMMARY

To summarize, to get to the future in which women are fully human, we must *abolish* prostitution, and *reset* pornography and altruistic/hierarchical sex. We can use law and policy to achieve the interventions on prostitution and pornography, but we may only use social movement (with a few exceptions) to achieve the intervention on altruistic/hierarchical sex. Social movement can also help evidence support for the legal interventions. This kind of intervention is a social/collective project, however, not an individual one. So our next question is, does the individual man who buys sex do anything wrong?

4 What's Wrong with Buying Sex?

4.1 Buying Sex as Unethical Consumption

In my book *Gender-Critical Feminism*, I argued that consuming the products of the sex industry is a paradigm example of unethical consumption (Lawford-Smith 2022a, ch. 4). Discussion of unethical consumption focuses on injustices in the supply chain of a product, anywhere from the extraction of raw materials through to the selling by the final retailer, and looks at whether consumers can be justified in purchasing those products given the injustices. It does *not* focus, generally, on the rights of the sellers to sell, although in some cases these rights are relied on by those objecting to the argument that it is wrong to buy particular products.

Think for a moment about the diamond industry, one of the industries whose injustices have been most comprehensively revealed. First of all there is the question of a country's natural resources, which political leaders may be selling off for their own personal aggrandizement rather than the people's benefit. Second of all, there is the question of all the physical harm done in the course of extraction, including murders, rapes, and beatings. Third, there is the issue of exploitation, paying workers unfair wages for their work, and/or making them work in unsafe and/or uncomfortable conditions for unreasonably many hours. It may be that a *particular* diamond avoids the worst of these injustices in its trajectory from the ground to the hand of the final buyer: perhaps no one was physically harmed in *its* extraction or along *its* journey through the supply chain; and perhaps the workers involved in its extraction were lucky enough to be employed by one of the companies that pay their workers fairly and ensure safe and reasonable conditions. Still, there is no getting around the fact that this diamond, along with all the others from the same country of origin, are being sold to the profit of corrupt leaders; that the natural resources belonging to the people are not being sold to the benefit of that people, and indeed may be being sold to the *detriment* of that people, helping to keep leaders in place who do harm to them, who keep them in a state of poverty or repression.

The same can be said for the sex industry (although we should take heed of Evelina Giobbe's claim, reiterated by Margaret Baldwin, that 'Prostitution isn't like anything else. Rather, everything else is like prostitution because it is the model for women's condition'—Giobbe 1990, p. 76; quoted in Baldwin 1992, pp. 47, 53). What are the injustices in the supply chain of commercial sex, specifically, the end product of a discrete session of sexual acts, paid for by a john? Depending on the individual woman, there may be any of a range of injustices, human rights violations, and other harms. There is human trafficking for prostitution. There are rapes. There are beatings. There is captivity / confinement. There is coercive control. There is psychological abuse. There is drug and alcohol addiction (whether a habit induced by pimps and traffickers, or a coping mechanism adopted by the sex worker herself). There are thefts, including refusals to pay. There is coercion/blackmail (e.g. police officers saying that they will arrest the sex worker if she does not service them for free). There is mistreatment by police and legal officials. There is social stigma, which may prevent sex workers in accessing physical and mental health services that are desperately needed, and which a woman not in sex work would be able to make use of. (Many of these are discussed in Phyllis Chesler's retelling of the life of the highway prostitute and eventual serial killer Aileen Wuornos—see Chesler 2020.) Anytime a man buys sex, he risks *having* sex with a woman who has had, or is having, any number of these experiences.

Of course *not every* purchase of sex, whether in prostitution or for pornography, involves the purchaser (or implicated third parties, e.g. the pimps, madams, traffickers, and brothel owners in prostitution; and the producers, film crew, and financers in pornography) in such harms to the sex worker. Similarly not every purchase is of someone working in exploitative conditions (or whose history, explaining her *being* in those conditions presently, is exploitative). But just as with diamonds, it is not to the benefit of *women* (the correlate of 'the people') that these purchases are made, and indeed may be much to their detriment, helping to keep sex hierarchy in place, both by securing the male 'right to sex', and by sustaining anti-feminist propaganda (most pornography). (If sex couldn't be bought, then pornography could only be made for free, and at least then it would be more likely to reflect the sex people are actually having, and so be a more plausible vehicle for change; disseminating awareness of changes on the ground rather than creating changes on the ground from high above.)

Furthermore, just as with diamonds, there's an epistemic issue: we know that *some* of the diamonds have serious injustice in their life histories, but we don't know which. As a consumer, we lack the information that might help us in making ethical choices about what we are willing to buy. In such cases of uncertainty, the best we can do is to gather information about the *ratios* of harm. If most diamonds have severe injustice in their life histories, then we're taking an enormous gamble in buying diamonds, because the chances are that we'll buy one that involved physical violence and exploitation. Similarly, if most sex workers (whether in prostitution or pornography) have severe injustice in their life histories, then a man who buys sex is taking an enormous gamble in buying sex, because the chances are that he'll buy sex from a woman who has been subject to physical violence and exploitation—either in the course of her work, or as part of the explanation for her being in that type of work. It is also important that she is not just highly vulnerable *in general,* but that she is vulnerable in ways related to hierarchical sex. With such a history, and with such a job, she may be less able to resist the ideology that tells her she is *for* fucking by men than a non- sex worker woman. Sex buyers always *risk* harm. In the book, I surveyed the evidence for harm to sex workers and argued that the odds are far from being in the sex buyer's favour (Lawford-Smith 2022a, ch. 4; see also Section 2.2 above). So it is likely that for any act of buying sex, the john not only risks harm but in fact does harm too.

One objection to the argument I made that buying sex is unethical consumption is that it's incoherent to claim that it's unethical for men to buy something which it is *not* unethical for women to sell. I tried to walk a fine line of making no judgement on the issue of women's selling of sex to men, whether in prostitution or in pornography, while yet indicting men's buying of sex from women. Can it really be forbidden for one person to buy what it is permissible for another person to sell? And if it *is* permissible for another person to sell something, then doesn't forbidding anyone else to buy it interfere with her freedoms in an unjustifiable way? There seems to be something not fully honest about saying that *she's* not doing anything wrong and *she's perfectly free to sell* while making it clear that *if he uses his freedom to buy* then *he is doing something morally wrong.* Can this fine line be maintained?

Here's a case that might help to show that it can. In 2017 I attended an event at the State Library of Victoria in Melbourne, launching the then-new book *Kiwi: The Australian Brand That Brought a Shine to the World* (see e.g. Webb 2017). The 'Kiwi' in the book's title refers to a wildly successful brand of shoe polish, invented by an immigrant to Australia and named after his New Zealander wife. At the event, mostly white, mostly older people milled about drinking wine and eating snacks. There was a shoeshine stand set up for people to try, as might have been seen on the streets of Australian cities throughout the late nineteenth century. The person who had been hired to work the stand was black. This struck me at the time as morally complicated. An individual black person looking for casual work in 2017 is absolutely free to accept the offer of a couple of hours of shining shoes. We can assume that the work was not overly taxing, and that the person was offered sufficient remuneration for it. Still, the *optics* of having a black person working to shine the shoes of a mostly white crowd were bad. Australia is a country with a largely unresolved violent colonial history and ongoing structural inequality between its indigenous population and its later migrants.

There is also global symbolism to the black person working literally at the feet of the white person, tapping into racial hierarchies in multiple countries where black people have worked in subservient positions relative to white people (e.g. as domestic help, or in service positions). It would seem odd to claim that the black person who accepted casual work at the Kiwi launch did anything morally wrong. That person is entirely free to sell their labour in such a way. But it doesn't seem odd to say that while *that* person didn't do anything wrong, any white person in the room taking up the offer of a shoeshine *would* have done, and that the organizers of the event should have been a little more aware of the racial optics of their casual hire. This looks like a case in which the seller is morally entitled to sell, and yet the buyer is not morally entitled to buy. And that remains true even if it is a casualty of the latter that the seller's freedom to sell cannot get uptake (after all, the seller's right to sell only gives the *possibility* of sales; if no one was interested in the product, then there would be no actual sales. The right to sell does not correspond to anyone's duty to buy. So if others don't buy for different reasons—not a lack of interest but rather a belief that it would be *unethical* to buy, then there is still no wrong done to the seller).

Under the heading of 'unethical consumption' arguments for why it's wrong to buy sex, we can distinguish at least seven distinct arguments. (There are versions of the second and the third in Dempsey 2010, p. 1752, under the headings of endangerment and complicity respectively, for what she calls 'the feminist-abolitionist call to criminalize the purchase of sex'.)

It is unethical to fail to treat other people as moral equals. Instrumentalizing others, without either also treating them as ends in themselves, or without the instrumentalization being mutual and reciprocal, fails to treat those others as moral equals. Violating the negative freedom of others fails to treat them as moral equals. Hierarchical sex fails to treat the woman as a moral equal in both of these ways. Therefore it is wrong to have hierarchical sex. All sex bought in prostitution is hierarchical sex, by definition: the man exercises his social power to *buy the use of* a woman's body. (This will apply to most, but not all, sex bought for pornography, too.) Therefore it is wrong to buy sex. This argument runs *a fortiori*: the case against *buying* sex follows from the stronger case against *having* sex.

Argument: It's Wrong to Have Hierarchical Sex

Premise 1: We must treat other people as moral equals.

Premise 2: Instrumentalization fails to treat other people as moral equals.

Premise 3: Violating others' negative freedom fails to treat them as moral equals.

Premise 4: Hierarchical sex is instrumentalizing and violates women's negative freedom.

Conclusion 1: It is wrong to have hierarchical sex.

Premise 5: All sex bought in prostitution is hierarchical sex.

Conclusion 2: It is wrong to buy sex.

Some of the women working in prostitution (including pornography) have been trafficked, or are subject to coercive control at the hands of violent pimps and/or partners. Having sex with these women, morally, is rape. It's impossible to know whether the woman you buy for sex is in this situation, and it's not okay to risk raping someone. The risk is non-negligible given the estimated proportions of trafficked women in prostitution, let alone the further numbers of women being pimped and otherwise controlled. Therefore it is wrong to buy sex (see also Dempsey 2010, pp. 1762–1769).

Argument: It's Wrong to Risk Rape

Premise 1: Having sex with a trafficked woman is rape.

Premise 2: Having sex with a woman coercively controlled into prostitution is rape.

Premise 3: It is impossible to know whether the woman a man buys for sex has been trafficked or is being coercively controlled.

Premise 4: It is wrong to risk rape.

Conclusion: It is wrong to buy sex.

Some of the women working in prostitution have been trafficked, sexually abused as children, raped as adults, and/or are subject to coercive control at the hands of violent pimps and/or partners. Having sex with these women makes a man morally complicit in the sexual and physical violence of other men, whose mistreatment has caused the woman to be in sex work. It's wrong to risk being complicit in another men's sexual or physical violence, therefore it is wrong to buy sex (see also Dempsey 2010, pp. 1752–1762).

Argument: It's Wrong to Risk Complicity in Another Man's Sexual/Physical Violence

Premise 1: Some of the women in prostitution are there as a result of the violence of other men.

Premise 2: Having sex with these women makes a man complicit in the violence of those men.

Premise 3: It's wrong to risk being complicit in the violence of other men.

Conclusion: It's wrong to buy sex.

As we saw in Section 2.2, a substantial proportion of sex workers have PTSD. Some of these women will be retraumatized by male sex buyers' use of them (which may be reminiscent of the way they have been abused by fathers, stepfathers, boyfriends, husbands, strangers). It's impossible to know whether the woman you buy for sex is in this situation, and it's wrong to risk retraumatizing someone. Therefore it is wrong to buy sex.

Argument: It's Wrong to Retraumatize a Person with PTSD

Premise 1: Many sex workers suffer PTSD.
Premise 2: Sexual use will retraumatize some of these women.
Premise 3: It's wrong to risk retraumatizing someone with PTSD.
Conclusion: It's wrong to buy sex.

As we saw in Section 2.2, sex workers are a highly vulnerable population. It's worse to do to vulnerable people what it's wrong to do to people generally, and especially when their vulnerability is related to the wrongdoing. Sex workers are vulnerable in ways typically connected to hierarchical sex, for example being survivors of rape, childhood sexual abuse, and domestic violence that includes sexual violence. It's wrong to have hierarchical sex with non- sex worker women. It's worse to have hierarchical sex with sex workers, given their related vulnerabilities. Therefore it's wrong to buy sex.

Argument: It's Worse to Do to Vulnerable People What it's Wrong to Do to People Generally

Premise 1: It's wrong to have hierarchical sex.
Premise 2: It's worse to do to vulnerable people what it's wrong to do to people generally.
Premise 3: Sex workers are especially vulnerable in ways connected to hierarchical sex.
Conclusion: It's wrong to buy sex.

Destitute people should be helped without being exploited. No one should be put in the position of having to trade sex in order to meet their most basic needs. A man confronting a destitute woman should simply help her; not exploit her by offering to trade her money for food or accommodation (or the drugs or alcohol she uses to cope) in exchange for sexual use by him. Most street-based sex workers are destitute. Therefore is it wrong to buy sex from street-based sex-workers.

Argument: It's Wrong to Respond to Destitution with Exploitation

Premise 1: Most street-based sex workers are destitute.

Premise 2: Destitute people should be helped without being exploited.

Premise 3: Buying sex from a street-based sex worker exploits her rather than helping her.

Conclusion: It is wrong to buy sex from street-based sex workers.

It's wrong to contribute to creating consumer demand for unethical products (with some exceptions). Some products are unethical, and yet there are no ethical alternatives available, and it is unreasonable to be expected to avoid using those products (personal electronic devices like cell phones, tablets, and laptops, were like this for quite a while in their use of conflict minerals). Use of such products contributes to creating consumer demand. Buying sex makes the same kind of contribution. The epistemic issues around knowing a sex worker's background and situation, and around the buyer's knowledge of how his buying of sex will contribute to his view of women, make 'ethical alternatives' unrealistic. So the question is whether it is reasonable for him to be expected to avoid using these products. I think the answer here is clearly 'yes' (and the same goes for pornography). Buying sex is *not* a situation where everyone is contributing to something bad and unilaterally opting out makes a man a 'sucker'. (Most men *do not* buy sex). Therefore, it is wrong to buy sex.

Argument: It's Wrong to Contribute to Creating Consumer Demand for Unethical Products

Premise 1: It's wrong to contribute to creating consumer demand for unethical products, unless it is unreasonable to be expected to avoid using those products.

Premise 2: Buying sex contributes to creating consumer demand for women (for sexual use).

Premise 3: It is not unreasonable to expect men to avoid the sexual use of women.

Conclusion: It's wrong to buy sex.

Note that with all these reasons taken together, it is *morally over-determined* that it is wrong to buy sex. Any one such argument would be sufficient alone; we have seven, and two more to follow.

4.2   Buying Sex as an Expression of Social Hierarchy

Pornography is propaganda for misogyny, it presents a very specific view of what a woman is for (Brownmiller 1975; see also McGlynn 2016). Rae Langton and Caroline West quote Ronald Dworkin on this point:

> Ronald Dworkin suggests that the pornographer contributes to the 'moral environment, by expressing his political or social convictions or tastes or prejudices informally', that pornography 'seeks to deliver' a 'message', that it reflects the 'opinion' that 'women are submissive, or enjoy being dominated, or should be treated as if they did', that it is comparable to speech 'advocating that women occupy inferior roles'.
>
> (Langton and West 1999, p. 1; quoting from Dworkin 1994, p. 13, and Dworkin 1991, pp. 104–105)

In R. Dworkin's view, pornography is political speech, as opposed to, say, 'psychological conditioning' (Langton and West 1999, pp. 1–2). Langton and West are dismissive of R. Dworkin's view: 'Dworkin's rhetoric in particular seems ludicrous. Pornography is designed to generate, not conclusions, but orgasms' (ibid., p. 2). Regardless of which of these views of pornography is more accurate, its view of women is one that vindicates the social hierarchy between the sexes, a hierarchy epitomized by the fact that a man can buy the sexual use of a woman. Debra Satz writes:

> If prostitution is wrong it is because of its effects on how men perceive women and on how women perceive themselves. In our society prostitution represents women as the sexual servants of men. It supports and embodies the widely held belief that men have strong sex drives that must be satisfied, largely by gaining access to some woman's body. This belief underlies the mistaken idea that prostitution is the oldest profession, a necessary consequence of human (i.e. male) nature. It also underlies the traditional conception of marriage, in which a man owned not

only his wife's property but also her body. Indeed until fairly late in the twentieth century many states did not recognize the possibility of 'real rape' in marriage.

(Satz 2010, p. 146)

What are the obligations of a person who finds themselves in a hierarchical society, and in the advantaged position in that hierarchy? I have argued elsewhere that while it is generally not possible to get rid of the privileges of these positions, there are ways to 'offset' those privileges (Lawford-Smith 2016; Dunham and Lawford-Smith 2017). At a minimum, men ought to refuse to act out the privileges of being male within sex-hierarchical societies. This gives us our seventh argument:

Argument: It's Wrong to Act Out the Privileges of Social Hierarchy When One Is in the Superior Position

Premise 1: Because social hierarchy is itself wrongful, acting out the privileges of sex-based social hierarchy is also wrong.

Premise 2: Consuming propaganda for sex hierarchy (pornography) is a privilege of sex-based social hierarchy.

Premise 3: Having hierarchical sex is a privilege of sex-based social hierarchy.

Premise 4: Making use of the possibility of buying hierarchical sex is a privilege of sex-based social hierarchy.

Conclusion 1: It is wrong to consume pornography, have hierarchical sex, or buy hierarchical sex.

Conclusion 2: It is wrong to buy sex.

4.3   Buying Sex as Risking Backlash against Movement for Equality

One of the arguments above was about one particular cohort of sex workers rather than all sex workers; this argument is about one particular cohort of sex buyers. I said at the end of Section 3 that it doesn't follow from showing that things could change for the better that each individual man ought to do his part in changing them for the better. Obligations relating to collective action are more complicated than that. Most relevantly, if *not everyone* needs to act in order for a change to be brought about, then it does not follow that each individual must act. Still, if a man is committed to the end of sex hierarchy (to the equality of the sexes), then *he* has obligations that other men do not. If he is publicly committed to women's equality yet uses prostitutes and is found out, then he risks incurring a social backlash for the movement (rooted in the claim that he is a hypocrite, saying one thing while doing another, and that maybe most men are like this, and do not really believe what they are saying). He at least has an obligation not to risk setting back the movement for women's equality. Leftist men tend to be publicly committed to women's equality, therefore it is not OK for leftist men—and any other men committed to women's equality—to buy sex. This gives us our ninth and final argument.

Argument: It's Wrong to Risk Setting Back the Social Movement for Women's Equality

Premise 1: Buying sex from women likely to be coerced, exploited, or otherwise vulnerable is antithetical to women's equality.

Premise 2: Acting in ways antithetical to women's equality while claiming to be committed to women's equality is hypocritical.

Premise 3: Hypocrisy by advocates for social justice causes risks setting their causes back.

Premise 4: Men who are committed to women's equality and also buy sex risk setting the cause for women's equality back.

Conclusion: It is wrong for men committed to women's equality to buy sex.

5   A Set of Likely Objections: Ideology about Male Sexuality

There's a collection of beliefs about men and sex that are likely to feed a lot of scepticism about how much change is possible when it comes to both commercial and altruistic sex. For example, it is not uncommon for people to believe that sex is a *need* (rather than a want, a mere pleasure); that men in particular are biologically promiscuous out of a desire to 'spread their seed'; that without prostitution, there would be more rape (of non-prostitute women); that sex is an outlet for men's aggression or pent-up emotion and without it there might be more violence of one kind or another. If some of these things are true they might be a reason to doubt that we could ever really do away with the sex industry or change what sex is like between men and women. If some of them are true, they might be a reason why we should not *want to* get rid of the sex industry even if we could. So it's important to address them head on.

First of all, whether sexual arousal creates a feeling that is intense enough to be described as a *need* rather than a *want*—the difference, perhaps, between *hunger* and *craving*—sexual relief/release for a man can be achieved without a woman, through masturbation. Sex itself cannot be described as a need, even if it is strongly desired. Second of all, while we can give an evolutionary explanation of the behaviour of males across the animal kingdom when it comes to what is reproductively advantageous, there is no ignoring of the fact that humans have culture, and this radically disrupts our merely acting out biological imperatives. Humans are *not* mere animals, slaves to their passions. They are capable of reason, and discipline, and respect. A man who chooses to cheat on his wife with prostitutes is not just an animal, doing what male animals do; he is also a rational and reflective being, making conscious decisions to lie, to deceive, and to betray. The ideas that sex is an outlet for men's aggression, or that without prostitution there would be more rape, are both myths that serve to perpetuate male sexual entitlement. They vindicate holding a class of women as separate, to be used by men for the greater good of other women. They vindicate women sexually servicing men, to avoid even greater calamities, like war. But rape is a tool of war, used to subdue enemy populations; and prostitution is often provided to soldiers in war. It is not that we trade one form of aggression for another, offering men sexual release *so that* we can avoid aggression in other forms. It looks more like one form of aggression breeds another; physical aggression breeding sexual aggression, sexual aggression breeding physical aggression.

The abolition of prostitution and reset of pornography (top-down; legal), and the reset of altruistic/hierarchical sex (bottom-up; social), are '**experiments in living**', experiments which might allow us to set these myths of male sexuality aside once and for all.

IT'S WRONG TO BUY SEX: LIST OF ARGUMENTS

1   *It's wrong to have hierarchical sex.* If it's wrong to *have* hierarchical sex, then it's wrong to *buy* hierarchical sex. All of the sex that is bought in prostitution is hierarchical sex. Therefore it's wrong to buy sex.

2   *It's wrong to risk rape.* Some of the women working in prostitution have been trafficked and/or are being coercively controlled. All of the sex that is bought in prostitution *risks* being rape. Therefore it's wrong to buy sex.

3   *It's wrong to risk complicity in another man's sexual and/ or physical violence.* Some of the women working in pornography have been trafficked and/or are being coercively controlled. All of the sex that is bought in prostitution *risks* making the buyer complicit in another man's sexual and/or physical violence. Therefore it is wrong to buy sex.

4   *It's wrong to retraumatize a person with PTSD.* Substantial numbers of women working in prostitution and pornography have PTSD and may be retraumatized by sexual use. Therefore it is wrong to buy sex.

5   *It's worse to do to vulnerable people what it is wrong to do to people generally*, especially when their vulnerability is related to the wrongdoing. It's wrong to have hierarchical sex (from 1.), sex workers are a vulnerable population, and their vulnerability is typically related to hierarchical sex. Therefore it is worse to have hierarchical sex with sex workers than with non- sex worker women. Bought sex is hierarchical sex. Therefore it is wrong to buy sex.

6   *It's wrong to respond to destitution with exploitation.* No person should be put in the position of trading sex in order to meet their most basic needs. If a man is confronted by a destitute woman, he should help her without fucking her. Most street-based sex workers are destitute, therefore it is wrong to buy sex from street-based sex workers.

7   *It is wrong to contribute to creating consumer demand for unethical products*, unless it is unreasonable to avoid using those products and there are no ethical alternatives.

Buying sex creates consumer demand for unethical products—the most unethical of all being trafficking into sexual slavery. Given background facts about sex inequality, there are no ethical alternatives. Therefore it is wrong to buy sex.

8   *It's wrong to act out the privileges of social hierarchy* when one occupies the superior position. Men occupy the superior position in sex hierarchy. Privileges include the consumption of propaganda for sex hierarchy (pornography), the ability to have hierarchical sex, and the capacity to buy sexual access to women. Therefore it is wrong to buy sex.

9   *It's wrong to risk setting back a social movement for equality.* Supporting women's equality while simultaneously using prostitutes risks an accusation of hypocrisy that sets back the movement. Therefore it is wrong for men who support women's equality to buy sex.

6   Conclusion

I opened this chapter with the following quote from Richard Rorty, in his paper 'Feminism and Pragmatism': 'Only if somebody has a dream, and a voice to describe that dream, does what looked like nature begin to look like culture, what looked like fate begin to look like a moral abomination' (Rorty 1991, p. 3). That women are *for fucking by men*, whether in commercial sex or in altruistic sex, looks like nature but is actually culture; that so many women were destined to be used by men in this way, for whatever form of remuneration—for money, in prostitution; for security, in so many marriages—or for no remuneration and just a frustrated desire, is the moral abomination. In Rorty's pragmatist view, women now and in the past *in fact* have less personhood than men, 'not because there are such things as "natural slaves" but because of the masters' control over the language spoken by the slaves—their ability to make the slave think of his or her pain as fated and even somehow deserved, something to be borne rather than resisted' (ibid., p. 8). It is not that women have full personhood but have been denied it by men, but that male dominance has created a world in which they do not have it. Still, they *might come to have it*, they are 'capable of being made into [full] persons' (ibid.). It is up to feminists to imagine (dream, prophesize) a future in which women are full persons, to articulate how things will need to be different for that to be so. Here I am interested in how things will need to be different when it comes to sex. Amia Srinivasan in her recent book acknowledged the importance of this topic, but then deferred that imaginative work to 'young people' (Srinivasan 2021, p. 71). The work is too important to be deferred, and it is not just for the young, but for all of us.

Chapter 2

It Is Not Wrong to Buy Sex

Angie Pepper

I Introduction

In my view, there is nothing inherently morally wrong with buying sex today. I'm not merely arguing for the moral permissibility of buying sex in a perfectly just society. Many philosophers defend (e.g. Fabre 2006) or accept (e.g. Satz 2010) this claim. Rather, I am going to defend the claim that buying sex in the imperfect liberal democratic societies of today's world—societies marked by inequalities and injustice that attach to sex, gender, race, class, and disability—can be compatible with the demands of morality. Moreover, I think that as autonomous agents we have a **moral right** to sell sexual services to consenting adults who want to buy, and a moral right to buy sexual services from consenting adults who are willing to sell. My argument is rooted in the values of freedom, choice, and the good of sex.

It should go without saying, but to be explicitly clear: this argument is not an attempt to legitimate sexual violence and exploitation. To that end, nothing I say here makes buying sex from children or trafficked adults morally permissible. Since consent is crucial to making the sale of sexual services non-wrongful, buying sex from people who are unable to give valid consent is morally prohibited. The issue of when consent is undermined is complicated and one that I will return to later in the discussion. But for now, I take it as uncontroversial that there is a moral prohibition on buying sex from children, people who are drunk or high, people who are mentally or cognitively impaired to the extent that free and informed choice is not possible, people selling sex under threat of violence, and people who dissent to selling sex or who withdraw consent to the provision of sexual services.

DOI: 10.4324/9781003169697-4

These caveats will of course make it **morally impermissible** to buy a significant proportion of sexual services available today. Take the sexual exploitation of trafficked women and girls, for example. The UN defines human trafficking as

> the recruitment, transportation, transfer, harbouring or receipt of persons, by means of the threat or use of force or other forms of coercion, of abduction, of fraud, of deception, of the abuse of power or of a position of vulnerability or of the giving or receiving of payments or benefits to achieve the consent of a person having control over another person, for the purpose of exploitation.[1]

The United Nations Office on Drugs and Crime states that 53,800 victims of human trafficking were detected and reported in 2020 by 141 countries (UNODC 2022, pp. 10–11). However, data on the true extent of human trafficking is hard to establish due to its criminal nature, and the number of actual victims is likely to be far higher than official figures. Of the detected cases of human trafficking, just under forty per cent of victims are trafficked for sexual exploitation (ibid., p. 17), and sex trafficking is markedly gendered with women comprising 64 per cent of victims and girls 27 per cent (ibid., p. 32). It should be clear that paying to have sex with trafficked individuals is morally wrong. These individuals do not freely choose to sell their sexual labour, and sex with trafficked children is doubly wrong since they cannot consent to sex in the first place.

In addition to trafficking is the problem of abusive pimping. A **pimp** is someone who manages the activities and income of one or more sex workers for financial gain. Abusive pimps may threaten, beat, and sexually assault the women whom they manage. They may also withhold the woman's earnings, control all aspects of her life outside of her work, and refuse to let her stop selling sex. Importantly, the problem of abusive pimping is most closely associated with **street work** where 'the evidence overwhelmingly suggests that the majority of street workers are funding class-A drug addictions, and are often involved with coercive dealer-pimps who

---

1. The definition is taken from Article 3(a) of the United Nations Trafficking in Persons Protocol to Prevent, Suppress and Punish Trafficking in Persons, Especially Women and Children. The full protocol can be viewed at www.unodc.org/res/human-trafficking/2021the-protocol-tip_html/TIP.pdf

control their prostitution, lifestyles and habits' (Sanders 2005b, p. 12). However, it is important to note that while all pimps make a living from someone else selling sex, it is not the case that all pimps are abusive. Moreover, some pimps work for their share of the sex worker's earnings by offering protection, managing accommodation and clients, and driving the worker to and from different establishments (Fabre 2006, p. 156). Nonetheless, when someone is the victim of *abusive* pimping, they lack a sufficient degree of control over their choices and are likely to be selling sexual services under duress. It is always wrong to buy sex from someone who is only selling under threat of violence from an abusive pimp.

Yet not all commercial sex transactions involve sex workers who are coerced or threatened into selling sexual services. And, though most sex buyers are men, and most sex sellers are women, the empirical evidence suggests that within the system of gendered oppression, of which the commercial sex industry as it currently operates is undoubtedly a part, an individual man buying sex from an individual woman does not always end in the man harming the woman. For instance, a Canadian study conducted by John Lowman and Chris Atchison (2006) found that of 77 self-identifying sex buyers 61 (or 80.3%) claimed they had not committed any violent offences against a sex worker, including refusing to pay and robbery. (One might worry about the truth of the testimony of the sex buyers in this case but there are reasons to think that these are honest reports. Importantly, the data was collected through self-administered mail-back questionnaires—displayed with pre-paid return envelopes in a variety of places, including a bookshop, sexual health clinic, and pubs and bars—which means that it was completely voluntary. Moreover, the questionnaire contained several internal mechanisms for checking the consistency of respondents' answers (Atchison, Fraser, and Lowman 1998, p. 199).) Lowman and Atchison conclude from their findings that while their study cannot support claims about the general population of sex buyers, 'much of the literature on the frequency and nature of sex-buyer violence appears to be empirically overestimated and theoretically underspecified' (2006, p. 292). The take-home point here is that although sex workers do experience high levels of violence—perpetrated by pimps, drug dealers, romantic partners, opportunistic criminals, vigilantes, law enforcement, as well as clients (Kinnell 2006)—it is misleading to think that commercial sex exchanges always end in violence. As Teela Sanders, suggests 'most

transactions go without incident; most clients are not sexual predators; most clients do not use violence, force or robbery. Crucially,
many clients respect the rules of sex workers and practise safe sex'
(Sanders 2008, p. 180; see also Sanders 2016).

It is within this space that my argument finds its place. I will
argue that it is possible, even in non-ideal conditions of gender
inequality, for a man to buy sexual services from a woman and for
it to be the case that the man does nothing **morally wrong**. I concentrate on the case of men buying sex from women for two reasons.
First, most sex buyers are men, and many men buy sex. Indeed, the
third National Survey of Sexual Attitudes and Lifestyles conducted
between 2010 and 2012, revealed that around 1 in 10 men in Britain have paid for sex (Jones et al. 2015, p. 118). Second, many
radical feminists regard sex industries to be the ultimate embodi-
ment of women's oppression by men and accordingly advocate for
their abolition (e.g. Dworkin 1993; MacKinnon 2011; Pateman
1988). For such critics, men who buy sex from women always do
something morally wrong and such exchanges are beyond moral
defence. This makes men buying sex from women both the most
commonplace and the most morally problematic form of exchange
of sex for money. Hence, by showing that exchanges between men
sex buyers and women sex sellers can be non-wrongful, I hope to
show that it is morally permissible for any of us (not just men) to
buy sex provided that we do so responsibly.

This last point is important. Though women's engagement as
consumers in sexual markets has been largely overlooked, there is
growing evidence that significant numbers of women are buying
sexual services. For instance, women's participation in sex tourism
and so-called **romance tourism** is well documented. This involves
travel to exotic locations in search of sex and romance typically
in exchange for meals, hotel rooms, and gifts such as clothes (see
Spencer and Bean 2017; Herold et al. 2001; and Pruitt and LaFont
1995). Moreover, recent empirical work in Australia and the UK
reveals that women are paying, directly and explicitly, for sexual
services covering a range of activities including massage and foreplay, oral sex, BDSM activities and penetration (Caldwell and de
Wit 2019, 2021; Kingston et al. 2020, 2021). So, while my argument focuses on the permissibility of men buying sex because
that is the most morally contested case, I am defending the right
of all of us—irrespective of our gender—to buy sex from those
who—irrespective of their gender—are willing to sell.

1.1   Commercial Sexual Exchange: Four Cases

To give you a sense of the kinds of exchanges I believe involve no moral wrong, I will now describe four fictional exchanges between sex sellers and sex buyers. Although these examples are fictional, they are informed by the first-person testimonies of both sex workers and sex buyers that have been well-documented by social scientists.[2]

Case 1: Adele and Chris

Adele is a 22-year-old student who has been **camming** for two years to financially support herself while she studies at university. A friend introduced Adele to camming, and she finds the work enjoyable and empowering, as well as better paid and more flexible than her previous work in a supermarket. Adele has a tipping menu detailing the prices customers can pay to see her perform certain acts. One of Adele's regular clients, Chris, is a 45-year-old man who works in computer programming. Chris enjoys chatting with Adele and he tips for personal messages, exotic dances, and to see Adele naked. Occasionally, Chris requests a private masturbation performance. For Chris, watching Adele is more exciting than watching standard pornography because of the level of interaction and the sense of emotional connection. Chris tips Adele for a two-minute nude display. Adele takes off her clothes and performs, sometimes responding to Chris's request to turn around, cup her breasts, and so on. The exchange passes without any further incident.

Case 2: Eva and Marc

Eva is 26 years old and employed as an erotic dancer at a strip club. Eva performs pole dances, lap dances, and striptease. Eva began working at the strip club after spending several years in the hospitality industry. She prefers dancing to waiting on tables and generally finds

---

2. See, for example, Bernstein (2007), Frank (2002), Jones (2020), Hester et al. (2019), and Sanders (2005a, 2007, 2008).

the work fun and sometimes even empowering. However, Eva knows that it will be difficult to make a living dancing as she gets older, so she is saving up to start her own business selling vintage clothes. Marc is a 35-year-old customer service manager, who visits the strip club once a week. The biggest draw for him is the beautiful women whom he loves to watch, and he feels that the club is a kind of fantasyland far removed from the stresses and demands of everyday life. Marc tips the dancers and occasionally he requests a private lap dance. He asks Eva if she will dance for him, and she agrees. He pays her to dance for the length of three songs. Even though Marc is not permitted to touch Eva, he enjoys the proximity of her body to his. Once the dance is over, Eva returns to the main stage, and Marc watches Eva and the other women without incident.

Case 3: Maria and Akira

Maria, aged 29, is a single mother who works in a massage parlour. Though the parlour does not explicitly advertise sexual services it is common for clients to ask the masseuse to masturbate them or to have penetrative sex with them for an additional fee. Maria doesn't have penetrative sex with her clients, but she sometimes masturbates them if they are polite and seem nice. Maria doesn't particularly like her work and she resents having to give 30% of her earnings to the parlour owner, but she feels like she can't leave because there is no other equally lucrative employment option available to her. Akira, a retired schoolteacher aged 66, has been visiting the parlour infrequently since his wife died. He does not want a new romantic relationship but desires physical intimacy. He asks Maria if she offers 'extra services' in addition to massage. Maria hasn't had much to do with Akira before, but she knows that he has frequented the parlour in the past. She decides he seems nice enough and she feels a bit sorry for him. Maria and Akira negotiate an additional fee for masturbation. Maria masturbates Akira, he pays and leaves without incident.

Case 4: Charlotte and Elvis

Charlotte is a 37-year-old independent sex worker. She has been in the industry for twelve years and though she started out working at a brothel she now works for herself and provides sexual services to clients who visit her in her home. Charlotte has a postgraduate degree in business management and wants to move out of the sex industry. However, Charlotte has found it difficult to move out of sex work because it is very hard to hide her time spent as a sex worker and potential employers refuse to hire her. Elvis is a 22-year-old student. Elvis prefers to pay for sex because he desires sexual intimacy and enjoys novel sexual experiences, but he doesn't enjoy dating or trying to persuade women to have sex with him for free. Charlotte advertises her services online, including the prices. Elvis visits Charlotte, pays his money, they have penetrative sex, and he leaves without incident.

Here I can offer only brief vignettes to illustrate the exchanges that regularly take place between sex workers and their clients, but I hope that these cases will make the subsequent discussion less abstract and more human. As I have said, and it's important to stress, these cases will not reflect the experiences of all workers in sex industries. I am not trying to suggest that all sex workers enjoy their work, that no sex workers are traumatized by their work, or that sex workers are always treated well by their clients. Rather, what I am trying to show is that sex market transactions may not manifest any obvious incidence of wrongdoing on the part of buyers.

What's important about the described cases is the variety. Each case differs in the sexual services provided, the degree of physical contact and intimacy, and the reasons that motivate the sellers and buyers of sex. It is impossible to capture the vast diversity in commercial sex exchanges, but these cases help to demonstrate that there is a wide range of services and circumstances where the discrete transactions between buyers and sellers involve no obvious moral wrong. In what follows, I argue that what makes these cases morally decent is that the rights of all parties involved are respected. That is, sex workers are permitted to sell sex and sex buyers do not violate the rights of those whom they pay to perform sexual services. To make my case, I begin by explaining the idea of **sexual autonomy**. I will argue that the basic human good of sexual autonomy is pivotal to explaining why consenting adults have a **moral right** to freely choose to exchange sexual services for money or like compensation.

MY MAIN ARGUMENT

Premise 1: Sexual autonomy is a fundamental human good.

Premise 2: Our interest in sexual autonomy is sufficient to ground rights to (i) refuse sex for whatever reason (or no reason at all) and (ii) form, revise, and pursue a conception of the sexual good, including conceptions that place value on selling and/or purchasing sexual services.

Premise 3: Our rights to sexual autonomy entail rights to (i) sell sexual services and (ii) buy sexual services from others who are willing, with valid consent, to sell.

Premise 4: When we have a moral right to do something, we are under no moral duty not to do that thing.

Premise 5: Since we have a moral right to buy sex (if people are willing to sell), we are under no moral duty not to buy sex.

Conclusion: It is not morally wrong to buy sex.

---

2   The Value of Sexual Autonomy

Our interest in **sexual autonomy** is one of our most basic and important interests and it is crucial to human well-being. Sexual autonomy has two dimensions. The first dimension covers our interest in having control over whether and when we permit other individuals to be sexually intimate with us. The idea that we have an interest in controlling the specifics of each sexual encounter, including our choice of partner(s), the location, the kinds of activities engaged in, and the use of contraception, is familiar and protected by law. You have a right against people having sex with you unless you give them consent. Moreover, while we may be prepared to negotiate with others over the specifics, we only have full sexual autonomy when we have the power to permit and forbid others in our sexual encounters with them.

The second dimension of sexual autonomy reflects our interest in being able to pursue our own sexual good. While there is no one sexual good life, there are several factors that may be important to a person's ability to determine, shape, and realize their own sexuality and erotic life. Among the things that will be important to many (though given variability in preference, desire, and values, not all these things will be important to all people) are the ability to pursue meaningful sexual experiences; the ability to experience sexual pleasure; the ability to engage in sexual experimentation; freedom in sexual orientation; and enjoyment of good sexual health.

To see why these things are important, consider practices that have limited people's sexual autonomy. Take female genital mutilation, for instance, which compromises sexual health and diminishes women's capacity for sexual pleasure. Or legislation that criminalizes homosexuality thereby thwarting freedom in sexual orientation and sexual experimentation and diminishing the ability of people to have meaningful sexual experiences with others of the same sex. Or poor provision of sexual education and sexual health services, which can threaten general health by failing to educate people about the risks of unsafe sex and disease, and leave sexual dysfunction untreated thereby diminishing the opportunity for sexual pleasure. When our sexual autonomy is limited in these ways, and many others, our lives go worse. The interest that we have in being able to determine and pursue a sexual life of our own choosing is crucial to our well-being.

The importance of sexual autonomy should be plain. Each of us has the capacity to determine, pursue, and revise our own view of what is valuable in human life and plan our lives accordingly (Rawls 2001, p. 19). In moral and political philosophy, this is sometimes referred to as our **conception of the good**. To elaborate, our conception of the good is the 'system of ends, aims, convictions, commitments and projects that provides the structure of values within which [we] make [our] decisions and plans' (Murray 2014, p. 130). Since sex is an important part of human life, it follows that we will each have, as part of our overall conception of the good, a view of what is good or valuable in the sexual domain. Let's call this our **conception of the sexual good**.

Our conception of the sexual good reflects our view on the sexual good life—what we value in the sexual and erotic domain. It covers a wide range of things including our preference for particular sexual partners, our sexual desires, the sexual activities (if any) that we enjoy and want to engage in, and so on. Moreover, given the diversity in desire, preference, politics, and taste, conceptions of the sexual good vary considerably and people disagree deeply about what is valuable in the sexual domain. There are, for example, debates over the value of monogamy and the promise of non-monogamous life-styles, such as polyamory; debates over whether BDSM is morally problematic because it eroticizes violence and oppression; debates over whether 'all feminists can and should be political lesbians' (Onlywomen Press 1981, p. 5); debates over the value of celibacy before marriage; and debates over whether the good life involves sex at all or rather transcends sex and sexual desire. In short, there is much variability in the sexual domain, and it is in our interest, as sexually autonomous beings, to determine for ourselves what kind of sexual life we want to pursue.

Conceptions of the good (and the individuals who hold them) can be **reasonable** and **unreasonable** (Rawls 2005, pp. 58–66, 144, 488–489). For our purposes, let's grant that a conception of the good is reasonable if it is compatible with the demands of justice. Conversely, a conception of the good is unreasonable if it is incompatible with the demands of justice. For example, a conception of the good that maintained that women were not equal to men, denied women basic rights, and permitted daughters to be sold by their fathers would be unreasonable because it is incompatible with what women are owed as a matter of justice: to be the full equals of men, to have the same basic rights as men, and to be treated as persons and not property.

I think the distinction between reasonable and unreasonable conceptions of the good similarly applies to conceptions of the sexual good. There is a plurality of reasonable conceptions of the sexual good that are compatible with the demands of justice because they fully respect the rights of all free and equal citizens. Arguably, most of the debates over the sexual good life that I just listed involve disagreement between reasonable conceptions of the sexual good: people disagree with one another about what the good sexual life consists in, but each of their views is consistent with the rights and just entitlements of others.

There are, however, unreasonable conceptions of the sexual good. Any conception of the sexual good that involves violating the basic rights of others is morally wrong and should not be tolerated in a liberal democratic society. People who, for instance, think that the sexual good life is one where we are freely permitted to have sex with infants or adults with severe cognitive impairments have an unreasonable conception of the good because it involves violating the rights of others to bodily integrity. Likewise, people who think that their view of the sexual good is the *only* legitimate view can creep into the bounds of the unreasonable if they try to impose that way of life on others. For example, those who endorse legal prohibitions on homosexuality act on a conception of the sexual good that is incompatible with others' basic interests in sexual autonomy. What this shows is that our interest in sexual autonomy is not always valuable or immune to interference. Our interest in sexual autonomy is only legitimate insofar as our conception of the sexual good is reasonable and our pursuit of it does not involve doing wrongful harm to others.

Importantly, everyone has an interest in sexual autonomy irrespective of their particular desires and preferences. This is so even when a person's idea of the good life eschews sex and sexual intimacy. For example, a person may choose to abstain from sexual activity despite their desire for sex or simply have no sexual desire or experience of sexual attraction. In cases such as these, where the importance of sex to a good life is minimized, the people in question nonetheless have an interest in being able to pursue their own conception of the sexual good without interference from others. Moreover, we all have an interest in being able to revise our view of what is good for us, sexually speaking. So, no matter how fixed our current preferences and desires may seem to us now, our interest in being able to revise our view of the sexual good and pursue an alternative sexual life is central to a good human life.

Hopefully, you agree with me that humans have a fundamental interest in sexual autonomy. Now I want to go one step further and say that our interest in sexual autonomy translates into a **moral right** to sexual autonomy. On one popular view about the function of rights, called the **interest theory of rights**, the function of rights is to protect fundamental interests—interests sufficiently weighty to ground duties on the part of others. Joseph Raz explains what it means to have a right in the following way:

Interest Theory of Rights

'Anne has a right' if and only if Anne can have rights, and, other things being equal, an aspect of Anne's well-being (her interest) is a sufficient reason for holding some other person(s) to be under a duty (Raz 1986, p. 3).

Let's assume that Anne is a human being who has rights by virtue of her capacity for well-being. To see how Anne's interests can ground rights, consider the following example. Anne has a significant interest in not being tortured because being tortured would seriously compromise her well-being. This interest is crucial to Anne's well-being and therefore is sufficient to place others under a **moral duty** not to torture her. Thus, Anne has a moral right not to be tortured.

As we have seen, our interest in sexual autonomy is essential to our well-being. When our sexual autonomy is supported and promoted our lives go well, and when our sexual autonomy is violated, thwarted, or diminished our lives can go very badly. Given the importance of our interest in sexual autonomy, we have, according to the interest theory of rights, a right to sexual autonomy that must be respected by others.

Since our interest in sexual autonomy has two dimensions, so too does the right. The first dimension is negative and grounds 'the right to safeguard and exclude, the freedom to refuse to have sex with any person at any time, for any reason or for no reason at all' (Schulhofer 1998, p. 99). The second dimension is positive and grounds 'the right to decide on the kind of life one wishes to live and the kinds of activities one wishes to pursue, including activities with others who are willing' (ibid.). These two dimensions of the right to sexual autonomy recognize that we have both an interest in refusing sexual relationships *and* an interest in pursuing sexual activities and relationships of our own choosing. When both rights are respected, then the capacity for sexual autonomy is protected and a person can be said to have meaningful control over their sexual life and choices.

The question we must now answer is what does it mean for these rights to be respected? Or put differently, what do these rights secure for those who possess them and what do they require of others? I now discuss each right turn.

2.1 The Right to Sexual Autonomy: Control and Consent

Let's start with the right to refuse sex. As we have seen, having control over whom we have sex with and under what circumstances is essential for the development of our sexual identity as well as the realization of valuable sexual goods. The idea that we have a right to refuse sex by withholding or withdrawing consent is familiar and does not stand in need of elaboration or further justification. If someone attempts to have sex with you without your consent, they morally wrong you by egregiously violating your rights.

Consent, then, is crucial to the exercise of sexual autonomy. In philosophical terminology, consent is a **normative power**, which means that by giving consent you can change the **normative relationship** between you and some other(s). This is a bit technical, so let's unpack what it means. When a claim is descriptive, it tells us how things are (i.e. what the world is like, what we are doing, what we have done, and so on). When a claim is **normative**, it tells us how things *should be* (i.e. how our social world *ought* to be organized, how we *ought* to act, what we *ought* to think, and so on). The normative relationship between us and particular others is made up of a set of rights, duties, and entitlements that determine how we *ought* to interact with one another. That others have a right not to be killed means that you *ought* not to kill them. Similarly, if you are entitled to social welfare, the state *ought* to provide it. Moreover, the set of rights, duties, and entitlements may differ depending on whom you are interacting with. For example, you may have duties to your friends that you don't owe to strangers such as visiting them in the hospital when they are unwell. And parents have special duties to their children, such as helping them with their homework, that they do not have to their neighbour's children.

Giving consent allows us to change the normative relationship that obtains between us and some other(s) by changing the duties that those others owe to us. Typically, as we have seen, you have a right that others do not have sex with you unless they have your consent—this right protects your interest in controlling whether you have sex and under what circumstances. This means that unless someone has your consent to sex, they will violate your right to sexual autonomy (as well as other rights, such as bodily integrity) by having sex with you without your consent. Yet sometimes you may want to engage in sexual activities with others and so you need to be able to give permission to some other(s) to interact with you in ways that they usually have a duty not to. When you give consent, you effectively waive the duty that others are under not to have sex with you and give them permission to do so. In this way you change the normative relationship between you and your sexual partner(s) by making morally permissible what would otherwise be morally wrong.

The idea that you need someone's consent before you have sex with them is relatively simple. However, and as we shall see later, precisely when consent is valid is more complicated. It is widely accepted that for consent to be valid, it must meet three conditions. Here I briefly sketch each condition, with a view to arguing (in Section 3.2.1) that Adele, Eva, Maria, and Charlotte (described above) give valid consent to their respective male customers.

2.1.1   The Individual Is Competent

Valid consent requires that the consent-giver have the *capacity* to give and withhold consent. The capacity to give consent has two key dimensions. First, an individual must be able to understand, form, and communicate complex intentions about normative concepts like rights and duties. This is because consent involves the waiving of rights by giving permission to others to do things that they are typically under a duty not to do. Accordingly, an individual only has the capacity to consent if they possess the capacities to know that they have rights, know that they can waive those rights, and can intend to give permission to others (Tadros 2016, p. 211). Individuals who lack these capacities, such as young children and people with severe cognitive impairments, are simply unable to waive their rights.

Second, an individual must have the capacity to understand information about the possible outcomes, risks, and costs associated with giving consent to some interaction or activity. If an individual lacks this capacity, then they cannot competently assess whether to take on risks and costs or have a sufficient understanding of what the proposed interaction or activity involves. The absence of the capacity to have a sufficient degree of understanding about the choices faced invalidates the ability to give consent since the would-be consent-giver is not a competent judge of their situation.

When an individual does not have the capacity to give and withhold consent, they are unable to transform the moral relationship between them and someone else. In the sexual domain, this means that incapacitated individuals—whether their incapacity is temporary or permanent—are simply unable to give someone else permission to have sex with them. Consequently, having sex with a person who is not competent to give consent will always violate their right not to have their body interfered with.

2.1.2   The Individual Gives Consent Voluntarily

For consent to be valid, it must be given freely. This means that consent is only normatively transformative when the consent-giver is not coerced into giving consent. For example, if Annika is threatened by Paul at gunpoint to engage in penetrative sex with him, then Annika's choice to have sex is not voluntary. The problem here is that the coercive threat ('have sex or be killed') 'puts pressure on [Annika's] will by making the two alternatives such that she must choose between evils' (McGregor 2013, p. 4). Importantly, in cases of coercion, the victim makes a choice, but their agency is severely limited because of the terrible options available to them.

When Annika is threatened at gunpoint to choose between having sex with Paul or being killed, the choice she makes is not morally transformative. Even if Annika chooses to comply, her choice does not make it permissible for him to proceed because her consent is coerced and not freely given. This example makes it clear that coercive threats will typically invalidate the consent given and thus make it impermissible for the threatener to proceed even when they have received what is called a **token of consent**, the words or deeds that communicate consent. So even though Annika may verbally agree, she does not give valid consent because the threat of death makes her options unjustly and coercively limited and her choice cannot, therefore, constitute the waiving of Paul's duty not to have sex with her.

The issue of which kinds of coercive conditions are sufficient to invalidate consent is a subject of much philosophical and legal dispute (e.g. Archard 1998; Wertheimer 2003). Some people think that threats are not necessary for coercion and that one can be coerced by other factors such as perceived threats (where no threat in fact exists), powerfully attractive offers, economic duress, conditions of gender inequality, and so on. This is a thorny and complex dispute that I do not have space to get into here.

That being said, given the kinds of commercial sex exchanges we're interested in here, there are a couple of things that need to be noted. First, in the kinds of morally decent exchanges that I have in mind, sex sellers are not threatened by sex buyers, abusive pimps, or other third parties: coercive threats are incompatible with morally decent instances of sex buying. Second, I take it as true that if their options were different, then many women would not choose to sell sexual services to men. However, it does not follow that these women's choices are not morally transformative. You can wish that you had better or different options, while nonetheless preferring to sell sex and intending to waive someone else's duty not to have sex with you. The idea that women are not capable of waiving their rights in existing societal circumstances is deeply problematic since it suggests that women do not have control over with whom, and under what conditions, they want to have sex.

2.1.3   The Individual Is Informed

'Consent must be voluntary to have the moral force of changing the moral relationships in the world and voluntariness requires knowing what one is doing' (McGregor 2013, p. 4). Thus, for consent to sex to be valid, the consent-giver must understand something of what they consent to. A person who thinks he is consenting to a wrestling match does not give valid consent to sex—even if his partner thinks that sex is what has been agreed to. This does not mean that the consent-giver must understand *everything* about what will take place. This would set the bar too high and make it difficult to consent to novel sexual interactions and activities that we don't yet have experience with. As we saw above, our ability to engage in sexual experimentation will often be important to the realization of our sexual autonomy, and so there must be space to give valid consent to unfamiliar people, activities, and circumstances.

In the context of commercial sex exchanges, for sex sellers, who are mainly women, to give informed consent, they must understand what they are consenting to. In the case of experienced sex workers, this condition is easy to meet because their experience will mean that they typically understand what they are offering, what is being requested, the risks involved, and so on. In the case of inexperienced sex workers, they may be less well informed about how the commercial exchange will play out, how they will feel about it and whether they are happy to engage in particular activities. While there is more uncertainty here, it is not that inexperienced sex workers know *nothing* of what they are offering to do. In general, we have a pretty good idea of what different sexual relations and activities involve even if we have never engaged in them ourselves. This is what makes it possible for us to be sufficiently informed about having sex for the very first time. Though it may be disappointing, boring, uncomfortable, or even painful, most of us understand what it is we're about to be engaged in, and who is putting what where, so to speak.

Valid Consent

For consent to be valid, the consent-giver must

i   be competent,
ii   give consent freely, and
iii be informed about what they consent to.

Each of these requirements is *necessary* for consent's validity. If an individual is incompetent, ill-informed or deceived, or coerced, then their attempt to consent will fail. In such cases, the fact that someone gives a **token of consent** is insufficient to morally transform the situation and the person soliciting consent cannot proceed without violating the other person's rights.

SUMMARY

To sum up the discussion of this section, the right to sexual autonomy involves the right to control whether we have sex and under what circumstances. To have full control within the sexual domain we must be able to (a) give valid consent to sex and (b) withhold or withdraw consent to sex. If we cannot give people normative permission to touch and interact with us in ways that would otherwise violate our rights to bodily integrity and privacy, then sexual interactions would always be wrongful. This makes consent a vital and necessary condition for morally decent sexual relationships, which means that our consent and dissent must always be solicited and respected in sexual interactions.

2.2   The Right to Sexual Autonomy: Freedom and Sexual Inclusion

Let's now turn our attention to the second right that protects our interest in sexual autonomy: the right to form, revise, and pursue our own conception of the sexual good. To be clear, this is not a right to have sex—there is no such right. This is because, as we have seen, each of us has the right to refuse sex and so we can never be under a duty to provide sex to satisfy someone else's right. The idea that people have a claim to sex is, therefore, perverse and at odds with the value of sexual autonomy.

That said, we have seen that sexual autonomy does require support and promotion if it is to be fully realized. Access to the goods associated with sex—such as pleasure, sexual intimacy, sexual expression, and so on—can be limited or blocked entirely. So, at the very least, the right to sexual autonomy requires that legal barriers to the pursuit of meaningful sexual experience be removed. But what other measures might our positive right to sexual autonomy demand?

It is easy to see how the right to sexual autonomy demands the removal of legislation that criminalizes homosexuality and the creation of legislation that criminalizes the genital mutilation of children. But sexual autonomy can be jeopardized in more subtle ways such as when people experience **sexual exclusion**—exclusion from meaningful sexual experience—which can occur for a range of reasons that have nothing to do with the formal mechanisms of the state (Danaher 2020, 2022; Flanigan 2020, pp. 232–237). For example, recent literature in disability studies shows how some people with disabilities have suffered sexual exclusion because of the nature of their impairment (Appel 2010), because they are assumed to be asexual (De Boer 2015, p. 73), and because social norms and mores to do with who and what is sexually attractive and desirable typically don't include disability. Similarly, people can be excluded from meaningful sexual experiences for more banal reasons such as being too old, too ugly, or too overweight. To access the goods associated with partnered sex you need others who are willing to engage in sexual activity with you. And when others are not willing to have sex with you or you find it difficult to find people who might like to have sex with you, that can seriously undermine your interest in sexual autonomy. If your conception of the sexual good places a high value on partnered sex, then it will be difficult for you to pursue what you value if no partners are available.

While no one is under a duty to have sex with you, that does not mean that your right to sexual autonomy has no corresponding positive obligations. John Danaher (2020) argues that meaningful sexual experience is integral to the good life and as such grounds a right to **sexual inclusion**. Again, this is not a right to sex. Rather, as Danaher suggests, the right to sexual inclusion places the state under an obligation to foster sexual inclusion by promoting equality of sexual opportunity. What this means is that the state should look at ways to diminish the causes of sexual exclusion and thereby create more sexual opportunities for those who currently find it hard to access meaningful sexual experiences.

For instance, Danaher argues, the state can increase our opportunity for meaningful sexual experience by reforming the laws that pertain to sexual and reproductive freedom, providing extensive and progressive sex education, providing free and widely available access to sexual health clinics, and providing sex aids and sex toys (ibid., pp. 479–480). Moreover, through education, the state can work to undermine some of the norms that contribute to sexual exclusion such as challenging hegemonic beauty standards, racialized sexual aversion, and the tendency to think of people with disabilities as 'not sexual persons whatsoever' (De Boer 2015, p. 74). Given the importance of sexual autonomy for human well-being, I agree with Danaher that the state should facilitate our ability to determine and pursue a sexual life of our own choosing.

SUMMARY

The right to sexual autonomy includes the right to form, revise, and pursue our own conception of the sexual good. This means that we must be free from interference to determine for ourselves what the good sexual life looks like and have adequate opportunities to access meaningful sexual experience. In practical terms, the state has an obligation to ensure that legislation and public policy governing the domains of sex and reproduction do not discriminate against or disadvantage reasonable conceptions of the sexual good. Moreover, the state must seek to promote access to opportunities for meaningful sexual experience by providing progressive sex education and dismantling the barriers to sexual inclusion.

2.3   Sexual Autonomy, Competing Conceptions of the Sexual Good, and Good Sex

Our right to sexual autonomy should not be confused with the right to qualitatively good sex. At the heart of the value of sexual autonomy is the idea that we should have freedom and control in the domain of sexual activity, not that we have a right to always (if ever) have good sex. Of course, good sex is, for many people, desirable and preferable to bad sex, but whether we desire good sex and whether we strive for it is essentially up to us. And, if we have the freedom to pursue our own sexual good in an environment that supports and promotes sexual autonomy, then we may in fact realize good sex with others. But the right to sexual autonomy protects our interest in sexual freedom and control even when the sex we *choose* is consistently terrible, unsatisfying, or even harmful to us.

Choice is key. When parties consent to sexual activity, those involved do not wrong one another. The sexual experience may be dreadful and those involved may choose never to engage in that activity again, but that is their choice. Indeed, the possibility of trying things out and deciding they're not for you is an integral part of shaping your own sexual good. If outside parties were to interfere with our consensual sexual choices, they would wrong us by diminishing our sexual autonomy. This is so even when our choices are likely to harm us or not lead to qualitatively good sex.

Given all this, we should see our right to sexual autonomy as protecting our interest in being able to have sex with any consenting adult(s) for *whatever* reason (Flanigan 2020, p. 179). It also protects our interest in refusing to have sex with any consenting adult(s) for *whatever* reason. These reasons may not always be particularly valuable or virtuous. One might want to have sex with another out of boredom, insecurity, pity, grief, a sense of duty, or to spite an unfaithful partner. Similarly, one might refuse to have sex with someone because of their race, disability, ethnicity, or class.

Some (if not all) of these reasons will strike many as pretty bad reasons to have (or not have) sex, but that judgment is insufficient to permit interference in someone else's sexual choices. Again, what matters is that each of us has a right to control and shape our sexual lives and having such a right comes with the risk of making mistakes about what is good for us, what is virtuous, and sometimes about what is morally right. For example, while most would agree that infidelity is morally bad insofar as it is a violation of trust, loyalty, and commitment, few would think that others have a right to prevent someone from being unfaithful or that we should have a law criminalizing infidelity. Crucially, sexual autonomy prevails and blocks interference from others who are disgusted by our sexual preferences and desires. It also blocks interference from those who might (perhaps even rightly) judge our sexual choices to be ill-judged, ill-fated, and perhaps even offensive (for a discussion of unjust sexual desires see O'Shea 2021). We have an interest in being able to freely shape our sexual identities and preferences even when doing so doesn't lead to good sex and when doing so leaves open the door to making moral mistakes.

SUMMARY

Our right to sexual autonomy is neither a right to sex nor a right to good sex. Rather it entails a right to have sex with consenting adults for whatever reason. This means that even when our reasons for certain kinds of sexual activity, or certain kinds of sexual partners, are ill-judged, lack virtue, or are offensive, others are blocked from interfering with our sexual choices.

3   The Right to Sell and Buy Sexual Services

We have seen that sexual autonomy is a fundamental human good and that we have rights to control whether we have sex and under what circumstances, and rights to freely pursue our conception of the sexual good. In this section, I go one step further and suggest that each of us has a moral right to sell and buy sexual services if we so choose. The importance of this claim to my main argument is simple: if we have a *moral right* to buy sex, then it cannot be *morally wrong* to buy it.

I want to be clear about the argumentative strategy here. When something is morally wrong, we typically have a duty not to do that thing. For example, it is morally wrong to break a promise, be unfaithful, murder someone, torture animals, pollute the environment, and so on. In each of these cases, since the action is morally wrong, we have a *prima facie* moral duty not to perform it. Now, if buying and selling sex are morally wrong, then we would similarly be under a duty not to buy and sell sex. So, in this section, I hope to convince you that we have a right to sell and buy sexual services and that we, therefore, do not act wrongly when exercising those rights responsibly. To that end, I finish by suggesting some guidelines for morally responsible sex buying (Section 3.3).

3.1   The Right to Sell Sex

I am going to argue that all competent adults have a right to sell sex. This is because such agents have a right to **sexual autonomy** and a right to **freedom of occupation** both of which are derived from our overall interest in living autonomous lives. Having these interests entails that we have a right to have sex with whom we want, that we have a right to have sex with people in exchange for money or other goods, and that we should be free to engage in such transactions as part of our conception of the good life and our rational life plan.

As we have seen, having control over whom we have sex with and the kinds of sexual activity we engage in is essential for the development of our sexual identities as well as the realization of valuable sexual goods. Moreover, our right to sexual autonomy protects our interest in being able to have sex with any consenting adult(s) for *whatever* reason (Flanigan 2020, p. 179). A person may, for instance, want to have sex for pleasure, to deepen their physical and emotional bond with their partner, to reproduce, to improve their sexual skills, to raise their self-esteem, to try and make some other person jealous, to get revenge on someone, out of boredom, pity, or a sense of duty. With this in mind, we can take the next step of suggesting that having sex to secure money or other goods is just one other reason why someone might want to have sex.

For some people, especially women, selling sex is more lucrative, flexible, and/or enjoyable than other ways of making money and that gives them a reason to engage in sexual activity with someone else. As we saw in the four cases I sketched in Section 1.1, Adele, Eva, Maria, and Charlotte all *choose* sex work as the best option *for them*. Being free to sell sex is, then, an important part of many sex workers' views about what is valuable in the sexual domain, but it also reflects their choices on how to use their bodies, what occupation to take up, and how to, most generally, live their life. Moreover, the choice to sell sex is compatible with respecting the rights of others and thus cannot be described as unjust and unreasonable. Thus, choosing to sell sexual services reflects not just a person's sexual autonomy but is a manifestation of their autonomy more generally. To have their choices criminalized, stigmatized, and interfered with represents a denial of their basic interest in sexual autonomy, and their right to determine for themselves whom they have sex with and under what circumstances.

One might try to argue that women who sell sex under patriar-chal conditions—as is the case in most societies in the world—are making a choice that is harmful to themselves and that, in gen-eral, we have no right to harm ourselves. This is implausibly **pater-nalistic**. Think of all the choices that we might make that could potentially harm us. We might, for instance, want to play contact sports, take up paragliding, drive a car, compete in ultramarathons, undergo cosmetic surgery, keep bad company, drink alcohol, eat fatty foods, swim in open water, complete home improvement proj-ects with power tools, and so on. The idea that we should not be permitted to engage in any of these potentially harmful activities is deeply unattractive. We should be free to decide for ourselves which harms or risks of harm we want to take up, which suggests that we often have a moral right—a right that protects us against paternalistic interference from others—to engage in activities that involve the possibility of harm. And, if we agree that we have a right to engage in potentially harmful or risky activities, then why wouldn't we also agree that competent adult women have the right to exchange sex for money?

Competent adult women can weigh up the benefits, costs, and risks associated with sex work and determine for themselves whether they are prepared to take on the costs and risks. To claim otherwise infantilizes women by suggesting that they—like young children—are not competent to make decisions in the sex-ual domain or at least are not competent to make decisions in the sexual domain when those choices involve the exchange of sex for money. This hardly seems compatible with the feminist ends of sex equality and women's liberation. The goal of gender justice can-not be invoked to justify legislation and social policy that thwarts women's rights to sexual autonomy and seeks to control women's bodies and what they choose to do with them. Instead of diminish-ing women's control in the sexual domain, we ought to concentrate on promoting it by ensuring that their choices are made against a backdrop of social justice and gender equality (Nussbaum 1998).

Though I think that the right to sexual autonomy is sufficient to ground a right to sell sex, the argument can be strengthened by appealing to the good of **freedom of occupation**. The freedom to choose our occupation is, like sexual autonomy, central to shaping our identity and our ability to form, revise and pursue our concep-tion of the good. Indeed, our choice of occupation will affect what skills and talents we develop, how we spend significant amounts of our time, and whom we spend time with. Moreover, our choice of occupation will reflect something of what we value, whether it be the role itself or the benefits that it brings, such as a steady income.

To see why occupational freedom is important to our well-being imagine that others, such as the state, were to decide your occupation for you. In such a world you would have no control over what skills and talents you developed, what kinds of ends you dedicated your labour to, what kinds of tasks you would be engaged in, what kinds of workplace values, ethos, or collegiality you would be made to endure, and so on. The state might decide, for instance, that you should be a surgeon when you want to be a teacher, or it may decide that you should go into finance when you want to work as a gardener, or it may decide you should be an electrician when you want to be a DJ, or it may decide that you should work in retail when you want to work in a nursing home, and so on. Being forced to do what you don't want to do is likely to make you feel miserable and unfulfilled. The idea that someone else would have the right to choose our occupations for us denies our basic freedoms and severely limits our ability to shape the course of our own lives. Since the good of freedom of occupation is central to our well-being, we have an interest in it that is sufficient to ground a **moral right** to freely pursue occupations of our own choosing. This right to occupational freedom is a right to choose our occupation 'without the interference of either legal or moral pressure' (Casal 2016, p. 383).

Of course, in the case of sex work, most critics argue that sex work should be *removed* as an option, and one might think that removing options is not as bad as imposing occupations upon people. When we only remove an option from the available option set, we leave the remaining options in place, so people may still have plenty of options to choose from. However, this misunderstands how our moral right to freedom of occupation functions. Our right to freely choose our occupation acts as a **presumptive reason** in favour of whichever occupation we choose and anyone who attempts to remove our chosen option must show that there is an adequate reason to do so. So, if someone wants to be a dog walker, they have a right to take up dog walking unless it can be shown that dog walking is not an occupation that they have a moral right to choose.

When might we not have a right to take up an occupation? I would argue that we are only free to exercise our right to freedom of occupation insofar as it does not wrongfully harm others. So, for example, you are not free to be a paid assassin, slave trader, or child pornographer because each of these occupations involves violating the rights of others. One key issue, then, is whether occupations within sex industries are the kinds of occupations that one has a right to choose. For example, can one legitimately choose to be a cam model, glamour model, lap dancer, stripper, escort, pornographer, sugar baby, or phone sex operator? Or are these occupations morally prohibited?

I can see no reason to think that these forms of occupation are akin to the morally prohibited occupations just mentioned. None of these occupations involves violating the rights of others. Think back to the exchanges described in Section 1.1 above. Adele does not wrong Chris or any third party by performing for him via webcam. Similarly, when Eva sells a lap dance, Maria sells masturbation, and Charlotte sells penetrative sex they do not violate anyone's rights. To strengthen the point, it's worth noting that what Adele, Eva, Maria, and Charlotte sell is the same as what many people do for free. If webcam performances, lap dances, masturbation, and penetrative sex are not inherently wrong, it's hard to see why selling them would be. This point is summed-up nicely by Jason Brennan and Peter Jaworski (2016) who argue more generally that 'if you may do something for free, then you may do it for money'.

Moreover, for many sex workers, their occupations offer valuable and meaningful employment. In their study of the experience of Canadian sex workers, Cecilia Benoit et al. (2021) provide numerous accounts of sex workers reporting higher levels of job satisfaction than in previous roles:

> Carleigh explained: 'I feel that I'm helping somebody'. Maci described her sex work as 'alternative sexual therapy' and stated: 'I'm very proud of my work'. Vaughn said that 'if you have a good person and you make them feel better, it's a good feeling inside'. Adeline spoke about satisfaction this way:
>
> I like one-on-one personal reactions. [...] I like the psychological aspects of sex work, I like the therapy aspects. I have several clients I know I've saved their life and I know I've changed their lives. And so, that's really valuable from a psychology/therapy point of view.
>
> For Krystal, sex work is 'the best work experience I've had. Because it's my own business [...] It taught me to be independent and take care of my needs.'
>
> (Benoit et al. 2021, p. 246)

These testimonies are not unusual. Similar sentiments are echoed by sex workers in Jade Bilardi et al.'s (2011) study of female brothel workers in Australia and Jane Pitcher's (2019) study of indoor sex workers in Great Britain. Yet the idea that sex workers might find their work meaningful is largely overlooked by those who look to eliminate sex industries.

Of course, the fact that some sex workers enjoy their work cannot serve to diminish the fact that other sex workers loathe what they do, but that is not my aim. Rather, I think that the positive testimony of sex workers about their work is further evidence of the value of sex work as an occupation that competent adults should be free to choose. Sex work is not for everyone but then neither is any occupation. The fact that sex workers do not violate anyone else's rights and they often value their work and choose it over other options is, I think, sufficient to protect it as an option.

Again, one might try to push the line that women who sell sex only do so as a last resort and therefore their choice is not a meaningful reflection of occupational freedom. Moreover, according to this line of thought, the language of 'sex work' serves to normalize and legitimize sexual violence and exploitation and the idea that people may have an 'occupation' to be exploited is nonsensical (Jeffreys 1997, ch. 6; Watson 2020). It would be like saying that a woman could take up the 'occupation' of being trafficked or being the victim of domestic violence. Consequently, since there are no 'occupations' in the sex trade (only exploited and prostituted people) women are not *free* to sell sex for money and have no moral right to do so.

To reiterate my earlier point, I agree that anyone forced to sell sex is wronged and such individuals might at best be described as non-voluntary workers. However, suggesting that all sex work is forced ignores the lived experience of voluntary sex workers and their testimony on how they think about their work. Take for instance the global political, social, and legal struggle that constitutes the sex workers' rights movement (Mgbako 2020). Sex workers across the globe have struggled to get their activities legally recognized as 'work' even though they, like other workers, use their labour to earn a living. By denying that sex work is work, sex workers are denied many of the protections and social benefits that come with having legally recognized employment such as labour rights, and the ability to pay taxes and access social welfare provisions. Moreover, it again ignores how sex work is a valuable employment option for many people.

The Global Network of Sex Work Projects

The Global Network of Sex Work Projects (NSWP) was founded in 1992 and is a global network of sex worker-led organizations. NSWP currently has over 280 member organizations in 82 countries and is composed of regional networks in Africa, Asia and the Pacific, Europe (including Eastern Europe and Central Asia), Latin America and North America and the Caribbean. The core mission of NSWP is to uphold the voice of sex workers and connect the regional networks that advocate for the rights of all sex workers. All NSWP members are committed to its core values, which are the acceptance of sex work as work, opposition to all forms of criminalization and other legal oppression of sex work, and support for the self-organization and self-determination of sex workers.

In 2013, the NSWP released a Consensus Statement on Sex Work, Human Rights, and the Law. This document details eight fundamental rights that sex worker-led groups from across sixty different countries identified as crucial targets for their activism and advocacy. Furthermore, the Consensus Statement stresses that these rights apply to all sex workers, irrespective of their gender, class, race, ethnicity, health status, age, nationality, citizenship, immigration status, language, education level, or disabilities (NSWP 2013, p. 1). Consequently, the Consensus Statement represents an important moment in the sex workers' rights movement and cements the idea that it is a movement that is truly global in scope.

The eight rights are:

1   The right to associate and organize.
2   The right to be protected by the law.
3   The right to be free from violence.
4   The right to be free from discrimination.
5   The right to privacy, and freedom from arbitrary interference.
6   The right to health.
7   The right to move and migrate.
8   The right to work and free choice of employment.

Nonetheless, one might worry, that even if we acknowledge that sex work is work, it is hardly freely chosen. According to this line of thought, limited employment options mean that a woman's 'choice' to take up sex work is not an exercise of her interest in occupational freedom, and, therefore, it ought not to be a protected option for her (i.e. an option she is free to choose). In response, it is worth emphasizing that this is not how all sex workers experience their decision to take up sex work: for some, sex work is their preferred option among a range of options, not a matter of last resort in dire economic circumstances.

But even when sex work might be a rational (but loathed) choice for a woman trying to survive in particularly difficult conditions, it does not follow that she ought to be prevented from taking up that option. Here I agree with Martha Nussbaum, who argues that

> a woman will not exactly achieve more control and "truly human functioning" by becoming unemployed. What we should instead think about are ways to promote more control over choice of activities, more variety, and more general humanity in the types of work that are actually available to people with little education and few options. That would be a lot more helpful than removing one of the options they actually have.
>
> (Nussbaum 1998, p. 712)

Removing the option of sex work, then, will not promote women's freedom of occupation and will likely make some women much worse off. While we should be concerned about the fact that many women do not have maximal occupational freedom, this does not give us a right to interfere with their choice to take up sex work. Rather, our focus should be on promoting fair equality of opportunity, fair wages, and creating different kinds of employment opportunities.

SUMMARY

In this section, I have suggested that competent adults have a right to sell sex. This right is grounded in our general interest in living an autonomous life and the derivative interests of **sexual autonomy** and **occupational freedom**. The fact that sex workers have a moral right to sell sexual services means that they do nothing morally wrong when they exercise that right.

3.2.1   Consent and Sex Work

As we just saw, one might try to argue that most people who sell sex do so under economic duress. People living in poverty or who have limited opportunities for employment would not sell sex if they had better options available to them. So, talk of the occupational freedom of sex workers is confused and misleading: women who 'choose' sex work do not make a choice in any meaningful sense since they do not have a real option to choose otherwise. Consequently, their sexual autonomy is undermined because they cannot exercise their right to refuse sex (without falling into abject poverty) and so do not, in fact, have control over whether they have sex. If this is correct, then it would mean that most sex workers do not consent to sell sex because dissent is not possible.

Of course, if it were impossible for sex sellers to give valid consent to sex buyers, buying sex would always be morally wrong: sex for money would always violate the rights of those selling because they would be incapable of waiving their rights to not have their body interfered with in that context. Here is that argument presented in standard form:

Argument: Valid Consent to Sex Work Is Not Possible

Premise 1: Sex without valid consent is morally wrong.
Premise 2: Coercion undermines valid consent.
Premise 3: Sex workers are coerced into selling sexual services.
Conclusion 1: Therefore, the consent of sex workers is not valid.
Conclusion 2: Therefore, sex with sex workers is morally wrong.

I can see no reason to think that it is *impossible* to give valid consent to selling sex. Consider the case of Adele and Chris, sketched in Section 1.1 above. Is Adele capable of giving valid consent to Chris? I think the answer is yes. Adele is a competent agent—she is not impaired or incapacitated—who knows that she has rights, that she can consent to waive those rights, and that she can withhold her consent to press those rights. Furthermore, Adele gives her consent voluntarily because she does not have to be a cam performer (there are other ways of earning money open to her, but camming is what she prefers), she does not have to perform for Chris on this occasion (she could say no), and she is not being coerced to perform. Lastly, Adele is able to make an informed choice about whether to perform for Chris: she understands what is being asked of her and so is sufficiently well-informed about what it is that she is consenting to. Indeed, in this case, she has determined what activities she is prepared to perform and how much their performance will cost.

Perhaps you think that while valid consent is possible between Adele and Chris, the unique features of their situation—the fact there is no physical contact, and the fact that camming is not Adele's only economic option—make this an easy case. Similarly, one might think that valid consent is easily present between Eva and Marc: Eva knows what she is doing, it's not her only option for employment, the exchange involves some physical contact but Marc abides by the no touching rule, and so on. But what about the case of Maria and Akira, or that of Charlotte and Elvis? In these cases, while Maria and Charlotte are clearly competent agents who understand what it is they are consenting to, one might argue that their consent is not freely given. Maria does not want to masturbate men for money; if there were a better option available to her, she would take that. However, all the other jobs available to her are less well-paid and would make it very hard, both in terms of money and time, to care for her child. Consequently, one might argue that Maria's economic circumstances are *coercive* and invalidate her consent to Akira. Similarly, Charlotte no longer wants to work in the sex industry and, by extension, would prefer not to sell sexual services to Elvis. Again, one might argue that Charlotte's consent to Elvis is invalid because she is coerced by her economic and social circumstances—if people were less prejudiced toward sex workers, then Charlotte may be able to get a job doing what she aspires to and that would be as lucrative as her sex work.

Though both Maria and Charlotte have limited options for employment, I am not persuaded that they are under the kind of duress required to make their consent void of its moral power to make Akira and Elvis' actions permissible. The first thing to note is that economic duress is not all or nothing but rather scalar: one can be more or less impoverished, one can have more or fewer employment opportunities, one can have more or less caring responsibilities, and so on. I don't want to deny that there may be very extreme cases of economic duress that perhaps invalidate consent. For example, cases where a person simply has no other option but to undertake sex work or starve, such as situations where people are homeless and/or suffering from drug addiction or live in countries with high levels of poverty and unemployment. As I mentioned in the introduction, the consent of some street workers may be invalidated by addiction and abusive pimping. However, unlike street workers, many indoor sex workers do not live in circumstances of extreme economic duress (Weitzer 2007, pp. 28–30). Indeed, both Maria and Charlotte have a choice about whether to undertake sex work or to engage in some other form of minimum wage labour such as working as a cleaner, carer, or in a bar. And it is worth noting that plenty of other people do those jobs instead of entering (or remaining in) the sex industry.

Moreover, it would be problematic to assert that Maria and Charlotte's consent to sex in these circumstances is morally redundant. Claiming that Maria and Charlotte are unable to give valid consent to Akira and Elvis would ultimately be autonomy-denying and would make the sexual interactions indistinguishable from rape. Not only does this infantilize Maria and Charlotte by denying them the power to choose to have sex for money, but it misdescribes the nature of their sexual encounters. Akira and Elvis do not threaten or compel Maria and Charlotte, and what is more Maria and Charlotte could withdraw consent at any point: these encounters, while not what Maria and Charlotte would choose in an ideal world, are not instances of rape. The idea that Maria and Charlotte's consent to sex for money is not morally transformative seems implausible.

The claim I am defending here is not that *all* people who sell sex are able to give valid consent to sex buyers. For the reasons noted at the outset, some people who sell sexual services are not capable of giving valid consent: women who are forcibly trafficked for sexual exploitation do not give their consent freely; children who are trafficked for sexual exploitation are not competent to give consent; people threatened with violence by abusive pimps do not give their consent freely; and people selling sex while highly intoxicated or suffering from serious mental illness are not competent to give consent. However, recognizing that some people are unable to give valid consent to commercial sexual exchanges should not be used to obscure the fact that others can.

Moreover, the importance of valid consent for morally decent exchanges between sex workers and their customers should not be overlooked. By giving her consent a sex worker waives her right not to have her body touched or interfered with in certain ways. She effectively *chooses* to give her customer permission to interact with her in ways that he would typically be under a duty not to. And she retains the right to withdraw consent at any point in their interaction. In this way, the giving and withholding of sexual consent enables and promotes the sexual autonomy of sex workers and their customers.

3.2   The Right to Buy Sex

So far, I've primarily been concerned with the right to sell sex. I have suggested that each of us has a right to choose how to use our bodies when doing so does not harm others. Having this right has important moral implications: if you want to sell a sexual service, then you do not act wrongly when you exercise your right. However, one might try to argue that even if each of us enjoys a right to sell sex, buying sex is nonetheless morally forbidden. In this section, I suggest that we have a **right to buy sexual services** from those willing to sell. This right is derived from our right to sexual autonomy.

The relationship between the right to sexual autonomy and commercial sex is simple. Commercial sex presents an important and valuable option for buyers as well as sellers. From the perspective of buyers, being able to purchase sexual services means being able to gain access to something valuable that it may otherwise be difficult to. Thus, having the option to pay for sex is important and valuable to many people's pursuit of their conception of the sexual good.

To unpack this in a little more detail let's look again at the case of people who are, for whatever reason, excluded from accessing meaningful sexual experiences. It might be that a person has physical or mental disabilities that make sexual relationships very difficult to establish (Appel 2010, p. 153). Or it might be that a person is perceived by others to be too fat, too old, too unattractive and that makes it hard for them to find willing sexual partners. Sexual exclusion is a real phenomenon and to pretend otherwise is to ignore the fact that there are people who, through no fault of their own, find themselves sexually marginalized and unable to access an important human good.

However, we must also tread carefully here. As Amia Srinivasan astutely writes 'talk of people who are unjustly sexually marginalized or excluded can pave the way to the thought that these people have a right to sex, a right that is being violated by those who refuse to have sex with them. That view is galling: no one is under an obligation to have sex with anyone else' (Srinivasan 2021, p. 86). So, while we can think that sexual exclusion is bad for people, and that many of the causes of sexual exclusion are unjust, this should not be taken to imply that people have a right *to* sex.

While not everyone who is sexually excluded will want (or can afford) to buy sexual services, the option to buy sex is for some currently the only realistic and reliable way to access meaningful sexual experiences. This means that purchasing sex may be the only way that some people can pursue their conception of the sexual good. Thus, the moral right to buy sex protects a valuable option to access the kinds of meaningful sexual experiences that may be crucial to one's view of what is valuable in the sexual domain.

If this is right, then claiming that the sexually excluded always do something morally wrong when they buy sex not only serves to further harm and stigmatize them but is, more importantly, false. As I suggested in the previous section, selling sex is something that people have a moral right to do if they so choose. If those who find it difficult to access sex in non-commercial ways are prepared to pay consenting sex workers for their services, then I can see no reason to think that a moral wrong has taken place.

So far, I've suggested that the interest we have in buying sex is rooted in our right to sexual autonomy. And I have argued that those who are sexually excluded have a moral right against others interfering with their purchasing sex from someone else who is prepared to sell. But I should not be read as saying that *only* those who are sexually excluded have an interest in buying sex. In reality, the reasons why people buy sex are more complex and these additional considerations are relevant to thinking about why we might have a right to buy sex. In her discussion of why men buy sex, Teela Sanders details several 'push factors'—reasons that men have for paying for sex that come from some lack in their own lives—and 'pull factors'—reasons that men have for paying for sex that have their origins in the appeal of the commercial sex industry (Sanders 2008, pp. 39–46; see also Hester et al. 2019, pp. 22–23).

With regard to the 'push factors', Sanders found from her interviews with male sex buyers in the UK that there were four main motivations for purchasing sex. First, some men said they paid for sex to satisfy their emotional needs such as desire for intimacy or wanting to dispel loneliness. Second, men sometimes seek commercial sex in response to lifestyle and relationship changes that occur at different stages of life. For example, 'some [older men] look to commercial sex because of their status as widowers, or after experiencing a lack of intimacy in a long-term marriage, while others were motivated by a final chance to experiment with different sexual relationships' (Sanders 2008, p. 81). Third, some men are motivated to buy sex because their long-term relationships are unsatisfactory insofar as they lack sexual and emotional intimacy. Fourth, some men seek out commercial sex because they find it difficult to navigate the world of dating and casual sex. For these men, the 'courtship rituals' associated with contemporary dating, such as drinking alcohol, going to dinner, or going to nightclubs, are intimidating, distasteful, and disappointing (ibid., pp. 43–44).

With regard to the 'pull factors', Sanders suggests that 'men are attracted to the nature of the sex industry, what it offers and the glitzy or gritty images and promises that emanate from adverts, websites, stereotypes, pictures and the allurement of fantasy created specifically for those who want to trade cash for pleasure' (Sanders 2008, p. 45). The opportunity to enter a fantasy world and pay for an experience that one would unlikely be able to access in real life—sex with a young, beautiful woman, for example—is part of the allure of commercial sex. Similarly, the ability to pay for sexual activities that it is difficult to find a non-compensated partner to engage in is also attractive to some as is the possibility of sexual experimentation. In addition, for some men, the social taboo of paying for sex can be a draw in itself.

That there are numerous reasons why people buy sex should come as no surprise. We have seen that there is much divergence and difference in conceptions of the sexual good, and buying sex can be a source of value in the sexual domain. Furthermore, what these various 'push' and 'pull' factors show is that men are motivated to buy sex for many different reasons that are not incompatible with respecting the rights of women sex workers. While some men who buy sex do so to degrade, dominate, and humiliate the women they buy sex from, for many buyers those motivations are absent. And many of the reasons that men have for buying sex make having the option to buy sex essential to the pursuit of their sexual good. Being able to purchase sex means being able to attain goods that one otherwise would not be able to access. Importantly, while I have focused on men it is worth pointing out that recent studies show that the factors motivating men to buy sex are shared by women sex buyers in the UK (Kingston et al. 2021). So, it isn't just men who benefit from being able to purchase sex. Buying sex can be a valuable option for people of any gender.

Our right to sexual autonomy means that we have a right to form, revise, and pursue a conception of the sexual good. Having the option to buy sex from people who are willing to sell may be a part of our conception of the sexual good because we desire sex that is paid for or because paying for sex enables us to access the sexual experiences that we desire. Either way, paying for sexual services is an important option for many and is crucial to their sexual autonomy. (I don't want to be misunderstood as suggesting that buying sexual services always contributes to the well-being of the buyer. In current social conditions, buying sex comes with many risks to buyers, including shame, sexual disease, being the victim of violence or theft, the often-disastrous consequences that come with being found out, and the financial and psychological harms associated with addiction to buying sex. Nonetheless, for many buyers of sexual services, purchased sex has value.) Consequently, our right to sexual autonomy, coupled with the seller's right to sell sex, entails a moral right to freely purchase sex from those prepared to sell. What this means is that it can be morally permissible to buy sex from those who are prepared to sell and one's choice to buy sex responsibly should not be interfered with by others.

SUMMARY

In this section, I have suggested that having access to meaningful sexual experience and sexual satisfaction is important to human well-being. And I have further suggested that, for all kinds of reasons, people may choose to purchase sexual services to satisfy their emotional and physical needs. As such, commercial sex might feature in a person's conception of the sexual good and it ought to be a protected option: an option that we can freely choose if it is available (i.e. there are people willing to sell). In this way, our right to sexual autonomy grounds a right to purchase sex from willing sellers.

3.3   Responsible Sex Buyers

Our moral right to buy sex, like all privileges, is a right that comes with certain responsibilities. We must exercise our right to buy responsibly. Indeed, the idea that sex buyers have a moral responsibility in their procurement of sexual services is not alien to existing sex buyers. As Teela Sanders argues, 'morality is often high on the agenda in the personal and public narratives of men who buy commercial sex' (Sanders 2008, p. 61). However, given legal prohibitions and social taboos surrounding buying sex, the moral conduct of buyers, though sometimes policed by the 'community' of sex buyers (ibid., pp. 58–59), is largely left to individuals to determine for themselves. This is obviously a problem because it shields troublesome behaviour and allows individuals to rationalize and justify preferences and behaviours that are morally wrong. Thus, without clear moral guidance on how to be a responsible buyer, individuals purchasing sex may well fall short of morally decent behaviour, and the risk of doing something morally wrong or lacking in virtue is increased.

When sex buyers act violently to sex workers or disregard their consent then their actions are not just morally wrong but also criminally wrong. Yet beyond the worst kind of wrongs that are prohibited by the criminal law, there are moral wrongs that though perhaps not sufficient for criminal punishment make sex work difficult, unpleasant, or frightening. Much of what is required to be a responsible sex buyer is not unique to sex markets but speaks more generally to consumer responsibilities. For instance, all workers have a right to be treated with dignity and respect, and consumers must never regard service providers as mere means. This means that consumers should not abuse, degrade, or belittle service providers, they should not try to get more for their money than is fair, and they should always remember that the person providing the service is just that: a person.

In addition to the basic requirements of interpersonal morality, some responsibilities are specific to sex market consumers. For example, while it is permissible for customers at bars and nightclubs to drink alcohol the same is not true for those purchasing sex. Responsible sex buyers should not try to procure sexual services while intoxicated. There are two very important reasons for this. First, when a sex buyer is drunk or high then their ability to consent is impaired, and if they are heavily intoxicated then their consent will be invalid. The sex worker in this case must refuse to provide sexual services to the buyer since they do not have the consent necessary to proceed. Second, trying to engage in sexual activity while drunk or high involves risks that one has a moral responsibility to avoid. When we're intoxicated, we're more likely to engage in unsafe sex, we're more likely to be disrespectful and aggressive, and, most importantly, we may be less sensitive to the withdrawal of consent. For these reasons, sex buyers have a responsibility to sex workers to refrain from trying to purchase sexual services while high or drunk.

As we have seen, the issue of consent is foundational to the ethics of buying sex and the responsible sex buyer must take steps to ensure that the sex seller has given them valid consent to touch and interact with their body. Given the discussion of consent in Section 2.1 above, several things are important here. First, buying sex from incompetent agents is morally wrong. This means sex buyers must ensure that the person selling sex is not incapacitated by checking that they are over the age of eighteen, that they are not intoxicated, and that they are not permanently or temporarily cognitively impaired. Second, consent to sex should be thought of as a process of mutual negotiation rather than a one-off contract. This means that sex buyers must make sure that they have sexual consent throughout the interaction by explicitly checking-in with the sex seller but also by being responsive to signs of discomfort and distress. Most importantly, sex buyers must respect the right of sex workers to withdraw their consent at any point. If this occurs, then sex buyers must stop touching or interacting with the sex worker. Third, if sex buyers suspect that a sex worker is the victim of trafficking or abusive pimping, then they have a responsibility (as does any citizen) to report the potential crime to the relevant authorities.

Sex buyers have a responsibility to sex workers, as well as other sexual partners, to always practice safe sex. Since sexual infection and disease can compromise sexual health and well-being, individuals have a responsibility to make sure that they are not either unwittingly or knowingly exposing others to unnecessary risk. In addition, since even safe sex is not without risks, sex buyers should undertake regular sexual health screening so that they are knowledgeable about their own sexual health and the risks they pose to others. Of course, this responsibility is not unique to sex buyers—all sexually active members of the community have a responsibility to avoid exposing others to infection and disease. It is in all our interests to live in a community where rates of sexual infection and disease are low, and so we each (everyone including sex buyers) have a responsibility to ensure that we are not taking unnecessary risks that may affect the community as a whole.

SUMMARY

In summary, if you're buying sex, then you have a duty to be a responsible consumer. At the very least, this means the following:

a   You must always make sure that you have the consent of the sex worker to touch and interact with their bodies. This includes making a determined effort to ensure that they are competent to give consent and that their consent is informed and freely given, which requires checking for signs of intoxication, mental impairment, and abusive pimping or other kinds of coercion.
b   You must always respect the sex worker's right to withdraw consent. Though sexual activity is paid for, that does not override the sex worker's right to withdraw consent at any point. If consent to some activity or interaction is withdrawn, then you must stop.
c   You must not attempt to purchase sexual services while under the influence alcohol or drugs.
d   You must agree with the sex worker in advance of the interaction how much will be paid, and you should pay the full price for the services agreed to (you should not try to get 'extras' for free).
e   You must always practice safe sex.
f   You must attend a regular sexual health screening. This is important because even safe sex carries risks of sexually transmitted diseases.
g   You must report cases of suspected trafficking, sexual exploitation, and abusive pimping, to the relevant law enforcement authorities or charities.

If you choose to buy sex and you ensure that you meet these ethical standards, then the act of buying sex is not morally wrong: you do no moral wrong to the sex seller.

4   Why Might it be Wrong to Buy Sex?

I hope to have persuaded you that both workers and consumers have important moral rights that make selling and buying sex in nonideal conditions sometimes morally permissible. However, the argument of the preceding sections is incomplete insofar as it faces several important challenges. In this section, I consider three problems with the position just sketched and show why none of these objections undermines my case. Given that I am trying to establish that buying sex is not always morally wrong, I will concentrate on criticisms that specifically challenge the moral permissibility of *ever* purchasing sex.

4.1 Purchasing Sex and Gender Injustice

I anticipate that many feminists will be unsatisfied with my general defence of the moral permissibility of buying sex. The most obvious complaint to the view I have sketched is that its narrow focus on the rights and interests of individuals obfuscates the structural dynamics that subordinate women. Moreover, it might be argued that the position I'm advancing reinforces the idea of the male 'sex right' and implicitly endorses the view that men are always entitled to the bodies of women (e.g. Pateman 1988; Jeffreys 1997). According to my opponents, no one can buy sex now (or perhaps ever) without doing something wrong, where the wrong is not to be thought of as violating someone else's rights but rather the contribution to a system of gendered exploitation and oppression that wrongs women and violates their rights. To see this objection more clearly, consider the following argument made by Christine Overall:

> Sex work is an inherently unequal practice defined by the intersection of capitalism and patriarchy. Prostitution epitomizes men's dominance: it is a practice that is constructed by and reinforces male supremacy, which both creates and legitimizes the 'needs' that prostitution appears to satisfy as well as it perpetuates the systems and practices that permit sex work to flourish under capitalism. What is bad about prostitution, then, does not just reside in the sexual exchanges themselves, or in the circumstances in which they take place, but in capitalist patriarchy itself. What is wrong with prostitution is not just that it is the servicing of sexual needs but, rather, that it is women's servicing of men's sexual needs under capitalist and patriarchal conditions. Those conditions create both the male needs themselves and the ways in which women fill them, construct the buying of sexual services as a benefit for men, and

make the reversibility of sex services implausible and sexual equality in the trade unattainable.

(Overall 1992, p. 724)

According to Overall, prostitution is both a product and a cause of male supremacy. In effect, prostitution creates a class of women whose purpose is to satisfy the sexual needs of men, which also serves to reinforce male privilege and dominance over women more generally. So, the problem is not simply with the individual exchanges that occur between sex sellers and sex buyers but rather the larger structures within which prostitution exists and that are sustained by aggregated patterns of individual exchange.

To reiterate my position, I accept that in current conditions sex work is gendered. I also accept that under ideal conditions of gender equality, one would expect there to be less gender disparity among sex workers and perhaps even fewer sex workers in total. But I don't think this is sufficient to show that individual men always do something *morally wrong* when they purchase sexual services from women. Individual sex buyers are not morally responsible for systemic gender injustice and, arguably, their actions do not even help to sustain it. Let's imagine that Elvis (Section 1.1, Case 4) decides against going to Charlotte's house in order to promote gender justice. While his ends may be admirable, his actions are very unlikely to have any impact on the sex trade or systemic gender injustice. Given that, can we really say that Elvis is under a moral obligation to refrain from going to Charlotte's house and purchasing penetrative sex? If Elvis's choice to buy sex does not violate anyone's rights and has no effect on systemic or structural gender injustice, then it is difficult to see what else might be morally wrong with his decision.

Maybe it's not so much that Elvis's actions contribute to systemic gender injustice but rather that his actions are an expression of the morally problematic beliefs and attitudes that sustain gender injustice. This doesn't quite seem right either. We can imagine that Elvis is a responsible sex buyer who has nothing but the utmost respect for Charlotte, that he regards her as a full equal, that he fully respects her rights (see Section 3.3. above), and that he values her work. Moreover, lets imagine that Elvis's respect for Charlotte extends to all women. In this case, it hard to see how Elvis's actions—exchanging money for sex with Charlotte—express morally problematic beliefs or attitudes.

Perhaps it's not that Elvis himself must have morally problematic beliefs and attitudes about women but that his actions unintentionally communicate or symbolize women's inferior status (Satz 1995). It's important to note that when Elvis buys penetrative sex from Charlotte his actions only communicate something about Charlotte's inferior status under certain cultural conditions. Imagine a world in which men were generally subordinate to women. In that world, Elvis's actions would not have the effect of communicating that Charlotte is subordinate by virtue of being a woman. So, the problem with buying sex in patriarchal societies like ours is that it reinforces women's unequal status and is, therefore, a barrier to achieving gender justice (ibid., p. 81).

I'm happy to cede that in current conditions sale of sex typically involves negative and harmful messaging about women. However, I'm not convinced that this always makes buying sex morally wrong or that commercial sex is incompatible with achieving gender justice. First, commercial sex acts—the exchange of money for sex—typically take place in private. This being so, it's not obvious that individual buyers communicate anything about the status of women since they often have no audience. In exchanges like the one between Elvis and Charlotte, there is arguably no moral wrong since it takes place in private and therefore does not communicate negative messages about women in a way that would serve to reinforce gender injustice.

Second, as Brennan and Jaworski (2015, p. 1058) argue, 'cultures sometimes impute meaning to markets in harmful, socially destructive ways. Rather than giving us reason to avoid those markets, it gives us reason to revise the meaning we assign to these markets or, if we can't, to conscientiously rebel against or ignore the meaning our society attaches to these markets'. So instead of thinking that there is a moral problem with buying and selling sex, we might argue that the problem is with the wider sexist culture within which sex markets are situated. Moreover, if we take rights to sexual autonomy seriously, this gives us a reason to favour trying to change the negative messages associated with sex markets rather than morally prohibiting buying and selling sex. This then generates different kinds of duties. We don't have moral duties to refrain from selling and buying sex but rather a political responsibility to support social and institutional changes that will alter the negative meaning imputed to sex markets by the wider culture. This creates a space in which we can recognize that our current institutional order is unjust and that we have an obligation to do something about that structural injustice. Yet it does not hold people in contempt for the decisions they make while trying to live their lives under that order.

4.2 The Complicity Argument

One other powerful challenge to my view is advanced by Michelle Dempsey, who defends a blanket prohibition on buying sex (Dempsey 2019, p. 610). Dempsey's challenge consists of two main arguments: (1) the complicity argument, and (2) the endangerment argument. Here I address the former before moving on to address the latter in the following section.

The complicity argument maintains that anyone who buys sex causally contributes to sex trafficking and abusive pimping. Since sex trafficking and abusive pimping involve wrongful harm to the victims, anyone who buys sex is implicated in that harm and therefore bears responsibility for it. Importantly, sex buyers are not the principal wrongdoers, rather we should think of them as *accomplices* or *accessories* to the wrong done (Dempsey 2010, pp. 1752–1753). In defence of the claim that sex buyers are complicit in the wrong done to the victims of sex trafficking and abusive pimping Dempsey offers the following argument.

The Complicity Argument: Prostitution

Premise 1: Sex buyers create market demand for prostitution.

Premise 2: Market demand creates a profit motive for pimps.

Premise 3: This profit motive makes a causal contribution to pimps procuring and maintaining a supply of people to sell for sex.

Premise 4: In procuring and maintaining this supply, pimps often engage in harmful conduct against these people (e.g. force, threats, and coercion).

Conclusion: Therefore, by purchasing sex, one makes a causal contribution to the harmful conduct of pimps against the people they sell for sex.

(Dempsey 2019, p. 610; Dempsey 2010, pp. 1752–1762)

This argument is straightforward. Sex buyers act wrongly when they buy sex because they causally contribute to the harm done to the victims of sex trafficking and abusive pimping. If sex buyers refrained from buying sex, the market demand for sexual services would evaporate and there would be no incentive for sex traffickers or pimps. While sex buyers may only be indirectly responsible for the wrong done to trafficked and abusively pimped individuals, they are nonetheless responsible, and they are therefore under a moral duty to refrain from buying sex.

Notice that Dempsey's argument applies to all sex buyers not just those who buy sex from the victims of sex-trafficking. This means that even if one were to buy sex from an independent sex worker and follow the guidelines for responsible sex buying that I suggested earlier (Section 3.3), one would still do something morally wrong. This is because *all* sex buyers are complicit in fostering the idea that sex is economically valuable, which in turn creates motives and opportunities for exploitation within sex markets.

One problem with Dempsey's complicity argument is that it relies on the questionable assumption that individual consumers make a significant contribution to market demand. Contrary to Dempsey's suggestion, I would argue that individual buyers do not in fact create a market demand for sex. If one person chooses to stop buying sexual services, then this is not likely to reduce demand. This suggests that if an individual chooses to purchase a sexual service, they won't similarly be causally responsible for increasing market demand. Thus, individuals do not on their own create market demand and they cannot stop market demand. The actions of individuals are in this context *causally impotent*.

If this is correct, then Premise 1 of the complicity argument is false: it is simply not true that individuals on their own create demand. But perhaps this is not the right way to interpret Premise 1. Maybe instead we should read Premise 1 as referring to the collective of sex buyers, so it is the collective of sex buyers that creates demand and not individual actors. However, interpreting Premise 1 in this way makes the overall argument invalid because it reveals that the argument relies on an equivocation between the meaning of 'sex buyers' as a collective and the meaning of 'sex buyers' understood as individuals. For Premise 1 to be true, it must be referring to the collective of sex buyers because it is the collective that creates demand, not individuals. Yet Dempsey's conclusion explicitly refers to the causal contribution made by individual sex buyers. And, as we have seen, individuals do not make significant causal contributions: the choices of individuals are causally impotent insofar as they do not increase or reduce market demand. This means that Dempsey's argument is invalid since her conclusion about the actions of individual sex buyers does not follow from the premises (which refer only to the collective of sex buyers).

A further problem with this argument is that it is overinclusive. This means that Dempsey's argument morally prohibits buyers from engaging in many more markets (perhaps even most markets) than those which involve the sale of sex. To see why, consider the fact that many of the markets that we participate in have exploitative elements that harm some workers in those markets. Obvious examples include the markets in care, coffee, chocolate, electronics, travel, hospitality, and so on. All these markets have exploitative and criminal elements. Consequently, while some workers enjoy various labour protections and fair remuneration for their work, others do not, and they may suffer many harms when providing services or producing goods. To illustrate, consider an analogous argument for the market in clothing:

The Complicity Argument: Sweatshop Labour

Premise 1: Clothing-buyers create a market demand for clothes.

Premise 2: Market demand creates a profit motive for exploitative clothing manufacturers.

Premise 3: This profit motive makes a causal contribution to exploitative clothing manufacturers procuring and maintaining a supply of people to produce clothes in sweatshop labour conditions.

Premise 4: In procuring and maintaining this supply, exploitative clothing manufacturers often engage in harmful conduct against these people (e.g. force, threats, and coercion).

Conclusion: Therefore, by purchasing clothes, one makes a causal contribution to the harmful conduct of exploitative clothing manufacturers against the people they employ to make clothes.

The conclusion here implies that whenever we buy clothes, we do something morally wrong. This is because *buying* clothes creates market demand, which, in turn, creates motives and opportunities for exploitation. Consequently, the morally right thing to do is to refrain from buying clothes (and all other goods produced in markets with criminal or exploitative elements).

This conclusion strikes me as counterintuitive: it is implausible to think that whenever we buy new clothes, we commit a moral wrong. Let's grant, for the sake of argument, that purchasing clothes produced in sweatshop conditions might contribute to the demand for clothes produced in *those* conditions (though of course, it's far from obvious that individual actors in global markets create demand). Why should we think that individuals who engage in a fair exchange of clothes for money contribute to *exploitative* elements of the market? Perhaps instead we should think that individuals who choose clothes produced in non-sweatshop conditions contribute to the promotion of fairer elements in the clothing market. Indeed, the idea that we can bring about social and institutional change through our consumer choices is at the heart of all consumer activist projects. For example, the anti-sweatshop movement calls upon us to buy clothes from manufacturers who do not impose sweatshop labour conditions on their workers (Young 2004). Interestingly, they do not call upon us to stop buying clothes altogether!

Dempsey anticipates the objection just raised and offers two possible responses. First, she suggests that 'markets for goods such as shoes and carpets introduce multiple actors into the supply chain, attenuating the relationship between the purchaser and the directly harmful conduct perpetrated against the forced or child laborers' (Dempsey 2010, p. 1757). One thing that's worth noting here, is that sex markets are not merely composed of sellers and buyers:

> Within each market there is an ever-increasing number of ancillary industries that profit from the sale of direct sexual services. The physical location of the indoor markets means that there are several benefactors from the secret liaisons between purchasers and sellers. At inflated prices, landlords rent rooms, houses or apartments by the hour, night, day, week or month to individuals or groups of women. Rooms are rented in motels and motorway service stations to cater for the mobile customer, and for the international clientele, airport hotels provide convenient meeting places. Owners of establishments and women who register as a 'hostess' with the Inland Revenue buy the expertise of accountants to manage income, reduce tax bills and balance the books. The safety of the sex industry is the responsibility of men who are employed as door staff to parade outside saunas, as personal minders for women who work alone, or drivers to take women on escorting jobs. Taxi drivers are indispensable to the constant ferrying of people to and from establishments and in between home and work.
>
> (Sanders 2005a, p. 20)

This is just the tip of the iceberg. Sanders goes on to detail numerous others who benefit from sex markets and contribute to the supply chain. For example, **maids** or receptionists, cleaners, beauticians, hairdressers, cosmetic surgeons, newspapers and magazines who charge for personal ads, photographers, webpage designers and administrators, and so on (Sanders 2005a, pp. 20–22). What this indicates is that sex markets are more complex and wide-reaching than is sometimes imagined and though sexual services may involve one individual purchasing sex from another, each transaction is supported by numerous other actors.

But let's grant for the sake of argument that there are fewer actors involved in the sale of sex than cheap clothes. Why does this fact mark a point of significant moral difference between the two cases? Remember, we are already on board with the claim that a person does something morally wrong when they pay to have sex with a trafficked or abusively pimped individual. What moral difference does having fewer actors in the supply chain make for a responsible sex buyer? The answer might be that when there are fewer actors in the supply chain it is much more likely that the purchaser makes a causal contribution to the wrong done to the victims. But, as we saw above, just as buying clothes from ethical manufacturers does not increase demand for clothes produced in sweatshop conditions, neither does responsibly buying sex from freely consenting sex workers increase demand for the victims of sex trafficking.

Second, Dempsey argues that the difference

> between buying sex and buying shoes or carpets lies in the relationship between the person who does the buying and the sorts of harms inflicted on the person who is subjected to force, threats, coercion, etc. In buying shoes or carpets, one does not inflict any additional, direct harm on the person who was forced to manufacture the goods. In buying sex, however, this additional harm—or at least the risk of it—is directly inflicted by the purchaser in the sexual act of prostitute-use. The infliction of this additional harm (or risk thereof) establishes another key normative link between the purchaser of commercial sex and the harms of trafficking and abusive pimping.
>
> (Dempsey 2010, p. 1758)

Again, it is hard to see how this argument applies to the responsible sex buyer. Recall the case of Charlotte and Elvis (Section 1.1., Case 4).

When Elvis buys sexual services from Charlotte, he does not directly inflict harm on any trafficked and abusively pimped individuals. Charlotte is an independent sex worker who determines for herself the conditions of her work. Moreover, we can imagine that this is known by Elvis because he has looked at Charlotte's website, on online forums where Charlotte's customers have testified to her independence and professionalism, and when he arrives at Charlotte's house he asks her explicitly about how long she has been in the sex trade and why she chooses to do it. Given all the evidence he has, it's quite difficult to see why Elvis is any more likely to harm Charlotte by having sex with her than he would be to harm someone he was not paying to have sex with.

4.3 The Endangerment Argument

The idea that sex buyers run the risk of harming sex workers is central to Dempsey's second argument against the moral permissibility of buying sex, which she labels the endangerment argument (2019, p. 610). The basic idea behind the endangerment argument is that buying sex is morally wrong because one cannot know for certain that the person providing the sexual service is genuinely consenting. Dempsey summarizes the argument as follows:

The Endangerment Argument

Premise 1: Even when prostitution is not pimp-controlled, the conditions that induce people to sell sex are frequently inconsistent with genuine consent to the commercial sex act.

Premise 2: Having sex with someone who is not genuinely consenting harms/wrongs that person (in a sense tantamount to rape).

Conclusion 1: Therefore, in having commercial sex, a buyer runs the risk of having sex with someone who is not genuinely consenting (and thus harming/wronging that person).

Premise 3: This risk of harm substantially outweighs the value of the buyer having sex.

Conclusion 2: Therefore, in purchasing sex, one engages in conduct that presents an unjustifiable risk of harm to the sex seller.

(Dempsey 2019, p. 610; Dempsey 2010, pp. 1762–1769)

Here the wrongness of buying sex attaches to the risk of egregious wrongdoing. Sex buyers run the risk of committing an egregious wrong if they assume that meaningful consent has been given when it in fact has not. As with the complicity argument, this argument applies to all sex buyers not just those who pay for sex with individuals who have been trafficked or coercively pimped. No sex buyer can know for certain that they have genuine consent to proceed, and so buying sex in our social world is *always* morally wrong.

In response, I think it's worth considering the plausibility of Premise 1. The basic claim is that sex sellers are often coerced into selling sex and that invalidates their consent. Note, however, the coercion is not that associated with pimp-controlled prostitution (although, in an earlier articulation of the argument Dempsey is only concerned with the consent of trafficked and pimped individuals—Dempsey 2010, p. 1762). We are all agreed that forced labour, violence, and threats of violence can invalidate a person's consent. So, what kind of coercion is Dempsey worried about? It's hard to say since she gives no examples. However, she does suggest that a free choice would be one made when an 'adequate range of valuable options' is available (Dempsey 2019, p. 610).

As I argued earlier, having few better alternatives to sex work is not sufficient to invalidate consent (Section 3.2.1). Many people don't have the luxury of a wide range of valuable employment options, but they can nonetheless give genuine consent to the terms and conditions of their employment, including the use of their bodies. Assuming a person is competent, no one is forcing them to take up one role rather than another, that they can withdraw their labour at any time, and that they are informed about what they are choosing, then that person can give valid consent to their employment. Put another way, some pot washers, bar staff, supermarket workers, and carers may not have a wide range of good employment options available to them, and they may resent the jobs they do or the terms of their jobs, but they can still give valid consent to perform those roles and by so doing make it permissible for their clients, customers, colleagues, and employers to interact with them and make certain demands of them (which they may or may not choose to satisfy). The same is true for sex work. Even when faced with a range of poor employment options, a woman can nonetheless consent to sell sexual services and have the normative power to morally transform others' duties while in her chosen work role.

All that said, I think we should be concerned about women who sell sex out of fear of violence, so Dempsey's argument has some force. Yet it seems implausible to suggest that responsible sex buyers are always unable to determine whether valid consent is given. As Sanders notes, one common theme in discussions between sex buyers online is 'that it is the individual's responsibility to make sure that they do their research in order to avoid unpleasant situations' (Sanders 2008, p. 78). Much of this research is self-serving—sex buyers are looking for the right seller—but the interests of the workers themselves do form part of the process. As an example, Sanders details a response from a sex buyer to a UK Home Office consultation in 2004:

> The internet has transformed part of the paid sex industry. There are websites with message boards where punters can exchange information. These message boards have an educative function, and among other things do set benchmarks. To give examples: Any mention of unprotected sex (bareback) will be met with a barrage of both criticism and informed argument. Just before the law was changed regarding sex with under 18 year olds someone attempted to advertise the availability of a sixteen year old; despite this being technically legal at that time strong negative responses were expressed, leaving any possible user in no doubt as to what the others would think of him. Message boards often contain links to Crime Stoppers or similar resources, encouraging users to report illegal activity such as the use of those underage. Boards often contain sections where both punters and providers can warn others about dangerous people or practices.
>
> (Quoted in Sanders 2008, p. 74)

What this suggests is that some sex buyers *are* aware when sex sellers are the victims of trafficking or abusive pimping, and they take active steps to avoid perpetrating the kind of harm that Dempsey is concerned with. Indeed, many men want a safe and consensual experience and online communities where sex buyers share information about sellers indicate that there is a general aversion to coerced commercial sex (Sanders 2008; Soothill 2004). Of course, this does not mean that all sex buyers care about the welfare of sex sellers—some don't, and their actions and attitudes are morally reprehensible. But I'm not arguing that all existing sex buyers do no moral wrong only that it is possible for a person to buy sex today and not do anything morally wrong.

Dempsey might suggest that even when sex buyers do their homework and ask sex workers explicitly whether they give their consent freely this does not entirely eliminate the risk of them having sex with someone who is coerced. According to this line of thought, the epistemic threshold for non-wrongful sex with sex workers is certainty and that's unattainable. But why should we think that that epistemic standard only applies in cases of commercial sexual exchange? After all, everyone who engages in partnered sexual activity risks perpetrating the harms and wrongs of non-consensual sex—arguably, we can never be *certain* that we have valid consent. This is especially the case for men having sex with women against the backdrop of patriarchal oppression, which undoubtedly increases the possibility that a woman's token of consent does not reflect her genuine consent. For example, it's not uncommon for women to signal consent to sex in noncommercial sexual interactions when they are afraid of their male partner, or they do not feel they can say no, or they are exposed to psychological pressure, or because they are socially coerced. In each of these instances, a man would risk harming the woman by having sex with her. If we grant these risks to be significant, then this argument implies that it's *always* wrong for men to have sex with women, not just wrong to have sex with women for money.

In response to this worry, Dempsey suggests that 'the likelihood that a prostituted person is not genuinely consenting to commercial sex is greater than the likelihood that there is a lack of genuine consent in noncommercial sex' (2010, p. 1768). Maybe this is correct, I confess to not being sure. But there is an implicit assumption that the likelihood of a *responsible* sex buyer buying sex from a prostituted person is equal to the likelihood of a *non-responsible* sex buyer buying sex from a prostituted person. This doesn't seem right. When one takes active and effective steps to reduce the risks of one's choices, then the likelihood of doing something wrong will decrease. And to my mind, the level of risk attached to responsible sex buying is much closer to the level of risk attached to noncommercial sex. Moreover, if the state ensured that sex workers' rights were protected and that women had good alternative employment options, then the risk of a sex buyer perpetrating a wrong would be even further reduced.

Another problem with Dempsey's endangerment argument is that it unjustifiably diminishes the sexual autonomy of sex workers by denying them normative control in the domain of commercial sex. Dempsey's argument entails that sex workers can no longer effectively change the normative relationship between them and potential clients by giving their clients permission to interact with them in ways that would otherwise be wrongful. This is because the endangerment argument demands that sex buyers treat all sex workers *as though* their consent is invalid. This is so, even when confronted with an independent sex worker who explicitly consents and for whom there is no evidence of incapacity, coercion, or ignorance about what is being consented to.

To avoid perpetrating the serious moral wrong of engaging in non-consensual sex, would-be sex buyers must err on the side of caution and assume that no sex worker's consent is valid. This means that there is no way for a sex worker to give meaningful consent to a potential buyer because the sex buyer must always doubt that meaningful consent has been given. Consequently, the sexual autonomy of sex workers is severely thwarted because they are denied the normative control needed to contract with sex buyers and consent to the provision of sexual services. They are now unable to exchange sexual services for money because they cannot make the buyer *know* that the interaction between them would be non-wrongful. It does not matter how free they are, how independent they are, how financially secure they are, how many other options they have available, how much they value the work, how much better the work is for them in comparison to other alternatives, they cannot, according to Dempsey's argument, provide sufficient evidence of meaningful consent. They, therefore, have no meaningful control in this domain.

The restriction on sex workers' autonomy is, to my mind, a completely unacceptable implication of Dempsey's endangerment argument. It infantilizes sex workers—the majority of whom are women—by denying them the ability to choose for themselves what kind of life they want to lead and what kind of work they want to do. Moreover, limiting women's control in the sexual domain looks like just another attempt to control what women do with their bodies and with whom. Contrary to what its defenders claim, the abolition of sex work is not a solution to patriarchal oppression but rather another means through which women can be unjustly coerced and denied their autonomy. Far from liberating women, abolitionism operates to reinforce women's subordination.

Dempsey might respond that this side-effect of the endangerment argument is regrettable but that the diminishment of sex sellers' agency is a necessary evil to prevent one of the worst kinds of harm: the harm of non-consensual sex. Indeed, she argues that women are free to choose to sell sex but 'their choice to sell sex does not justify the risk of harm posed to other prostituted people who are sold against their will' (2010, p. 1769). Thus, according to Dempsey, while women in economic need may be morally permitted to sell sex, the men who might pay for such services are nonetheless morally prohibited from buying.

One thing that's worth noting at this point is that Premise 4 of Dempsey's argument has to be revised to include the value of commercial sex to buyers *and* sellers. It should read:

> Premise 4: This risk of harm substantially outweighs the value of the buyer having sex *and the value to the sex worker of selling sex*.

Recast in this way, it is likely that many more commercial sex transactions stand to benefit *both* the buyers and sellers. Indeed, in our four imagined cases, Adele and Chris, Eva and Marc, Maria and Akira, and Charlotte and Elvis all stand to benefit from their respective transactions. And it is not clear that the risk of harm outweighs the benefits of each transaction to those involved. Moreover, I think we should be wary of compromising the rights of individuals simply because some people are wronged by exploitative elements of the market. The better solution, it seems to me, is to invest more resources into preventing trafficking and sexual exploitation and regulate the sex trade in ways that benefit sex workers and minimize the risk of sex buyers harming them.

5 Conclusion

To conclude, I have argued that morally permissible commercial sex exchanges between men and women are possible in liberal democracies marked by sex inequality and gender injustice. Central to my argument is the claim that each of us has a fundamental interest in sexual autonomy, which grounds rights to buy and sell sexual services if we so choose. I have further suggested that the right to buy sex from those who can give valid consent to sell is accompanied by a set of moral responsibilities, which must be met if buying is to be morally decent. Ultimately, while one may find the idea of purchasing sex distasteful or think that it somehow devalues the good of sex, such concerns are the subject of reasonable disagreement about what the sexual good life is. Insofar as responsible sex buyers satisfy their moral duties, they do not wrong those with whom they transact.

Throughout I have accepted that there is much that is problematic about existing sex industries and morally bad behaviour is rife. But it is important to see that 'the violence and exploitation that sex workers face from a range of sources including the state, police, communities, partners, pimps, clients and those pretending to be clients [...] occurs not because of the exchange of cash for sex, but because of the circumstances and regulation around such exchanges which make it harder for sex workers to operate safely' (Kingston et al. 2021, pp. 542–543). The moral problems associated with sex work, then, are not because sex is paid for, or because men buy sex from women, but because we fail to organize our social, legal, and political life in a way that protects sex workers and promotes all our rights to sexual autonomy.

Part II

First Round of Replies

Chapter 3

No Such Thing as a Good Sex Buyer

First Reply to Angie Pepper

Holly Lawford-Smith

1 Choice, Agency, Autonomy

A familiar gloss on the difference between a **liberal feminist** and a **radical feminist** is that a liberal feminist cares about choice and agency *within* the social structures that we have, and a radical feminist cares about the social structures *that* we have. Take the question of a woman who resigns from her meaningful and well-paid job in order to stay at home with her children in the early years of their lives. The liberal feminist will tend to ask whether that was her choice; to make sure that she was not coerced by her husband, her mother-in-law, the state. The radical feminist will tend to ask what the background structure is like such that she has that set of choices rather than another. If it is one in which childcare is expensive, female-dominated industries have on average lower salaries, and there are strong social norms in favour of mothers rather than fathers putting their careers on hold for family reasons, then the radical feminist may refuse to accept the woman's choice as the end of the matter. (On the other hand, if the background is not characterized by any such inequalities, she may agree with the liberal feminist that the woman's choice *is* the end of the matter.) This difference between the liberal and the radical is my first disagreement with Angie.

In her essay 'Sexuality' in *Toward a Feminist Theory of The State* (1989), Catharine MacKinnon wrote powerfully about the concepts of choice, agency, and autonomy when they are used without taking account of the conditions in which they are allegedly exercised. She starts by comparing women's sexuality to black culture, acknowledging both that forms of culture can emerge in conditions of oppression, and that such culture 'can be experienced as a source

DOI: 10.4324/9781003169697-6

of strength, joy, expression, and as an affirmative badge of pride' (MacKinnon 1989, p. 153). Still, the conditions matter. She writes:

> Both [forms of culture] remain nonetheless stigmatic in the sense of a brand, a restriction, a definition as less. This is not because of any intrinsic content or value, but because the social reality that is their shape, qualities, texture, imperative, and very existence are a response to powerlessness. They exist as they do because of lack of choice. They are created out of social conditions of oppression and exclusion. They may be part of a strategy for survival or even of change. But, as is, they are not the whole world, and it is the whole world that one is entitled to. *This is why interpreting female sexuality as an expression of women's agency and autonomy, as if sexism did not exist, is always denigrating and bizarre and reductive, as it would be to interpret Black culture as if racism did not exist.* As if Black culture just arose freely and spontaneously on the plantations and in the ghettos of North America, adding diversity to American pluralism.
>
> (MacKinnon 1989, p. 153, my emphasis)

In the world as we know it, there is restricted choice, restricted autonomy, restricted agency. Women are forced to operate under conditions of oppression and exclusion. Of course, *within* those parameters, they may act in ways that are highly rational, securing for themselves as individuals the best of what is available. Female sexuality, for example its experience of dominance as exciting, may be an adaptation, a 'strategy for survival' (on these strategies see also Hoagland 1988, ch. 2). Just as we have no idea what black culture would be like, and indeed whether there would even be a distinctively black culture, under historical conditions of racial equality, we have no idea what women's sexuality would be like, and whether there would even be a distinctively women's sexuality, under historical conditions of sex equality. Calling her sexuality 'autonomous' because she exercises choice within these limiting conditions misses something important precisely about the range of choices that she has because of those limiting conditions.

MacKinnon's criticism applies to Angie's approach to buying sex: Angie focuses on the actions of individual sex sellers and sex buyers under our current conditions, rather than looking at the relationship between those actions and the conditions. In her cases, it is enough that the women choose sex work, and that the sexual inter-actions pass 'without incident', by which she presumably means, without physical violence. This is true even though in Case 3 'Maria doesn't particularly like her work … but she feels like she can't leave because there is no other, equally lucrative, employment option available to her', and in Case 4, 'Charlotte … wants to move out of the sex industry. However, Charlotte has found it difficult to move out of sex work because it is very hard to hide her time spent as a sex worker and potential employers refuse to hire her.' She offers no comment on why camming and stripping are things that Adele in Case 1 and Eva in Case 2 see as a reasonable use of their human potential. MacKinnon's point bites here: these options *are not the whole world, and it is the whole world that one is entitled to.*

I think Angie will say, to take autonomy seriously is to give people the right to shape their own lives, in the conditions that they find themselves in, whatever those are. In some kinds of conditions, this clearly can't be right, but in others, it does look appealing. Imagine for a moment that instead of sexualized violence against women—and sexualized treatment that many people struggle to even *recognize* as violence—there was simply targeted and arbitrary physical violence. If a woman were to leave her house, she would be at risk of being shot or stabbed, the same risk she is currently at of being raped, being subject to domestic abuse, or being coerced or blackmailed into pornography or prostitution. Suppose that some women, higher in risk-taking in the face of this violence, do well out of the reduced competition for resources (because women lower in risk-taking remain in their homes). Now suppose some feminists came along and proposed new laws that would 'set a high price on our blood', to borrow Andrea Dworkin's phrase from *Scapegoat* (2000, p. 246). Would Angie then criticize these laws for failing to respect the autonomy of women, who after all have the right to shape their own lives in the conditions they find themselves in? If we take male violence to be a fixed feature of their lives, then it does look like women's choices are between more safety and less freedom (remaining in the home), and more freedom and less safety (going out and running the risk of violence). Either of these choices might be rational. But is that the end of the matter?

I do not believe that Angie would criticize those laws that put a high price on women's blood. And if I am right, then this establishes that it is not true *in general* that we should always take social conditions as fixed and ask only about autonomy within them. Even if autonomy is our ultimate concern, some social conditions have too negative an impact on autonomy, by restricting people's choice sets to unacceptably few options, or options of unacceptably poor quality. In such a case we have a conflict between two different groups of women's autonomy; or, between violations of the autonomy of one group of women to take up *this specific option* now, versus increased autonomy for all women to take up *these new and/or better options* later. This means we first have to settle the question of when option sets are good enough for us to ask only about the autonomy of the people who have them. But then our disagreement becomes live again: I say that because society has been **androcentric** for thousands of years, men's ideas about women's nature and function have had undue influence on a woman's own ideas about herself, including her ideas about her sexuality; and that this means her choice set contains unacceptably few or unacceptably poor-quality options. (Or less universally, but at the very least: the choice sets of *many* women contain unacceptably few or unacceptably poor-quality options, because of the way that men's ideas about her and men's treatment of her—e.g. childhood sexual abuse, rape, sexual assault and harassment, sexual objectification—have impacted her.) I say that what happens to her in the conditions under which she lives *is* 'targeted and arbitrary physical violence', we just don't think of it as violence because we think of it as—confuse it with—sex. A not insignificant proportion of commercial sex *is* violence in the form of sex.

More significantly, virtually no one thinks that autonomy is the *only* moral value that matters. Even way back in *Two Treatises of Government* (1689) it was not liberty alone, but 'life, liberty, health and goods' that John Locke thought couldn't be secured for every person in the state of nature, and which therefore made it in their interests to consent to government (see discussion in Clack 1999, p. 112). But what of women's lives, health, and goods? If these are all sufficiently negatively impacted by the current conditions in which she sells sex, then they trade off unfavourably against autonomy *even if* autonomy supports taking the conditions as fixed.

Finally, what of the autonomy of the feminists? Members of oppressed groups will have competing interpretations of their situation. Consider a contrast to another group. MacKinnon talked about black culture, noting that it would be bizarre to proceed as though it 'just arose freely and spontaneously on the plantations'. Suppose that some black people living in conditions of slavery thought that slavery was unjust, that there was violence, there was social hierarchy, there was the frustration of human potential. Let's call those people black liberationists. Would we take seriously the complaints of other black people—acclimatized to their situation or having internalized white people's view of them as inferior—that *they* accepted slavery, and that the black liberationists' agitations for black equality *undermined their autonomy*? Surely we would not; surely we would say, the 'autonomous' choice to accept slavery keeps all black people in a state of oppression. Why, then, do we accord so much respect to the 'autonomous' choices of women to act as objects and instruments for men's sexual pleasure? At the very least, we should not care about the autonomy of sex workers to the exclusion of the autonomy of feminists, especially considering that only the feminist attempts to speak to the interests of her whole class.

Angie might reply that it is unfair to use MacKinnon's analogy in application to sex work in particular (rather than women's sexuality in general), because all slavery is forced, while only some sex work is. But her point could be made for a group whose daily activities are not forced. Consider caste hierarchies as existed in India, for example. Suppose members of the Waishya caste (ranked third of the five main caste groups) had competing interpretations of their situation, with some simply glad not to be in the lower castes (Shudras and Dalits), and some resentful of the greater status and opportunities afforded by being in the higher castes (Brahmins and Kshatriyas), and desiring an end to the caste system (see e.g. BBC 2019). We might agree that those Vaishyas happy to make the most of the choices they had were exercising autonomy, and yet disagree that Vaishya 'caste abolitionists' were *undermining the former's autonomy* by working to bring about a society in which they would not be limited to just those choices. It's not that the choices previously available would necessarily disappear after the social structure changed. Vaishyas were farmers, traders, and merchants, and even in an egalitarian India there would likely still be farmers, traders, and merchants. The point is rather that the range and quality of choices would change for *everyone*, and that means different people making the choices that were previously limited to one social group. In the case of slavery, reform of the social structure does remove any choices made *within* the practice of being a slave, because that practice is abolished. (I leave open whether sex work is more like slavery, and so would disappear, or more like farming, and so would remain, the change being only who does it, so as not to beg any questions against Angie.)

I'm not saying that those who speak in the language of liberation are always getting it right, and those who don't are not. I agree with Janet Radcliffe Richards in *The Sceptical Feminist* that we should be cautious about this. But her test for 'the true liberator' is too strong. She says: 'there is never any justification for taking a choice away from a group you want to liberate unless it is demonstrable beyond all reasonable doubt that removing it will bring other, more important, options into existence' (Radcliffe Richards [1980] 1994, p. 108; see also discussion in Lawford-Smith 2022a, pp. 188–190).

Merely giving sex workers another option, like a social welfare payment insufficient to cover her bills, or menial work insufficiently flexible to let her care for her child, is not likely to transform the choice sets of women who opt for sex work. Thinking *merely* in terms of alternatives, whatever they are, plays into the hands of those who are not opposed to sex hierarchy; for they can say, look, she had another option, and she did not take it. She *prefers* sex work. But this establishes nothing. She is rational to prefer whatever choice will give her the most of what she wants. If she wants more money and more time with her kid, then she may choose sex work. That may be a rational choice. But what if we think that option should not exist, because *women are not things for men to fuck*? What if, once men truly understand that women are not things for them to fuck, women's options transform radically, for she is finally, fully, human? Radcliffe Richards suggests that this would have to be 'demonstrable beyond all reasonable doubt'—the same standard as for a criminal conviction under the law. But how could the feminist future be *demonstrable* now, let alone beyond all reasonable doubt? Instead, we might think the 'true liberator' is the one who can make a compelling argument that eliminating one option will increase options overall. And this is precisely what I am arguing: the existence of markets in sex makes a significant contribution to sustaining sex hierarchy (in both senses: the social hierarchy of the biological sexes; and hierarchical sexual intercourse).

2   Always Wrong versus Generally Wrong

It appears from our opening statements that Angie and I have already converged on the view that quite a lot of the sex that is currently bought is such that it is morally wrong to buy it. I agree with

Angie that it is wrong to buy sex from underage girls, women who are drunk or high, women who have mental or cognitive impairments that affect their ability to consent, women who are selling sex under threat of violence, women who do not agree to sell sex or who withdraw their consent during a sexual interaction, and women who are subject to violence at the hands of the man who buys sex (Chapter 2, Section 1). This rules out all trafficking and all abusive pimping (ibid.). That means it is likely to rule out most street-based sex work, which tends to involve both abusive pimps and drugs. It leaves in non-abusive pimping, if there is any, and the sex that is bought without violating any of those other conditions and also does not end in violence. This will be some indoor sex work. (If Angie is employing a broader definition of sex work than I am, including no-contact work such as camming and OnlyFans, then this will also be in the category that is left in as not morally wrong for her. I have been focusing on contact sex, particularly penetrative sex.)

Angie and I agree that there is a lot of violence in sex work, but she thinks 'it is misleading to think that violence in sex work is inevitable or that sex work is inherently violent'. We agree that some sex workers don't enjoy their work, are traumatized by their work, and are not treated well by those who buy sex from them (Section 1.1). It is not clear to me how large the pool of remaining sex buying is. That, in turn, makes me wonder what we are really debating, in the proposition 'it is morally wrong to buy sex'. Are we asking whether it is *always* wrong to buy sex? Or are we asking whether it is *generally* wrong to buy sex?

If it's the former, then Angie will win the argument so long as she can provide a single counterexample, one case where buying sex is morally permissible. Perhaps it doesn't even need to be an actual or likely case, just a possible case—possible in light of current social conditions. If this is all it would take, then it could be true for most of the men who buy sex, and most of the sex that they buy, that they are doing something morally wrong. To me, it would be better to articulate this position as 'it is not *necessarily* wrong to buy sex', or 'it is not *always* wrong to buy sex', rather than 'it is not wrong to buy sex'. To agree that much, if not most, of the sex that is currently bought is morally wrong, and yet to argue that it is not morally wrong to buy sex, is somewhat confounding. If it generally is wrong, then colloquially, it is wrong.

When I argue that it is morally wrong to buy sex, I mean to defend both disambiguations of the claim. It is generally wrong for a man to buy sex, and he is always wrong to buy it. He is wrong to buy it whenever she is unable to consent to sell it: Angie and I agree on this. He is also wrong to participate in the social practice that is a market in sex, because of what that market means and does against a background of sex hierarchy—because it is wrong *that there is* that market. And finally, he is wrong to risk harm to the individual woman he buys sex from, in all the ways I explained in my opening statement. Angie and I disagree about these last two, I think. (Or perhaps, we disagree about the background conditions, and we disagree about whether my arguments for individual wrongdoing in specific sex-buying interactions cover *all* cases or only *some* cases.) For me, the wrongness of buying sex is overdetermined. There can be no counterexamples to the structural claim, because there are no cases of sex buying that operate without the background of sex hierarchy. But if we set the structural claim aside, and focus on the conditions of the individual interactions, then perhaps we would agree that buying sex is only generally (usually) wrong rather than always wrong.

Here, then, is my summary of where we are at in terms of agreement and disagreement: Angie and I disagree about the significance of the background conditions, and this disagreement leads me to think all sex-buying is wrong, and her to think that it is not. We agree about inability to consent, and we probably disagree about whether my arguments for individual harm within sex-buying interactions cover all cases or only some. (I would be surprised if she thinks they cover none.) Thus, we are really arguing, at this point, over a relatively small proportion of all the sex-buying that there is or could be, given roughly the present social conditions. This is likely to be some brothel prostitution and some elite prostitution. The open question is whether all of *that* is wrong too.

3   Moral Wrongness

This takes me to my third issue. Angie and I have a disagreement over whether it is morally wrong to buy sex. I say it is, she says it is not. It is impossible to mediate this dispute without considering what moral wrongness consists in, and neither of us have been explicit about that. (For that reason, this part of the rejoinder is a rejoinder to both of our contributions.) That is to say, we have both cited particular values, her citing autonomy and rights to sexual freedom; me citing a rather eclectic collection of things including harm and risk of harm, risk of complicity, exploitation, acting out privileges of social hierarchy, contributing to demand for unethical products, and risking backlash against movements for equality. But neither of us have said whether we think these are the only values, the most important values, or values that have **lexical priority** over others (which means, they take precedence when there is any potential conflict). Neither of us have said whether in the background there is a more holistic theory of moral wrongness, which we are using these more specific terms to point at, perhaps some version of one of the 'big three' moral theories: **virtue theory, consequentialism,** or **deontology**. (Virtue theory tells us that the right thing to do is whatever the virtuous—courageous, wise, benevolent, etc.—agent would in fact do; consequentialism tells us to consider the consequences of our actions, and to choose the action with the best consequences according to our preferred metric, for example, acting in the way that will secure the most happiness; and deontology prescribes a set of categorical rules or imperatives that we must follow if we are to do what morality demands, for example 'do your fair share in producing public goods'.) What does moral wrongness consist in? Do we agree on that, but disagree on what that means for buying sex? Or do we disagree on that, and that's *why* we disagree about the morality of buying sex?

One clue that we disagree on what moral wrongness consists in comes from what Angie says at the end of Section 4.1: 'we can recognize that our current institutional order is unjust and that we have an obligation to do something about that structural injustice … [and yet] not hold people in contempt for the decisions they make while trying to live their lives under that order'. I don't think that taking someone's action to be morally wrong entails holding that person in contempt. I think that almost everyone is doing moral wrong surprisingly often, and it would be counterproductive for us to all go about holding each other in contempt for what most of us are doing. This misunderstanding points to the need for further clarification. Trying to work out how we disagree about moral wrongness might help us to make progress on our disagreement about buying sex.

Before I say more about that, it is worth noting a further way that we might disagree about what is morally wrong. That is not by having different background theories of what moral wrongness (and rightness) consist in, but by having different ideas about what we can realistically expect of people. Most people think that 'ought

implies can', which means that we have an obligation to do some
thing only if we can actually do that thing. Things get even more
complicated when it comes to what we can do as a community, a
society, a nation, because there we need to coordinate the actions
of many people, and we may or may not have the infrastructure in
place to do that. Here's one way to think about things: we can tell
a story about what is morally good from the *absolute best* set of
actions all the way down to the *absolute worst*. Let me explain this
using an individual, instead of a social group, to keep things simple.

Let's say the *absolute best* way that Perry can treat Celeste is
with love, care, and respect. One implication of this is that he never
lays a hand on her except in ways that she desires. The next best,
still pretty good but not ideal, is that he sometimes gets angry and
puts his hands on her, but he just grabs her by the shoulders and
shakes her. He doesn't leave a mark, and she isn't very scared; more
annoyed. The next best, and you probably see where this is going, is
that he gets angry quite often, and he hits her, but he makes sure to
hit her on the parts of the body that can be hidden under her clothing, so that it's not embarrassing for her with her friends, inviting
awkward questions. He is considerate, within the fixed conditions
of being a wife-batterer. Keep going on down the chain until you get
to about the worst that you can imagine (if you can't imagine, you
might consult the television adaptation of the novel *Big Little Lies*,
from which the names 'Celeste' and 'Perry' are taken; or Andrea
Dworkin's description of the character 'Andrea's first marriage, as
told in *Mercy*—Dworkin 1990).

The point of spelling out some of these steps is to note, first, that
we could decide that what morality requires is the *absolute best*
thing, and therefore anything else, *even if it is better than some
other action*, is still morally wrong. Or, we could think about which
of the options we think is the most realistic best, better than the
status quo but not 'idealistic' or 'utopian', and settle there, and then
the morally wrong actions would be all the actions worse than *that*.
Both of these would be compatible with acknowledging that there
is better and worse in moral terms. In terms of evaluative claims
(claims about what is good and bad), Angie and I might agree on
the scale from worse to better; but in terms of normative claims
(claims about what should be done), we might disagree *because* we
disagree about which is the most realistic best option.

We could use language in a way that makes this explicit, for example, saying 'given that the best we can expect from Perry is that he hit

Celeste in ways that don't leave bruises she can't cover up with clothes, it is morally wrong for him to hit her in ways that leave bruises on her forearms, lower legs, or face'. Maybe I am saying that buying sex is wrong because for the man who does it *there's a better realistic thing that he could do* when it comes to women, and Angie is saying that buying sex isn't wrong, *because there are no better realistic things he could do*. In fact, the disagreement may be even more pragmatic than that: as a purely descriptive matter he *is going to* continue to buy sex and she *is going to* continue to sell it, *therefore* we should focus on clearly communicating that the worst ways he can do that are morally wrong, so that at least she is spared those. But then I have to ask, what justifies these assumptions about what the world will be like, and will remain like? *Why* is that the best we can hope for?

Let's return to the question of moral wrongness. The 'big three' approaches differ in how easy they make it to establish moral wrongness. I don't have the space to run through all of the available versions of each of them, but I will run through a few, to illustrate. With act consequentialism, a version of consequentialism focused on a particular individual's actions at a particular time, it is the easiest. Among all the actions available to you, the right action is the one that will have the best consequences measured in the relevant metric. Moral theorists disagree about the metric: it might be happiness, well-being, flourishing, transcendence; it might be the minimization of misery, pain, ill-health, suffering. Once we have figured out the action with the best consequences, we know what we should do. Doing that thing is morally right, doing anything else is morally wrong. So one way that I could defend the claim that buying sex is morally wrong is to commit to some form of act consequentialism and a corresponding metric like flourishing, then argue that buying sex is never the option available to a man that will have the best consequences in terms of flourishing. Consequentialists care about global consequences, not individual ones: so he cannot ask only what will contribute to *his own* flourishing, but must also take into account what will contribute to hers. From there we plug in everything we know about her vulnerability and how being sexually used might impact it, and it will come out as unlikely that this interaction will increase her flourishing, or that what he gets out of it will counterbalance what she loses in it. Buying sex is not the best thing he could do, so it is not the morally right action, and doing anything other than the morally right action is morally wrong. Therefore, buying sex is morally wrong.

With virtue theory, it is similarly easy, because we do not need to think about anyone other than the sex buyer himself. We defend a set of virtues, and we assess sex buying in light of them. Suppose we think it is virtuous to be kind, fair, caring, generous, compassionate. What a person with these virtues would do is what is morally right, and anything else is morally wrong. It is hard to see how it could be the case that a compassionate person would risk retraumatizing a sexual assault survivor; how a generous person would respond to destitution by offering money in exchange for sex (instead of just helping); how a fair person could fail to notice the sex inequality of who tends to buy sex and who it tends to be bought from. Even if Angie thinks it can be *not wrong* to buy sex, I doubt that she thinks buying sex is *virtuous*, is something that a virtuous person would do (although perhaps I am wrong about this).

Perhaps the most challenging approach for establishing the moral wrongness of sex-buying is deontology. One helpful set of distinctions when it comes to thinking about the morality of our individual actions in deontic terms is:

forbidden | permissible | obligatory

When an action is forbidden, you must not do it. When it is permissible, you may do it, or you may not do it. It is up to you. When it is obligatory, you must do it. Here are some uncontroversial examples from 'folk morality', which means, the set of moral beliefs that most people subscribe to. It is forbidden to abuse an animal, it is permissible to drink a cup of coffee, it is obligatory to pay your taxes. Wherever there are moral claims, there is the prospect of disagreement: we might want to talk about whether it's really permissible to drink a cup of coffee if the beans were supplied with exploited labour; we might want to argue about whether it's obligatory to pay your taxes if your state is using them to fund an unjust war. This set of distinctions is helpful, though, because it makes clear that there is a large set of actions that have no important moral status, being neither forbidden nor obligatory, but merely permissible. This is presumably where Angie locates sex buying: so long as it is done in a particular way (with consent and 'without incident') then it is permissible. The obligatory and the permissible combined are a very large category of actions, the actions that it is not morally wrong to do. This flips the verdict of the first two approaches, where one thing is the best action, or a few things are what a virtuous person would do, and everything else is morally wrong. I want to locate buying sex in the rather narrow category of the forbidden. What are some of the familiar strategies for determining which actions belong to that category?

Some of the best-known strategies will be no use to us, for example one that asks only whether the action is 'universalizable', meaning, such that everyone could do it (this is one of the three formulations of Immanuel Kant's 'categorical imperative'). Presumably everyone *could* buy sex from someone else, it's simply that in practice, it's men who buy it from women. So we won't get forbidden actions, and thus moral wrongness, in this way. Another common way to determine what goes into this category is to look at what does harm. It is forbidden to do harm. Other ways to say this are, it is obligatory that we do no harm; the only actions that are permissible are the ones that do no harm. Gratuitous physical violence is an uncontroversial harm, so gratuitous physical violence goes into the category of the forbidden. Several of the arguments I gave for the wrongness of buying sex fall into this category: risking rape, retraumatizing a person with PTSD, doing to vulnerable women what it is wrong to do to any women, and exploiting a destitute person (helping conditional on receiving sex, and not otherwise). These are the most straightforward because with his action *alone*, the sex buyer either does harm or risks doing harm to the woman selling sex.

Risking complicity in another man's violence is slightly more complicated, because it is about the harm that a few men do together. But we are used to thinking about these kinds of harms from 'joint enterprise' cases, for example where a group of friends decide to rob a bank (see further discussion in Lawford-Smith 2018). Just as we might think that all contributors acted wrongly because in the course of the robbery a bank teller was killed, even if only one of them did the actual killing, we might think that the sex buyer and the husband who pimped out his wife to the buyer harm the wife, and so their actions are wrongful for that reason.

More difficult are the cases where the group gets bigger, so that there is not plausibly a joint enterprise even though there is a causal impact of what everyone is doing. It might be that women *are harmed*, and yet harder to say *who* harmed them. Contributing to creating consumer demand for unethical products/practices, and risking a backlash against the movement for women's equality, both fall into this category. When enough of the sex buyers buy sex, they create a demand that may be filled with trafficked and otherwise coerced women. When enough of the men who say they are for women's equality are revealed to be sex buyers and therefore hypocrites, they create a backlash that may set back the women's rights movement. We can't say that a sex buyer does harm here, whether alone or in joint enterprise with other men. We can say only that he contributes to the harm that he and many other men do together. Some may think this is not enough to establish the moral wrongness of his action.

(For what it's worth, I think that in some cases, the wrongness of the practice is enough to make participation in the practice wrong. I *don't* think carbon emissions are like this: most people participate, but it's the practice that does harm, and is wrong, not the individual participants' contributions. But I *do* think slavery is like this. The practice does harm, and is wrong; *and* participation in the practice is wrong, quite aside from any further harms inflicted on slaves by slave-owners. Slavery as a social practice is wrong; it is wrong for individuals to own slaves; violence and brutality by slave-owners toward slaves is additionally wrong. Similarly, markets in sex are wrong; it is wrong for men to buy sex (off-camera and on-camera, for themselves or for other men); and violence and brutality by sex-buyers toward women who sell sex is additionally wrong.

The arguments most difficult to accommodate in terms of what is forbidden being what is harmful are the argument that it is wrong to have hierarchical sex, and the argument that it is wrong to act out the privileges of social hierarchy when one occupies the superior position. People will struggle to see these actions as harmful precisely because they are so ordinary. There is social hierarchy and men act out the privileges of maleness every day (to anticipate a common objection, this does not mean there are no disadvantages to maleness). The sexes have been organized like this for thousands of years, and sexual intercourse has gone roughly like this since *Homo sapiens* emerged. Perhaps one can make a revisionary case that the apparently ordinary is in fact *wrong*, but one can't so easily make the case that the apparently ordinary is *harmful*, especially when it does not cause any of the things we usually think of as harms, like physical or psychological suffering. I think this is correct. For those two arguments in particular, the source of the wrongness is *inequality*, and *frustrated potential*. When men act out the privileges of social hierarchy, and when they have hierarchical sex, which is one of those privileges, they accept and perpetuate inequality between persons (men and women, boys and girls), and they together sustain a world in which women struggle to be seen as—struggle to *be*—full human persons, because they struggle perpetually against men's sexualized ideas of what women are. Philosophers have certainly noticed these things and thought that they matter; the **Aristotelians** were concerned with flourishing (which is precisely to *not* have one's potential frustrated) and the **existentialists** were concerned with 'transcendence' (which is not exactly the same thing, but somewhere in the neighbourhood). But whether they'd go so far as to say that actions *against* flourishing or transcendence are morally wrong is another question.

To come back to something I mentioned at the start of this section, the reason moral wrongness in terms of doing harm doesn't justify holding the wrongdoer in contempt is that most of us are wrongdoers in this sense, and for some of us we are wrongdoers a lot of the time. A lot of ordinary actions do harm, or contribute to doing joint harm; whether to poorer people in other countries (through supply chains), to future people (through climate change), to animals (through the agricultural industry), or to the environment (through unsustainable use of land and resources).

None of these approaches settle the matter of what is and isn't morally wrongful action. Once you settle on an approach, you still need to make the case for or against an action in terms of its relationship to good and bad consequences (in your preferred metric), to virtues (however you fill in what those are), or to what is obligatory and/or forbidden (whatever you think determines an action being each of these). But setting them out will hopefully be helpful, in allowing us to see which approach is most accommodating of our respective views about buying sex. To justify my conclusions, I will have to say either that buying sex has bad consequences, or that it is not something a virtuous person would do, or that it causes harm (or I will have to propose some novel moral approach, or a hybrid of the big three approaches, that gives me the conclusion I want). I suspect that a deontic view built to accommodate inequality and frustrated potential alongside harm will be the most congenial to my position. Once we know what Angie thinks is the most congenial framework for her view, we will be in a position to answer the question of whether we agree about what moral wrongness consists in but disagree about its implications for buying sex, or disagree about buying sex *because* we disagree about what moral wrongness consists in.

4 'Good' Sex Buyers

Angie's Section 3.3 is called 'Responsible Sex Buyers', and there she lays out 'clear moral guidance on how to be a responsible sex buyer' so that the men who buy sex don't 'fall short of morally decent behaviour', and 'risk doing something morally wrong or lacking in virtue'. (Her mention of virtue here suggests that I may have been wrong in Section 3 when I predicted that she would not believe sex buying could be virtuous.) It is revealing of our different views of what the sex industry is like from the perspective of sex workers that Angie thinks it is sometimes morally permissible to buy sex, and yet also says 'all workers have a right to be treated with dignity and respect, and consumers must never regard service providers as mere means'. In what I have read (and watched, and listened to), so many sex workers say that they are *not* treated this way that to me it is virtually inherent to the practice of buying sex that one treats the sex worker as a means. She is exactly a means to his sexual pleasure.

I do not deny that Angie's directives are useful, and would make the world *better* for sex workers if they were followed. We can make use of the discussion from Section 3 above to understand this: there are better and worse ways the world can be. I think Angie and I probably agree that things as they are now are bad, and that things would be better if the men who buy sex followed her list of directives. It's just that I don't stop there. I think there's something even better than that, which would be if men didn't—and *couldn't*—buy sex at all. I think it would be better if Adele, Eva, Maria, and Charlotte from Angie's cases had other options, options that were well-paid and that respected their full humanity, rather than turning them into objects or instruments for men's sexual pleasure. I agree that the men who follow Angie's list of directives are morally better than the men who don't, but I don't think that following her list makes them morally *good*—or makes them *not moral wrongdoers*. They will be morally good when they see women as fully human, and on my view you cannot see a class of people as fully human *and* pay for sexual access to them.

Chapter 4

Why It's Still Not Wrong to Buy Sex

First Reply to Holly Lawford-Smith

Angie Pepper

This reply is divided into three sections. In Section 1, I start by setting out more precisely the moral framework that underpins my position. I do this for two reasons. First, because Holly invites me to do so in her response to my opening statement. Second, because making my own view transparent helps us to see more clearly why I and Holly disagree and why I think that Holly's view is unpersuasive. In this Section, I elaborate on the central features of my view, which include a commitment to the **separateness of persons** and **normative individualism**, a commitment to the distinction between wrongness and badness, and a commitment to the idea that rights are 'trumps' (Dworkin 1984).

In Section 2, I address Holly's opening statement and her first argument that men buying sex from women is morally wrong because under current social conditions men having sex with women is morally wrong. It is worth spending time on this argument because Holly devotes considerable space to it and because it is a controversial and radical critique of things as we know them. In Section 2.1, I discuss what Holly calls hierarchical sex and in Section 2.2 I address what she calls altruistic sex. I ultimately argue that though there is a lot of bad sex, it does not follow that the parties involved wrong one another. Since Holly's first argument against commercial sex depends on her view about the ethics of non-commercial sex, I use the arguments from Sections 2.1 and 2.2 to show that even if commercial sex were always bad, it does not follow that it is always morally wrong (Section 2.3). I also suggest that there are some differences between commercial and non-commercial sexual exchanges that might help to mitigate some of the disvaluable elements of hierarchical sex. In Section 2.4, I look at Holly's suggestion that morality demands a sex reset: the legal abolition of commercial

DOI: 10.4324/9781003169697-7

sex, and a moral prohibition of hierarchical/altruistic sex. I argue that a reset for sex conflicts with our rights to sexual autonomy, is infeasible, and likely to do more harm than good.

In Section 3, I respond to the remainder of Holly's argument. Specifically, I address Holly's claim that buying sex is (in current conditions) *always* a form of unethical consumption. In Section 3.1 I argue against the claim that sex is a non-essential good, like sneakers, that can easily be forsaken. In Section 3.2, I argue against the claim that buying sex is comparable to the purchase of blood diamonds. In Section 3.3, I argue that buying sex is not the same as a white person getting their shoes shined by a black person in a racially charged context.

1   My Ethical Framework

In this section, I clarify the **normative ethical framework** that underpins my view that it is morally permissible to buy sex in current societal circumstances. In her first reply, Holly helpfully distinguishes between the three dominant normative ethical frameworks: consequentialism, virtue theory, and deontology (see Chapter 3, Section 3). To be clear, the position I develop in my opening statement is a form of deontological ethics: it is concerned primarily with *what* moral agents do, as opposed to the consequences of our actions or how virtuous we are. In my view, the rightness and wrongness of our choices is determined by whether we have succeeded or failed in satisfying our moral duties. Of particular importance is the idea that many of our moral duties correspond to the rights of others. These are called **directed duties** and are the 'duties that an agent owes to some party—a party who would be wronged if the duty were violated' (May 2015, p. 523).

Critically, my deontological perspective locates moral wrongs in the choices and actions of **moral agents**. Moral agents are those agents with the ability to reflect on their reasons for actions, apprehend moral principles, determine what morality requires in any given situation, and choose to act (or not) in accordance with the demands of morality. While moral agents can act wrongly or rightly, and have obligations to perform particular actions, non-moral agents or states of affairs cannot. This means that bears who eat humans do not act wrongly, tornados that destroy houses do not act wrongly, and cancer does not act wrongly. These things may all be bad for someone (i.e. the person eaten, the person whose home is destroyed, and the person with cancer), but there is no moral agent who has perpetrated a wrong.

A further important feature of my approach, and deontological approaches more generally, is that right and wrong actions are not merely a function of good and bad consequences. For sure, the fact that a choice is bad (or has bad features) can sometimes contribute to a case for its being morally wrong, but it does not follow from the fact that it is bad (or has bad features) that it *is* morally wrong. For example, pain is bad, but it might be permissible, or indeed obligatory, for a surgeon to perform painful life-saving surgery on her patient. Similarly, it may be bad for me to eat nothing but chocolate brownies, but I am not morally prohibited from doing so. Nevertheless, the bad consequences of our choices may give us reasons to act in certain ways: the negative impact of pain on the patient's well-being gives the surgeon a reason to perform the surgery in the least painful way possible, and the negative impact of my brownie consumption on my health gives me a reason to eat fewer chocolate brownies.

I do not have space here to defend my commitment to deontology but it's worth pointing out a few details that make it especially attractive in the context of sexual ethics. For starters, my framework recognizes the **separateness of persons**, which is the basic fact that our minds and bodies are our own and not shared with anyone else. People are, therefore, distinct entities who experience life from their own unique physical and psychological perspectives. It is this uniqueness that makes us different from one another in terms of our capacities, abilities, wants, needs, and conceptions of the good. It also makes our vulnerabilities personal: the pain we feel is *our* pain, not the pain of someone else.

The separateness of persons calls for a commitment to **normative individualism**. This means several things. First, individuals are equally worthy of moral concern and respect. This means that all human beings are owed equal respect and consideration irrespective of sex, gender, race, ethnicity, sexuality, nationality, and so on. Second, every human being is an end in themselves. This means that every person should be valued for their own sake and never used as a *mere* means to some other person's ends. Third, when we're thinking about how to organize our social and political institutions, the basic interests of individuals must be prioritized over those of other collective entities such as families, religious groups, communities, or the state. To be clear, my commitment to normative individualism means that I *always* prioritize the interests and rights of individuals, including individual women, whereas Holly sometimes prioritizes the interests of women as a group or class.

In the context of sex, recognizing the separateness of persons and being committed to normative individualism is crucial. We have seen that sexual autonomy is an important good *of individuals* that grounds rights against others (Chapter 2). It is vitally important that these rights are respected and that individuals have control over what happens to their bodies in the sexual domain. Rights in my view should be regarded as 'trumps' (Dworkin 1984). This means that when a person has a right she may be permitted to act in certain ways or others may be required to treat her in certain ways, even when respecting the right does not yield maximally good consequences. So, for example, according to my framework, we are under a moral duty not to kill people and we cannot justify killing an individual by appealing to the fact we could harvest her organs and save five other people. Sure, it might be good that five other people would live instead of just one but that does not make it **morally permissible**. This is because the individual has a right not to be killed and her right 'trumps' any good consequences that might be secured by killing her. (This is not to say that good consequences can *never* justify infringing a person's right. For example, it may be morally permissible to sacrifice one person to save a million people. Precisely where we set the threshold for rights infringements is the subject of much disagreement among deontologists, but most agree that the threshold will be very high.)

Accordingly, our rights to sexual autonomy act as trumps, which means that we cannot justify overriding a person's rights to sexual autonomy by appealing to good consequences. Consider Robert Nozick's famous example of the **utility monster** (Nozick 1974, p. 41): the utility monster is an individual who gets extremely high levels of satisfaction from acts that directly or indirectly cause suffering or displeasure in others. Indeed, the utility monster is so efficient at converting others' suffering into his own pleasure that on balance his pleasure outweighs his victim's suffering. Thus, the good consequence (i.e. the utility monster's satisfaction) outweighs the bad consequences (i.e. his victim's suffering), which means that the utility monster is morally required to make others suffer for his own benefit. In my view, rights block this kind of consequentialist calculation. Just because one person would get more pleasure out of nonconsensual sex than the suffering of their victim, it does not follow that this person is morally permitted (or indeed, following consequential-ism, morally required) to engage in non-consensual sex. The rights of individuals to control whether and with whom they have sex 'trump' the potential pleasure of sexual utility monsters. Similarly, though many people in a society may feel displeasure that others are engaged in same-sex sexual activity, the rights of individuals to pursue their sexual conception of the good trumps others' displeasure by protect-ing same-sex sexual relations from interference.

Having spelt out my view in more detail, I'd like to raise a chal-lenge to Holly's normative ethical framework. Holly borrows insights from the big three approaches—consequentialism, virtue theory, and deontology—but I am not convinced that she can help herself to arguments from each and have a consistent position. As we have seen, Holly agrees that we have rights to sexual autonomy but her reliance on consequentialist arguments raises questions about the status and function of these rights in her argument. I have argued that rights are trumps—they cannot be overridden by appeal to good or bad consequences. Yet Holly believes that our rights to sexual autonomy can be overridden by bad consequences such as the (potentially) harmful consequences of commercial sex for indi-vidual women and women as a class, and the negative impact of commercial sex on the social movement for women's equality. If that is the case, then what does it mean to have a right to sexual autonomy in Holly's view? Can our rights to sexual autonomy be overridden by sexual utility monsters? Can our rights to sexual autonomy be overridden when the majority dislikes our sexual preferences and desires? I invite Holly to address these questions in her final reply.

2   Hierarchical, Altruistic, and Commercial Sex

2.1   Hierarchical Sex

Holly argues that it is always morally wrong for men to buy sex-ual services from women in current conditions of sex inequality. This is because all bought sex is **hierarchical sex,** and it is always morally wrong to have hierarchical sex (p. 53). Hierarchical sex, according to Holly, is sex that men *impose* on women, and it has three key features: (1) it involves an unequal distribution of plea-sure that privileges the pleasure of the man; (2) it involves the man instrumentalizing the woman by treating her as a mere means to sexual pleasure; and (3) it is dominating in the sense that the man has the ability to arbitrarily inflict sex on women, and face few (if any) negative consequences. Importantly, Holly implies that all heterosexual sex is hierarchical (p. 28; p. 48), which means that heterosexual sex is generally morally impermissible: all men who have sex with women are doing something morally wrong.

This radical hypothesis should give us pause. If Holly is correct, then the scale of wrongdoing is morally catastrophic. Almost every instance of sexual activity involving a man and a woman (across space and time) will involve moral wrongdoing, and all children conceived through penetrative sex would be the result of a morally wrongful act. The only exceptions are instances of sex between men and women that occur in fully egalitarian social conditions and it's doubtful that any such conditions exist now or that many have existed in the past. Moreover, her account casts all heterosexual men as moral wrongdoers by virtue of their sexual activity with women. In this section, I want to rescue (some) sex between men and women, and (some) men from being morally condemned simply for having sex with women. More precisely, I argue that while hierarchical sex may frequently be *bad* it is not always *wrong*. Establishing this claim is important to defending the moral permissibility of buying sex because even if turns out that all bought sex is hierarchical, it would not follow that all bought sex is morally wrong.

I agree with Holly that there is a lot of bad sex out there. I agree that hierarchical sex as she describes it does exist and is disvaluable: in an ideal world hierarchical sex would not exist. I also agree that in current social conditions, the disvalues associated with hierarchical sex are patterned—they are not idiosyncratic features of discrete sexual interactions but rather a common feature of heterosexual relationships. However, I think we can grant all of this without concluding that (1) *all* sex between men and women is hierarchical, or that (2) *all* sex between men and women is wholly disvaluable, or that (3) *all* men who engage in sex with women do something morally wrong.

Let's begin by considering the following question: is hierarchical sex *bad* in a way that makes it *morally wrong?* Holly contends that sex between men and women is hierarchical and therefore disvaluable. However, while we might agree that there is a lot of bad sex out there, it is doubtful that *all* sexual interactions between men and women are disvaluable in the ways that Holly suggests. Indeed, the empirical evidence that Holly appeals to suggests that plenty of women find some pleasure in the sex that they have with men. Specifically, the study estimates that 30% of British women (not an insignificant number) orgasm *every* time they have sex and 27% of British women (again, not an insignificant number) orgasm most of the time they have sex (Nolsoe and Smith 2022). This means that 57% of British women frequently experience sexual pleasure, in the form of orgasm, when they have sex. This suggests that although there is inequality in men's and women's experience of sexual pleasure in the form of orgasms, the majority of women experience orgasms, and if we assume that many of those orgasms are pleasurable, then sex with men is not wholly disvaluable for many women.

Of course, as Holly herself notes, assessing sexual pleasure purely in terms of orgasms is problematic. First, not all orgasms are pleasurable, they may be painful or experienced as bad if they occur during coercive sex (Chadwick et al. 2019). Second, 'positioning orgasm as the ultimate symbol of sexual satisfaction and sexual health constrains perceptions of satisfying sexual pleasure and pathologizes orgasm absence' (ibid., p. 2436). There is much to enjoy about sex beyond orgasm so reducing positive sexual experience to orgasm is harmfully reductive. Though some men and women don't experience orgasms, it does not follow that they do not experience sexual pleasure. I think this observation is overlooked by Holly and it suggests that there is more to the good of sex (and good sex) than the occurrence of orgasms. Human sexuality is complex, and the sources of sexual pleasure and enjoyment are incredibly varied. People may find pleasure in touching another's body or having their own body touched, they may find pleasure in meeting their partner's sexual needs, they may find pleasure in a sense of connection and emotional intimacy, they may find pleasure in utilizing their own body in distinctive ways to achieve sexual ends, they may find pleasure in sexual creativity and experimentation, and so on. None of these pleasures depends on the presence of orgasms and we must not lose sight of the varied and multiple goods of partnered sexual interaction.

Holly might argue that any pleasure garnered by women in the sexual domain occurs in spite of men's involvement rather than as a result of anything that men are doing right as sexual partners. Moreover, she might counter that a small majority of women frequently experiencing orgasms is perfectly compatible with a large majority of men instrumentalizing their sexual partners and having more control over whether sex occurs. This may be correct, but Holly needs more evidence to establish this as truth. In Holly's view, all hierarchical sex is bad (i.e. all heterosexual sex is bad), which suggests that under current conditions it is impossible for men and women to have mutually respectful, reciprocal, and satisfying sexual interactions. This claim strikes me as implausibly strong. It is incredibly unlikely that there are *no* cases of men and women having non-hierarchical sex.

While I think that the possibility of mutually respectful and pleasurable interactions between men and women is not merely wishful thinking, it's difficult to prove beyond appealing to mere anecdotes. So, let's concede that few sexual interactions involve the kind of mutuality needed for optimally or ideally good sex. Does the fact that sexual interactions lack these good-making features mean that sex absent mutuality is bad all the way down? I think the answer here is no. Specific sexual interactions might be bad in some respects and good in others. For example, a woman might find a particular sexual interaction with a man bad because he privileges his own physical pleasure, but good because it creates the opportunity for emotional intimacy. This suggests that whether sex is all things considered bad is not as straightforward as pointing to the ways that it may be disvaluable. We must also consider the positive or desirable effects of an interaction before we can reach an **all things considered judgement** about the goodness or badness of the sex in question.

The idea that hierarchical sex can be more or less bad is important because it puts pressure on the claim that *all* men who engage in hierarchical sex **morally wrong** their sexual partners. To see why, let's think about hierarchal sex and non-hierarchical sex as appearing at two polar ends of a spectrum. At one end of the spectrum, are men who impose sex on women that is very bad because it is disvaluable in the ways that Holly contends: it is selfish, inegalitarian, instrumentalizing, and coercive. At the other end of the spectrum, we have non-hierarchical sex where men who engage in sex with women do so in a genuinely respectful and mutual way. And between those two ends, we have men who are doing more or less well at having sex *with* women as opposed to imposing sex *on* them.

It is my view that not all the bad sex on this spectrum involves moral wrongdoing. For sure, sex at the very bad end of the spectrum may be bad *and* morally wrong. This is because the men involved violate the **directed duties** that they owe with regard to their sexual partners. In the sexual context, women have rights to sexual autonomy and bodily integrity, which, as I have argued, include a right to control whether and under what circumstances they have sex.

Insofar as a man forces or coerces a woman into sex, he violates his duties to respect her rights to sexual and bodily autonomy and thus acts wrongly. So, this is not merely a case of bad sex but a case of egregious moral wrongdoing.

What to say of bad hierarchical sex that is not forced or coerced? Though this sex will have the bad-making features that Holly describes, two important things make it **morally permissible**, which is to say that people are morally permitted to engage in hierarchical sex if they so choose. First, merely bad hierarchical sex does not violate any directed duties, we do not have moral rights to pleasurable sex, mutual pleasure in sex, or reciprocity. Moreover, though a man who engages in hierarchical sex may treat his partner as a means to sexual gratification, if he ensures that he has his partner's valid consent then he arguably does not treat her as a *mere* means. It is perhaps worth stressing at this point that though one may believe that good sex necessarily involves mutuality, respect, and reciprocity, that is an evaluative ideal as opposed to a deontic requirement. And as

> an ideal, or even the ideal, of human sexuality, rather than an account of moral norms pertaining to it, it will tell us what is best in sex and what is less than best. It will ground appreciation or praise of those who attain to the former. But it will not justify moral condemnation of those who do not. It will not tell us how to distinguish between sex acts that are unacceptable, illegitimate, wrong, and need to be condemned as such, and those that are merely permissible, legitimate, not to be morally condemned.
>
> (Primoratz 2001, p. 215)

Bad sex is not always morally wrong because we do not have a **moral right** to qualitatively good sex (see Chapter 2, Section 2.3). This is because though qualitatively good or morally virtuous sex is desirable, it is not something that others are under a duty to provide. Recall the interest theory of rights that I introduced on p. 74. There I said that every moral right is underpinned by an interest that is sufficient to place some other(s) under a duty. In the context of partnered sex, we have no right to sex, no right to qualitatively good sex, indeed, no right to sex of any kind. This is because each of us has a basic interest in sexual autonomy that grounds a right to determine whether we have sex, with whom we have sex, and the terms of the sexual interaction. The idea that one might be morally compelled to deliver on respectful, mutual, and reciprocal sex is at odds with our interest in sexual autonomy.

Moreover, each of us is psychologically and physically different which makes any kind of right to good sex both hard to specify and hard to satisfy. One may find it difficult to derive as much pleasure from sex as one's partner, one may not desire mutuality at all, one may happen to be an incompetent or inexperienced sexual partner, one may find it hard to sustain interest beyond orgasm, one may have a lower or higher sex drive than one's partner, and so on. As Holly herself notes, inequality in the ability to achieve sexual pleasure is not morally wrong per se (p. 21–22). So, implying that we have a moral right to sexual pleasure, mutual pleasure in sex, or reciprocity (because partners who would deny us those things act wrongly) is overly demanding.

This brings us to the second reason why bad sex is morally permissible, namely that our rights to sexual autonomy include a right to have bad sex. One might wonder why we would have an interest in having bad sex, or sex with some bad-making features, but you don't have to think too hard to come up with some legitimate reasons: sex that has some bad-making features may also have some good-making features; sometimes sex that has the promise of being good turns out to be bad; sometimes the good-making features of sex are what others would argue are the bad-making features of the interaction (e.g. pain, dominance and subordination, some kinks and fetishes such as coprophilia); and so on. There are plenty of reasons why bad sex, or sex that others judge to be bad, may nonetheless have value for us as sexually autonomous beings. This makes bad (but not morally wrong) sex an option that is morally protected for us and one that others are prohibited from interfering with.

Holly might wish to maintain that even though hierarchical sex does not necessarily involve rights violations and may have some value for all parties involved, it is nonetheless morally wrong for men to engage in sex of this kind. But why should we accept this? What is the story that explains precisely why hierarchical sex is morally prohibited? As I have been arguing, it is not sufficient to assert that hierarchical sex is bad. Inegalitarian, dull, and unsatisfying sex may be disvaluable in some respects, but that doesn't show that a woman's male partner wrongs her. Yes, the sex may be bad, and yes maybe he could do better, but having a lousy time does not entail moral wrongdoing.

At this juncture Holly might press the thought that hierarchical sex isn't just lousy sex but *harmful* sex, and as such it is wrongful because it is wrong to do harm to others. In response, it's worth restating that the right to sexual autonomy protects our interest in being able to pursue our conception of the sexual good even when it harms us. So, there is a countervailing reason—our right to sexual autonomy—that morally permits individuals (in this case individual women) to consensually engage in activities that may be harmful to them. Specifically, we can consent to sexual interactions that may make us worse-off by giving permission to others to do things to us that are harmful.

Moreover, many of the harms associated with the normative expectations of heterosexuality cannot be tracked back to the actions of individual men. As I argued earlier (Chapter 4, Section 1), for an action to be morally wrong, it must be performed by a moral agent. The harms perpetrated by the normative expectations of heterosexuality are reproduced by both men and women who internalize and act upon those norms, but no individual man is responsible for the norms themselves or the harm that such norms may do in the sexual lives of women. To make this clear consider the following cases.

Case 5: Betty and George

Betty wants to be a good wife and believes that in order to be a good wife she must always have sex with George whenever he asks, even when she does not desire sex herself. George never tries to persuade or manipulate Betty into having sex. From George's perspective, Betty always seems to welcome the attention and the invitation. During sex, Betty frequently fakes orgasms, thinks about other things, and deploys sexual tricks to make George orgasm quicker. The sex they have is fully consensual.

Case 6: Camilla and Diego

Camilla and Diego watch a lot of pornographic films together. They particularly enjoy **inegalitarian pornography** in which the sex is rough, and the man debases and humiliates the woman. Once a week, Camilla and Diego make time to watch a film and then act out what they saw in the film. Camilla enjoys playing the submissive and when Diego physically and verbally humiliates her she finds it sexually exciting. The sex they have is fully consensual.

In both cases, we may worry about Betty and Camilla's preferences, desires, and choices. One might, for example, argue that their desires and choices are harmful both to themselves and the cause of feminism. Yet should we think that either George or Diego does anything morally wrong? Since they do not violate anyone's rights it's very difficult to see how they wrong their sexual partners. This suggests that even if we agree with Holly that Betty and Camilla's situations are bad in some way, we cannot say that they are the victims of a moral wrong perpetrated by their partners. First, neither George nor Diego is under a directed duty to their respective partners not to have sex with them. Second, neither George nor Diego is responsible for any non-rights violating harms caused by the normative expectations of heterosexuality.

2.2 Altruistic Sex

According to Holly, men who have sex with women in current conditions are having *hierarchical sex*, while the women having sex with these men are having *altruistic sex*. As we have seen, hierarchical sex is sex inflicted or imposed on women by men. By contrast, altruistic sex covers non-commercial sex with men that women submit to (p. 21). In this case, women regularly gift sex to men out of a false sense of duty, fear, economic dependency, social expectation, and so on. Despite the positive connotations associated with the word 'altruism', Holly urges us not to think of altruistic sex as positive since it may be abusive, unpleasant, and is always characterized by submission. Utilizing this distinction between hierarchical and altruistic sex, Holly suggests that present heterosexual interactions involve men having hierarchical sex and women having altruistic sex.

If all heterosexual sex is hierarchical—all men who are having sex with women are imposing sex on them—then it follows that all women who have sex with men are having altruistic sex: they submit to sex. One limitation of this analysis of existing heterosexual relations is that it denies women's sexual agency, empowerment, desire, or pleasure. Women are effectively rendered the passive victims of the institution of heterosexual sex: women don't fuck, they get fucked. And the sexual selves of existing women are viewed as the maladapted, inauthentic, consequence of masculinist desire and male supremacy.

The trouble is that this is not how all women experience their own sexuality or (all) their sexual encounters with men. For sure, there are staggering rates of sexual assault and harassment, and most women will not make it through life unscathed by sexual wrongdoing. Moreover, for some women, the trauma of such events will make it very difficult, if not impossible, to ever feel safe and secure in sexual relations with men. Nonetheless, as we saw in the previous section, many women do have sexual relationships with men that they desire, enjoy, and value. Moreover, many women do not see themselves as always 'gifting' sex or submitting to the sexual demands of their male sexual partners.

This concern is not new. Sex positive feminists have long been responding to the anti-sex arguments of radical feminism. They have been especially keen to point out that not all women are sexually submissive and that male-female sexual interactions are not always initiated or led by men. However, this kind of response is routinely met with the objection that *those* women's desires have been hijacked by men, and more generally, whatever women desire is a product of patriarchal domination. This suggests that we can put little stock or value in what women do, want, or value in the sexual domain. Put another way, women's testimony on their sex lives is unreliable (unless they agree that sex with men is bad).

To illustrate the objection and the sex positive feminist response, here is Ellen Willis discussing the dispute in the context of pornography:

> To the objection that some women get off on porn, the standard reply is that this only shows how thoroughly women have been brainwashed by male values [...] And the view of sex that most often emerges from talk about 'erotica' is as sentimental and euphemistic as the word itself: lovemaking should be beautiful, romantic, soft, nice, and devoid of messiness, vulgarity, impulses to power, or indeed aggression of any sort. Above all, the emphasis should be on relationships, not (yuck) organs. This goodygoody concept of eroticism is not feminist but feminine. It is precisely sex as an aggressive, unladylike activity, an expression of violent and unpretty emotion, an exercise of erotic power, and a specifically genital experience that has been taboo for women. Nor are we supposed to admit that we, too, have sadistic impulses, that our sexual fantasies may reflect forbidden urges to turn the tables and get revenge on men.
>
> (Willis 1993, p. 355)

The worry that Willis articulates here is that feminist views like Holly's reinforce certain norms about women's sexuality that cast women as sexually passive, undercut women's sexual agency, and make taboo women's desires for power and domination in the sexual context. Moreover, by dismissing women's sexual desires and preferences as the product of a maladaptive process, radical feminists typically discount and devalue experiences that many women value positively. Consequently, women's desires are not to be celebrated or pursued but rather condemned and overcome. This view of women's sexuality leaves little space for women who find their sexual relations with men to be liberating, empowering, and generally positive, and is at odds with women's felt experiences. Furthermore, it problematically endorses the view that women have false desires and that they do not know what is good for them.

All this said, the idea that women's sexual preferences, desires, and fantasies are a reflection of patriarchal values is not without persuasive force. We grow up in patriarchal societies with deeply entrenched systems of gender that dictate how men and women should be and it is against that backdrop that all of our wants and desires are formed. However, though our desires and preferences may be the outcome of unequal social conditions, they are nonetheless *our* desires and preferences: our sexual selves and conception of the sexual good are our own. This means that while we can and should be worried about the societal and cultural pressures that shape men's and women's sexual preferences, we must respect the rights of individuals to live out their lives in accordance with their own judgments about what is good for them.

2.3 Commercial Sex

Part of Holly's argument against commercial sex depends on her arguments about the moral wrongness of hierarchical/altruistic sex. In my opening statement, I suggested, following Brennan and Jaworski (2016), that if it's ok to do something for free, then it's ok to buy it. What Holly argues is that it is *not* ok to have hierarchical/altruistic sex and, therefore, it is *not* ok to buy it. In brief, her central argument is that since it's wrong to have hierarchical sex (and all paid-for sex is hierarchical), it's wrong to buy hierarchical sex. On top of this, Holly claims that buying sex contributes to the continuance of hierarchical sex because it reinforces the idea that men have a right to use women's bodies for sexual gratification and contributes to women's inferior social status.

I addressed some problems with Holly's conceptualization and moral evaluation of hierarchical and altruistic sex in the previous two sections. In this section, I do two things. First, I argue that even if all commercial sex is hierarchical, it does not follow that commercial sex is always wrong. Second, I suggest that commercial sex and non-commercial sex are different in important ways, such that commercial sex has more resources to evade the model of hierarchical/ altruistic sexual relations that Holly is worried about. Beyond this, I want to emphasize a claim that I made in my opening statement, that it is difficult to see how an individual man buying sex from an individual woman causes or perpetuates the inferior social status of women *as a class*.

I earlier argued that even if hierarchical non-commercial sex is bad, that does not make it morally wrong. I believe that argument extends to commercial sex. One might think that commercial sex lacks the virtues or values of good sex, one may also think that commercial sex is disvaluable in the ways that Holly suggests that hierarchical sex is, but, as we have seen, judging commercial sex to be bad is not the same as establishing that it is morally wrong. Since responsible sex buyers respect the rights of sex sellers, it is far from obvious that the (alleged) disvalue of commercial sex constitutes a wrong. Again, bad sex may be all things considered disvaluable but that doesn't in itself make engaging in it morally wrong.

Moreover, I think that commercial sex has the potential to be less hierarchical (and therefore less bad) than non-commercial sex. The reason for this is that responsible sex-buying men must explicitly *negotiate*, *contract*, and *pay* for sex. In these commercial exchanges, sex is not something that men assume that they can get for free. On the contrary, sex comes at a financial cost and women's bodies are not something that they can expect to have access to without first negotiating with the sex worker. This casts doubt on Holly's repeated claim that commercial sex grants 'unconditional sexual access to women'. Accessing a woman's body through a commercial sexual exchange is very much conditional: sex workers may choose to turn down a client, or they may choose to limit the kind of access on sale, and clients must have the sex worker's valid consent, as well as be able to pay the agreed price. Moreover, since the arrangement involves an explicit discussion about the services and activities that may be bought, women sex workers potentially have more control and clarity over what they are willing to do and how interactions will play out. It's also the case that in the context of commercial sex, many of the gendered norms and expectations governing women in romantic relationships are absent. For example, sex workers are unlikely to feel any *obligation* to consent to sex with their clients because they are not bound to them by a pre-existing intimate relationship.

2.4   A Sex Reset

The final part of Holly's argument that I want to speak to is her claim that morality requires a sex reset: the legal abolition of commercial sex, and a moral prohibition of hierarchical/altruistic sex. According to Holly, a sex reset is required to address the moral wrongs associated with sex in current social circumstances. In practice, this means that men are morally required to forgo sex (or at least penetrative sex) with women until hierarchical/altruistic sex has all but disappeared, leaving in its place only good sex. Once our sexual lives have been 'reset', Holly anticipates that the world will look very different. In this feminist sexual utopia

> there is *less sex*, the *meaning of 'sex' has changed* (no longer centring penetration), and *women are in control* of the sex that they have. Sex is not something that is *done to them for the benefit of a man*, not something that they endure or passively accept, but something that they actively desire and direct (or simply do not have).
>
> (p. 44)

The utopian vision that Holly sketches is for me a dystopian nightmare. Though I have no real qualms with the endpoint, the journey is incredibly troubling. Holly says that 'a social movement against sex as we know it would have men commit, and signal their commitment, to not using prostitutes. It would have people commit, and signal their commitment, to not watching pornography, and to not having altruistic/hierarchical sex' (p. 45). This suggests that for Holly the sex reset will be achieved by a social movement in which men and women make various public avowals or pledges thereby signalling their commitment to not use pornography, to not buy sexual services from prostitutes, to not have heterosexual penetrative sex, and so on. Those initial activists who publicly commit to the transformation of existing sexual relations through public pledges of abstinence will be at the forefront of the movement. Their actions will give rise to more discussion and critique of hierarchical sex, and more people will join the movement and publicly pledge their allegiance to the cause. And so on, until we reach a state of feminist utopia and sex has been reset.

So far so good, but like all social movements presumably Holly's movement for a sex reset will involve tactics that harness the power of social shame and guilt. In effect, the utopia that Holly envisages makes men and women the legitimate targets for moral condemnation just for having sex with one another: heterosexual couples should forsake penetrative sex and all heterosexual sex and sexual reproduction (since this is how most babies are made!) should be morally shamed. If you are a man having penetrative sex with a woman, or a woman having penetrative sex with a man, then you are failing to do what is morally required and can expect to be socially chastened (if discovered). Moreover, people who make public pledges of abstinence but are then later discovered to have engaged in heterosexual penetrative sex will likely be the targets of even harsher social sanctioning.

Importantly, it is not only men who are affected by these proposals but the women who desire sex (especially penetrative sex) with men. For women too, heterosexual sex is now morally forbidden. Presumably, this means that women who have sex with men are also liable to social condemnation in Holly's view (with pregnant women being the most vulnerable targets of attack because pregnancy may plausibly be perceived as evidence of consensual penetrative sex). This looks to me like just another form of **slut-shaming**, where girls and women are publicly criticized and shamed for being sexually provocative, having multiple sexual partners, and/or simply acting on their sexual desires. In my view, no feminist should tolerate women being shamed for their sexuality and the idea that the bodies of pregnant women could be the legitimate object of social scorn is deeply antithetical to feminist ends. Whatever one thinks about the harms of heterosexuality, being made to feel guilty for one's sexual desires and being socially shamed for acting on them is not a morally decent solution to the problem.

In addition to worries about sexual conservatism and threats to sexual autonomy, I think that demanding that men (and by implication women) forgo heterosexual sex is implausible and likely to do more harm than good. There are several reasons for this. First, there is a gamut of empirical evidence in the context of sexual health which shows that those initiatives which are sex-negative and focused on risk-reduction tend to produce effects opposite from those intended (see Ford et al. 2019 for a review of the literature). By contrast, 'health programs that incorporate sexual pleasure consistently produce improved attitudes and knowledge about sexual health, partner communication, condom use, and safer sex behaviors' (Ford et al. 2019, p. 219). Similarly, one might worry that the demands of a sex reset cast heterosexuality in too negative a light and ultimately deny people something that, while flawed, they nonetheless find valuable. This suggests that the sex reset strategy is likely to be met with much resistance and might serve to reinforce the norms of hierarchical sexual relations rather than serve as a catalyst for their transformation. If we want to diminish the patterned disvalue of hierarchical sex it would be far better to develop and implement a sex-positive strategic vision for women's empowerment, mutuality, and equality in the sexual domain.

A second reason to be doubtful of Holly's proposed sex strike is its infeasibility. Holly points to people who are celibate as a matter of faith to show that her idea of a reset for sex—where men and women stop having sex with one another—is not infeasible (p. 40). However, celibacy in religious orders is notoriously fraught and vows of celibacy are frequently broken. If the most devout of humans find it difficult to abstain from sex for God or religious enlightenment, then it's unlikely that the average man (or woman) is going to find the strength of will to abstain from sex. Moreover, there is plenty of evidence to suggest that abstinence-only policies in the context of adolescent sexual activity do not work (Kantor et al. 2008). Both observations suggest that abstinence is not as easy for us as Holly suggests.

This brings us to a third reason against the proposal for a sex reset, which is that we need a detailed account of how sex between men and women will improve as a result of abstinence. The story Holly offers is vague and idealistic: we stop having hierarchical/altruistic sex and hopefully cultivate better sexual habits, desires, preferences, and attitudes. But what reason do we have to be hopeful about this? Given that our sexual lives and selves are constructed through a myriad of wider social norms, expectations, and practices, I doubt that a sexual revolution will occur through abstinence alone. More specifically, it seems unlikely that we will see more equality in the sex between men and women without wider societal change.

This last point suggests that we should see bad sex as a *symptom* of systemic gender injustice as opposed to the *cause* of gender inequality. I would further argue that focusing on sex as the linchpin of sex inequality draws our attention away from other more pressing matters of feminist concern such as securing women's basic rights and liberties, and their equal social status. For sure, sex is a part of the story but arguably it is a relatively small cog in the ubiquitous patriarchal machine. For this reason, it is more likely that securing social justice for women will lead to women's equality and empowerment in the sexual domain, rather than the other way around.

3   Defending the Moral Permissibility of Buying Sex

3.1   The Value of Sex: Not Like Food, Not Like Sneakers

The argument I made in my opening statement rests on the claim that sexual autonomy is a fundamental human good. As such, we have basic interests in being able to control whether others are sexually intimate with us, and an interest in being able to determine, shape, and realize our conception of the sexual good. I think that Holly agrees that sexual autonomy is an important part of the human good: no one should be forced to be sexually intimate with others and people should be free to develop reasonable conceptions of the sexual good. However, whereas I think that having meaningful sexual experiences with others is an important component of human well-being, Holly rejects this. She says: 'Food is a basic need, sex is not (despite a large amount of propaganda claiming that it is)' (p. 38). Similarly, in developing her argument against sex-buying she suggests that the pleasure one might get from cheap sneakers cannot justify the harm done to sweatshop labourers, which implies that she views the value of sex as akin to the value of cheap sneakers (p. 38).

How should we understand this claim? I agree with Holly that unlike food no one is going to die if they do not have partnered sexual interactions. But that does not mean that meaningful sexual experience is something that people can easily forego, or that those who have experienced sexual exclusion and felt terrible about it are simply in the grips of propaganda. Being able to have meaningful sexual experiences with others is valuable in the same way that having children, free speech, and the right to vote are valuable. No one is going to die if they don't have children, are unable to speak freely, or are unable to vote, but it does not follow that these things are not of central importance to people's lives and that the absence of these things can very seriously impede a person's capacity for well-being.

Perhaps sex is not like these other valuable things. Perhaps sex is not important to human well-being at all. As I noted in my opening statement, this is certainly true for some human beings who are indifferent to sex or perhaps loathe sexual intimacy. However, I think that outside of this minority, sex continues to be important to many people across the course of their adult lives (Satcher 2001, p. 1) and there is a growing body of evidence that links sexual pleasure to human well-being (Ford et al. 2019). This suggests that purchasing sex is not the same as purchasing 'cheap sneakers'. We might really want the cheap sneakers, but we can easily forgo them in favour of uglier but more ethical options. Sex is not like this. As we have seen, the reasons why people buy sex are varied but the importance of the option of purchased sex should not be downplayed.

3.2   Why Buying Sex is Not Like Buying Diamonds

One of Holly's central arguments is that buying sex is a form of unethical consumption. To make this case, Holly compares commercial sex with the trade in diamonds. It is now well-documented that diamond mining is often bound up with corruption, organized crime, violence, and exploitation. Consequently, buying diamonds is morally problematic because purchasing diamonds only serves to profit and bolster corrupt leaders, deprive the people of the profit from the natural resources of their state territory, and perpetuate the many harms associated with diamond mining.

For Holly, buying sex is like buying diamonds:

> What are the injustices in the supply chain of commercial sex, specifically, the end product of a discrete session of sexual acts, paid for by a john? Depending on the individual woman, there may be any of a range of injustices, human rights violations, and other harms. There is human trafficking for prostitution. There are rapes. There are beatings. There is captivity/confinement. There is coercive control. There is psychological abuse. There is drug and alcohol addiction (whether a habit induced by pimps and traffickers, or a coping mechanism adopted by the sex worker herself). There are thefts, including refusals to pay. There is coercion/blackmail (e.g. police officers saying that they will arrest the sex worker if she does not service him for free). There is mistreatment by police and legal officials. There is social stigma, which may prevent sex workers in accessing

physical and mental health services that are desperately needed, and which a woman not in sex work would be able to make use of. [...] Anytime a man buys sex, he risks having sex with a woman who has had, or is having, any number of these experiences.

(p. 50)

In sum, Holly concludes, that the risk of doing harm by buying sex is so great that there is a moral imperative against buying sex.

I don't want to deny that sex industries can involve the kinds of harms detailed by Holly. (Although, as we have seen, vulnerability to violence and exploitation is very much conditioned by the kind of sexual service being sold and the circumstances in which it is sold.) But I do want to resist the claim that the risk of doing harm is sufficient to make it always morally wrong to engage in buying sex. There are two reasons for this. First, as I argued in my opening statement, the risk of harm can be mitigated by being a morally responsible sex buyer. As I suggested there, if a sex buyer takes active and effective steps to reduce the risks associated with buying sex, then the likelihood of them doing something wrong will decrease (Chapter 2, Sections 3.3 and 4.3). So the risk of having sex with someone without their valid consent or retraumatizing someone with PTSD can be significantly reduced by acting responsibly. I also argued that the level of risk attached to responsible sex buying is much closer to the level of risk attached to non-commercial sex. Therefore, if we allow that some level of risk is morally acceptable in non-commercial sex, then we can grant that there will be some similar level of risk in commercial sex without concluding that buying sex is morally wrong.

Second, the sale of sexual services is not like the sale of diamonds in one important respect: unlike diamonds, sexual services are not sold to profit corrupt leaders. Though some individuals may take a share of a sex worker's earnings, she ultimately sells sex to profit herself. Sex workers are autonomous agents with the capacity to make decisions about how they want to live their lives and the right to live in accordance with their own **conception of the good**. This means that sex workers (or, for that matter, any of us) have a right to sell *their* sexual labour for *their* benefit. The right to undertake sex work, even sex work that is in some ways bad for the seller, is underpinned by their interest in autonomy, sexual autonomy, and freedom of occupation.

3.3   Why Buying Sex is Not Like Getting One's Shoes Shined

Some people argue, and I gestured at this myself, that if it's morally permissible for someone to sell something, then it's morally permissible for another to buy that thing. Let's call this the **symmetry argument**.

Symmetry Argument

When a person is morally permitted to sell something, then it is morally permissible for another person to buy that thing.

Holly rejects the symmetry argument. She argues that even when someone has a right to sell something, it may not be permissible for another to buy that thing. Importantly for Holly, there may be some circumstances where buyers are under a **moral duty** not to buy from ethical sellers. In this kind of scenario, would-be buyers must refrain, for moral reasons, from purchasing. Moreover, by not purchasing they do not wrong sellers because 'the right to sell does not correspond to anyone's duty to buy' (p. 52). The example that Holly uses to illustrate this point is a launch event for the book *Kiwi: The Australian Brand That Brought a Shine to the World*. The event involved a shoeshine stand with a black employee tasked with shining the shoes of a mostly white audience. Holly contends that though the shoeshiner in this scenario has a moral right to sell his shoeshining service, white members of the audience have a moral duty to abstain from purchasing.

I think this is an interesting case that successfully undercuts the symmetry argument. I agree with Holly that just because someone has a right to sell, it does not follow that there aren't *any* moral reasons against purchasing from them. There are many moral reasons that might demand that we refrain from purchasing something. For example, we might have a duty to refrain from purchasing things in order to leave enough and as good for others. Think for example of how, at the beginning of the COVID-19 pandemic, some people bulk-bought essentials, such as pasta, toilet rolls, and hand sanitizer, which caused national shortages of these products. Arguably, these people did something morally wrong by purchasing more than their fair share of these essential goods. Similarly, if a parent were to spend all their disposable income on expensive handbags instead of essential items for their child such as toothbrushes, shoes, and school uniforms, then we might reasonably believe that their purchasing habits are morally wrong. In general, we might think that parents have a moral responsibility to forgo luxury items if purchasing those items would prevent them from providing the essentials for their children. Both these cases, and the others discussed by Holly, show that sometimes there are moral reasons against buying even when the person selling has a right to do so.

How should we think about the right to buy in such cases? Typically, we think that people have a right to buy toilet rolls and handbags but the right to buy is not the only relevant moral reason for determining the moral permissibility of purchasing. In the scenarios just described, we can make an **all things considered judgement** that the bulk purchase of toilet rolls, and the purchase of expensive handbags are morally wrong. This is because there are moral reasons that, when taken together, eliminate the moral right that one typically has to make purchases. When there are moral reasons that make buying something morally wrong, then one is under a duty not to buy that thing.

The important question is whether buying sex is like getting one's shoes shined (or any of the other cases discussed). That is, are there moral reasons that make men buying sex from women who are entitled and willing to sell all things considered impermissible? An affirmative answer has to show that there are moral reasons—either individually sufficient or, when taken in combination with others, jointly sufficient—that support an all things considered judgement that it is *always* morally wrong for men to buy sex from women in current conditions.

In response, I again appeal to the idea that the right to sell sex is grounded in a person's sexual autonomy. When a person has a right to sell sex, selling sex is a morally protected option: it would be wrong for others to interfere. Remember, in my view, there may be lots of circumstances in which a person is unable to give valid consent to sell sex. For example, a person may be drunk or high, acting under threat of violence, or underage. In such circumstances selling sex is not a morally protected option for them. Since the right to sell sex is grounded in the value of sexual autonomy the right does not extend to cases where one's ability to exercise sexual autonomy is absent or impaired. So, only those sellers able to validly consent to sex have a moral right to sell sex. Why might it be morally wrong to buy sex from those individuals? In response to this, Holly offers nine reasons. I will briefly mention each reason and indicate why it does not apply or is insufficient to outweigh or 'trump' the right to buy. Note that many of the responses I mention here are given at length in my opening statement and in the earlier parts of this reply.

	Holly's Reason	My Response
Reason 1	It's wrong to have hierarchical sex.	Hierarchical sex is bad but insofar as sexual partners respect one another's rights they do not wrong one another (see pp. 142–143).
Reason 2	It's wrong to risk rape.	Responsible sexual partners, both in non-commercial and commercial sexual exchanges, can reduce the risk of rape to a morally permissible level by ensuring that they have ongoing consent from those with whom they have sex (see p. 100; pp. 112–113).
Reason 3	It's wrong to risk complicity in another man's sexual and/or physical violence.	Responsible sex buyers are not complicit in the sexual violence perpetrated by other men (see pp. 107–110).
Reason 4	It's wrong to retraumatize a person with PTSD.	Responsible sex buyers have a duty to ensure that they have the free and informed consent of the sex worker and that they stop the sexual activity if there are any signs of distress (p. 100).
Reason 5	It's worse to do to vulnerable people what it's wrong to do to people generally.	Responsible sex buying is opposed to wronging vulnerable people. Hierarchical sex is not wrong if it is rights-respecting and having that kind of sex with consenting sex workers does not wrong them (p. 149).
Reason 6	It's wrong to respond to destitution with exploitation.	This is compatible with the demands of responsible sex buying (see p. 101). Responsible sex buyers do not have sex with destitute sellers.
Reason 7	It's wrong to contribute to creating consumer demand for unethical products (with some exceptions).	Individual sex buyers do not create consumer demand (see p. 106).

Reason 8	It's wrong to act out the privileges of social hierarchy when one is in the superior position.	Buying sex is not something that only men have the privilege of doing. Both men and women are morally permitted to buy and sell sex. Moreover, some forms of commercial sex, by making contract and consent explicit, have the resources to avoid replicating hierarchical/altruistic sexual relations (p. 149). Responsible sex buying is not premised on men's unfettered access to women's bodies but rather on women's rights to decide what they do with their bodies, including negotiating payment for the provision of sexual services and the terms of the interaction.
Reason 9	It's wrong to risk setting back the social movement for women's equality.	Responsible sex buying is compatible with a commitment to women's equality (p. 103). Consequently, a 'leftist' man who is committed to sex equality may permissibly purchase sexual services and not be a hypocrite. Responsible sex buying does not, therefore, set back the social movement for women's equality.

The above table captures the arguments of my opening statement, and this first reply, and explains why I think the nine reasons Holly offers against purchasing commercial sex are insufficient to show that buying sex is **all things considered** morally wrong. As you can see, I think that *responsible* sex buying is not guilty of the charges that Holly puts forward and where I agree with Holly, I agree with the argument as it applies to *irresponsible* sex buying. In short, I do not believe that Holly has shown that men have a moral duty not to buy sex.

You may be unpersuaded by some of my responses here. That's not necessarily a problem for my overall position. Even if you think that some of Holly's arguments have force, you need to be able to show that those arguments are sufficient to outweigh or trump the rights of individual men and women to buy and sell sexual services. This is no easy task. Remember, in Section 1 of this first reply, I explained that rights are 'trumps' which means that they typically cannot be overridden to bring about good consequences. So even if you think that some good may come from men not buying sex, that will be insufficient to show that men have no moral right to buy sexual services from those who wish to sell.

Before I end, I want to briefly highlight an important disanalogy between buying sex and the shoeshine example. Part of what makes Holly's description and analysis of the shoeshine example compelling is that the shoeshiner is (arguably) not terribly wronged. Though they might not shine many shoes at the book launch—perhaps only the shoes of white moral wrongdoers and non-white patrons—they are free to sell their shoeshining service in other, less racially charged, environments and people will be morally permitted to buy.

Compare that with the case of sex work. According to Holly, it is never morally permissible for a man to buy sexual services from a woman in current conditions. In effect, Holly is calling for a boycott on purchasing sex. This means that, unlike the shoeshiner who may still be gainfully employed as a shoeshiner in other contexts, a woman sex worker will have her employment options severely limited if men do what Holly alleges is morally required. Since it is *never* morally permissible to buy sex in our social world, this effectively demands an end to the sale of sex.

As I mentioned in my opening statement, I find the indirect attempt to remove the option of sex work for women morally pernicious. Not only does it violate women's rights to choose for themselves whether they have sex and under what circumstances, but it also violates their right to freedom of occupation. Whether one likes it or not, many sex workers prefer sex work to other forms of labour and they have, as I have argued, a right to freely pursue such work.

Part III

Second Round of Replies

Chapter 5

What Women Owe to Each Other

Second Reply to Angie Pepper

Holly Lawford-Smith

I What Women Owe to Each Other

In the 10 January 1913 issue of *The Suffragette*—a newspaper edited by Christabel Pankhurst, and whose printer Edgar Whitely was charged with 'inciting people to join the Women's Social and Political Union' (National Archives undated a)—Emmeline Pankhurst wrote to her suffragist and suffragette readers that their militancy should not be put on hold simply because the Prime Minister at the time had announced that the House of Commons would discuss amendments to the 'Manhood Suffrage Bill' that might give women the right to vote. Pankhurst wrote:

> every member of the W.S.P.U knows that the defeat of the Amendments will make militancy a moral duty. It will be a political necessity. We must prepare ourselves now. There are different levels of militancy. Some women are able to go further than others. To be militant in some ways is a moral obligation. Every woman owes this to her own conscience and self-respect, and to future generations of women. If any woman does not take part in militant action, she shares in the crime of the Government.
>
> (Quoted in Webb 2011, ch. 10)

British historian Fern Riddell writes that the WSPU 'acted like a regulated army with professional soldiers, seeing the Edwardian period as a civil war between the sexes' (Riddell 2018). The militant tactics of the suffragettes included 'a nationwide bombing and arson campaign', physical assault ('a suffragette attacked a young Winston Churchill with a horse whip on the platform of

DOI: 10.4324/9781003169697-9

Bristol railway station'), and destruction of property ('armed with a catapult and missiles, [they] attacked Prime Minister Asquith's car in Liverpool') (ibid.). They attempted to set fire to a theatre 'during a packed lunchtime matinee attended by Asquith' (ibid.). They smashed glass cases in art galleries and bank and post office windows, and they cut telegraph wires (ibid.). One estimate of the damage the suffragettes did to property during 1913 alone put it at £510,150 (National Archives undated b, p. 19). By the end of 1912, '240 people had been sent to prison for militant suffragette activities' (Riddell 2018).[1] Some of those militants went on hunger strike in prison and were subjected to torture in the form of force-feeding (see e.g. Cook 2018).

Why am I talking about the militant tactics of the suffragettes in a book about whether it's wrong for men to buy sex from women? The reason is that one of the most important challenges Angie made to my view in her first rejoinder is that it *violates the autonomy rights of individual women to sell sex*. Angie writes 'I find the indirect attempt to remove the option of sex work for women morally pernicious. Not only does it violate women's rights to choose for themselves whether they have sex and under what circumstances, it also violates their right to freedom of occupation. Whether one likes it or not, many sex workers prefer sex work to other forms of work and they have, as I have argued, a right to freely pursue such work'. One way to answer that challenge is to ask *what women owe to each other* when it comes to achieving sex equality. Perhaps they owe each other enough that this loss of autonomy is justified, and perhaps thinking in Pankhurst's terms can help us to fill that idea out. (Note that the WSPU were just one suffragette group; there were others, including the Women's Freedom League, and the East London Suffragettes, and different groups differed in their commitment to militancy—see discussion in Jackson 2015.)

What obligations do women have, and what costs can we reasonably expect them to bear, in the name of women's liberation? This is just a specific version of a question that can arise for any oppressed group of people at any time in history. Individual members of those

---

1 Riddell says 'people' rather than 'women', because although the WSPU was a women-only organization, there was also a counterpart organization for men, the Men's Political Union for Women's Enfranchisement, and some of those men also went to prison for militant action, including one who *also* 'took a whip to Home Secretary Winston Churchill' (Cook 2018).

groups can simply accept the background conditions and try to get the best outcome possible for themselves within those parameters, or, they can find a way to coordinate with others to fight for better conditions.[2] Once we know what it would take to change the background conditions, we can start to work out what members of the group might owe to each other: what each (or most, or some) would have to do in order for that change to be realized, and how they would need to coordinate those individual contributions. Coordination may appear virtually impossible. Some members of the oppressed group may have internalized their own oppression and not believe they deserve anything better than what they have. Some members of the oppressed group may have aligned themselves with the oppressors in order to get a better deal for themselves. Potential supporters from outside the group may be clueless, or complacent. There is always the possibility of being betrayed, being disappointed, of finding oneself completely isolated, of facing retaliation. Nonetheless, it has been done. The suffragettes, together with their male supporters, are one dramatic illustration of this.

Most of my focus earlier in the book has been on men, and what wrong they do when they buy sex. My focus in this section is on women. In the last rejoinder, I argued *within* the parameters of Angie's assumptions about individual rights, even though I do not share those assumptions. Angie thinks there is a trumping right to autonomy. I said, even if that is true, there can be cases in which there is a conflict between some people's autonomy and other people's autonomy, and then simply pointing to *the right to autonomy* won't settle the conflict. In such a case, we should surely look at how to achieve the most autonomy. (Which I understand to mean, having more options, and having options of better quality. If Angie understands this only as avoiding violations of autonomy—stopping people from doing something they have been doing or actively desire to do—then this may further explain our disagreement. For on my view, people who say they care about autonomy should care about oppressive conditions that lead to

---

2 On one very interesting hypothesis about the origin and persistence of patriarchy (as male dominance), women's subordination is *explained by* men's success in coordinating, which came as a result of their hunting together. This is not exactly to say that women's failure to coordinate is the cause of their oppression, but it is to relate coordination intimately to the fact of sex-based social hierarchy (see discussion in Jackson undated).

people having unacceptably few options, or options of unacceptably poor quality.) Applied to women who want to do sex work, in conflict with women for whom it would be good if there were no sex work (which, I have argued, is *all women,* including those women who want to do sex work), we'd get the most autonomy out of settling the conflict in favour of the latter. In this rejoinder, however, I will take a different approach. That is to reject the *individualism* of the rights-based approach that Angie advances, in favour of a form of *collectivism*[3] concerned with the social structures that perpetuate sex inequality, and with how we might break free of those structures. When we try to think about what is good for women together on the liberal individualist view, we are forced to classify any conclusions as merely 'evaluative'. The only thing the liberal individualist can countenance as 'normative' is what is good for individual women. Taking a collectivist approach means that questions about the normative shift to the level of the group.

Pankhurst seems to have been viewing things in this way. She lived in a world in which women were second-class citizens, and lacked the voice in politics that would enable them to use the formal channels available to advocate to change that fact. It is important that Pankhurst said not only that women owe militancy to themselves, but to 'future generations of women'. She had a conception of women as a group: a collective; a community; a people. She saw that carefully coordinated collective action was required to change women's situation. And for that reason, she saw inaction by women as complicity: 'If any woman does not take part in militant action, she shares in the crime of the Government'. That is, she is just as bad as those in power who were wilfully denying women the vote.

At this point one may object—why are we only talking about women? We might accept for the sake of argument the shift from individualism to collectivism, but what determines that the relevant collective is *women,* rather than *everyone?* The restriction is merely pragmatic: those who are advantaged by hierarchical social arrangements—here men—can be expected to work to retain that advantage (Jackson undated). That means they cannot be relied upon as supporters. That does not mean that some of their number *won't* in fact be supporters, they probably will, just as some men

---

3 Some people who use the term 'collective', especially within the philosophical subfield of social ontology, mean by it that the group is organized. I do not intend that meaning here. Women are a group, but not an organized group.

were supporters of the suffragettes. But in strategizing about how to change social hierarchy, it is prudent to consider what the disadvantaged can do to free themselves. So the question becomes, *if* we accept that it is in women's interests to disrupt the social structure that perpetuates their inequality, and that key parts of this social structure are altruistic/hierarchical sex, prostitution, and pornography, then what obligations does that confer on individual women, what kinds of costs can we reasonably expect each woman to bear?

Once we frame the issue this way, Angie's assertion of the individual sex seller's *right* to sell sex, as an exercise of her autonomy against the background conditions of sex hierarchy, starts to look a lot less compelling. The sex-selling woman may lose an option, and that is a cost. But that is not an objection in itself. The objection shifts, perhaps to worrying when she is asked to take on *disproportionate* cost relative to other women, or when she is asked to take on an *unreasonable* amount of cost (one that impacts too severely on the rest of her life plan). It may be regrettable that *any* woman has to take on costs; but what is ultimately regrettable is that there is social hierarchy, and that those who benefit from it can't be relied upon to cede their position, in the name of equality. Members of the disadvantaged group taking on costs is just the price of ending oppression. So the question now is, in losing the option to sell sex, are individual sex sellers being asked to take on disproportionate or unreasonable cost?

Angie might want to insist that a violation of the sex-seller's right to autonomy is something distinctive, not just a 'cost' she can be asked to bear for the greater good of the group. But it is worth noting that she is defending a liberal position, and other liberals are not so categorical even about the values they take to be most fundamental, like liberty. John Stuart Mill, for example, gave a passionate defence of the liberty of the individual, but still thought that individuals could be compelled to do things to the collective benefit, including to give evidence in court, to bear a fair share of the country's military defence, and to save another person's life or intervene to stop a wrong being perpetrated against another person (Mill [1859] 1978, p. 10). If an individual can be compelled to give evidence in court, because having courts that hear evidence is the best way to secure justice for the society, then surely a woman can be asked to give up the option of selling sex, because eliminating the possibility of men buying sex from women is one necessary step along the pathway to a world where the sexes are equal.

The point may be clearer if we think about someone deliberately acting *against* a liberation movement, rather than just continuing to participate in practices that seem ordinary to us but which the liberation movement is trying to reframe as morally unacceptable. Suppose an individual woman in Britain in 1912 took to the streets in *counterprotest* of the suffragettes and their supporters. Her opinion on whether women should have the vote is a matter of her freedom of thought and expression, so she should not have been prevented from doing this. But we can still ask whether she was *morally wrong* (or right) to do this. Other women at the time were taking on very serious costs—mostly in the form of risks, e.g. of being arrested and sent to prison—in order to increase women's equality. Their sacrifices stood to increase autonomy for *all* women, not just at the time but into the future. If the individual woman we are thinking about acts so as to compromise the suffragettes' project, then she acts *against* the interests, including the autonomy interests, of women. In doing so, she acts wrongly.

It may be unsettling to accept this as a parallel to the sex worker, for that may feel like putting blame in the wrong place. It's true that if we were just approaching the topic of sexuality's role in sex inequality, considering women as a collective and asking where to start in distributing obligations and asking individual women to take on costs, we wouldn't be likely to start with sex workers. Indeed, perhaps we'd make so much progress with other women that we'd never even get to sex workers. It's a familiar thought that the most privileged women should be asked to take on the most cost, and while I don't agree with mainstream approaches to understanding the concept of 'privilege' in conjunction with women, this thought is otherwise correct. But we're *not* approaching the topic that way. Rather, I'm responding to a very specific objection that Angie has made, and which it is common for liberal feminists who take roughly Angie's position on sex work to make. They object that the radical feminist undermines the autonomy of the sex worker by taking options away from her. The radical feminist can respond to that objection that *all* women will have to take on costs to escape sex oppression, and this undermining of the sex worker's autonomy in the form of a narrowing to her set of options is the cost that she is asked to take on.

The advantage of this response is that it *acknowledges* that it's a cost, but simply responds that it's not an unreasonable or disproportionate cost. It would be great if we could change the world by reducing the options *only* of those with the most numerous and high-quality options, as might be the case when we argue for income equality by way of higher taxes to the top income brackets. But unfortunately that's not how the world works. We cannot get rid of markets in organs or markets in pregnancy without also reducing the options of some of those with the fewest and lowest-quality option sets (see also Satz 2010).

The feminist who insists upon the autonomy rights of the individual woman *not* to contribute to the project of women's liberation, rather than on the interests of the class—including that individual member—in escaping their current conditions, may be functioning, however noble her intentions, as a propagandist for the status quo. If we were to exaggerate for dramatic effect the disagreement Angie and I have over buying sex, we might say that I see her as a *propagandist* and she sees me as an *ideologue*. I worry that she is using the language of feminism and liberalism in a way that ultimately upholds sex oppression; and she worries, I think, that I use the language of feminism and utopia in a way that ultimately harms real women in the here and now by limiting their opportunities to improve their circumstances. Whether I'm an ideologue or just a dreamer (or perhaps, an optimist) is the subject of the next section.

2   One Woman's Utopia as Another's Dystopia?

In Section 2.4 of her first rejoinder, talking about my idea of a sex reset, Angie writes 'The utopian vision that Holly sketches is for me a dystopian nightmare'. We might think this reveals something about the nature of utopia and dystopia. Just as one man's trash is another man's treasure, one woman's paradise is another woman's purgatory. But this is not quite the disagreement, for Angie continues: 'Though I have no real qualms with the end point, the journey is incredibly troubling. In order to achieve this utopia, men and women are the legitimate targets for moral condemnation just for having sex with [one] another.' A little later she says 'attempts to socially shame people into doing the right thing rarely work'. So we do not, necessarily, have a disagreement over what the feminist utopia is. Angie's problem is with the journey, not the destination. The question for this section is, do we at least disagree about the journey?

I think we do not, but I can see that the way I made my case *left open* an interpretation of the tactics I think it is acceptable to use, and Angie has an objection to certain tactics. Her response suggests that I endorse a strong form of moralism in individual action and attitudes, where people go about delivering 'moral condemnation' and attempting to 'socially shame' one another, in order to bring about the sex reset that I advocated for. So I should be clear about what tactics I endorse, and what I see myself as doing.

Feminism is a democratic project in the colloquial sense that every woman has a say in what it is and what it does. It cannot be democratic in the formal sense because there is no infrastructure to coordinate all women globally, but it also cannot be just for *some* women, because those women will be vulnerable to the criticism that it does not represent the rest. The process works by *uptake*, with ideas being put forward, considered, and either rejected or accepted. The role of feminist thinkers, then, is to come up with these ideas. Some may hold most of the present background fixed, focusing on the most urgent problems of the present, offering diagnoses and solutions. Some may take a little more of the background to be up for grabs, conceiving of reforms to law and policy, spaces and services and provisions, that would advance women's interests and remove some of the current obstacles to equality that she faces. And still others may refuse to hold much of anything fixed—at least without strong evidence as to its necessity or permanence—and instead speculate about the way that things might be very different, and very much better, for women. Merely considering that things might be different may be enough to start *wanting* them to be different, and working toward achieving that. Utopian thinking can change our sense of what is possible and what is desirable. I do not deny that I have been a utopian thinker in this book. I do deny that there's anything wrong with that.

I'm explaining all this in order to say how I see what I have done in this book, which is that I have *offered* a picture of a feminist future, one where there is sex equality (the equality of the sexes), and where there might be good sex (or there might be no sex; in any case, where there is not altruistic/hierarchical sex, and where our relationship with sex has transformed entirely). And I have also offered a pathway to that future. It may not be the only path, and it may not be the best path, but I suspect it is the fastest and least circuitous. I am a feminist academic, explaining my ideas, and asking people to consider them. If they reach enough people, and are attractive to them, then maybe they will get uptake. If enough people give the ideas uptake, then a social movement will grow, and that movement will put pressure on law-makers to pass the relevant laws. None of this involves moralistic tactics.

Perhaps Angie was less worried about *my* licencing of moralistic tactics, and more worried that the mechanism for the sex reset is a social movement, and *the way that* social movements grow and spread is with interpersonal moralism of the kind she is worried about. If that is right, then in advocating for a social movement I am thereby advocating for interpersonal social shaming. This is an empirical question, and I am happy to be answerable on this point if it turns out to be right. But from the armchair (as philosophers like to say) I'm not sure it's right. Social movements have lots of different tactics for drawing people in. There's no getting around the fact that *some* are highly moralistic, attacking opponents, vilifying apostates, and dogpiling minor transgressions. The question is whether a social movement *has* to operate this way, so that merely advocating for a social movement as a means to a desired end entails endorsing tactics of social shaming. 'Calling in' (admonition done in private and 'with love') has been defended as a superior alternative to 'calling out' (admonition done publicly—social shaming, or 'cancelling'), for example (Bennett 2020). Elizabeth Anderson gives a long list of the practices of 'contentious politics' in her discussion of social movements, including things like publicity campaigns, theatrical performances, candlelight vigils, and litigation (Anderson 2014, p. 9). Of course, those involved in such politics are likely to have a strong moral view on what they are advocating for, but their *tactics* need not be moralistic in the pernicious way that Angie has in mind.

For the sake of argument, though, suppose it were the case that a successful social movement to disrupt altruistic/hierarchical sex, and to bring about the legal abolition of prostitution and pornography, *would* require moral condemnation and social shaming. These tactics were used in the second-wave feminist movement over the issue of feminist women's involvement with men, and created severe tensions between heterosexual and (politically-) lesbian feminist women. The Leeds Revolutionary Feminists, for example, wrote in their pamphlet *Love Your Enemy?* 'Any woman who takes part in a heterosexual couple helps to shore up male supremacy by making its foundations stronger' (Leeds Revolutionary Feminist Group 1981, p. 6). Their reasoning was different to mine. They saw the heterosexual couple as a unit that put individual women under the control of individual men, as part of an efficient system that kept *women* in service to men and thus upheld male supremacy (ibid.). But their tactics were divisive, and alienated some heterosexual women from the feminist movement. Perhaps Angie is asking, if these kinds of tactics were the *only* means to my desired social ends, would I stand by the ends at the cost of the means, or would I repudiate the ends?

I have to say that in this case I *would* stand by the ends. That is because while this kind of moralism—let's call it *nasty* moralism—is deeply unpleasant for those at whom it is directed (at least when it is not transformative, when its targets disagree with it and resist it), I think it still falls on the 'remonstrating... reasoning ... persuading ... entreating' side of John Stuart Mill's distinction between the ways society can interfere with individual liberty (and for which he thought compulsion could only be justified to prevent harm to others), rather than falling on the 'compelling' side (Mill [1859] 1978, p. 9). It *can* be resisted, and we have no right against others' moral attitudes, including their moral attitudes expressed strongly. I do not personally approve of these tactics, and in some current social movements I think they are used reprehensibly. I have first-hand experience of just how unpleasant they can be, and yet I *still* stand by them, at least when the alternative is the continuation of the sex-hierarchical status quo. Some instances of cancelling and social shaming do cause harm, such as loss of livelihood and serious and sustained psychological suffering,[4] and in those cases could be shut down by compulsion, or at least sanctioned after the fact. In particular, when the social movement's cause is not just, then these tactics are considerably less acceptable. But given the seriousness and scale of injustice against women, I would not throw out the end that I imagined in my opening statement *because of* the nature of the means, supposing that nasty moralism is the worst of the means.

3   Returning to Moral Wrongness

At the end of Section 1, Angie invites me directly to answer several questions. The first is whether I have 'a consistent moral position', given that I borrow insights from across different moral theories. Another is what my view is of the 'status and function' of 'rights to sexual autonomy' given my 'reliance on consequentialist arguments'. In particular, do I think 'that our rights to sexual autonomy

---

4 As opposed to transient negative emotions.

can at least be overridden by bad consequences such as the (potentially) harmful consequences of commercial sex for individual women and women as a class, or the negative impact of commercial sex on the social movement for women's equality'. Angie asks whether our rights to sexual autonomy can be overridden by 'sexual utility monsters', or 'when the majority dislikes our sexual preferences and desires'. These are two separate challenges, one to do with my overall moral position and the other to do with how autonomy fits into my view. I will take them in that order.

I said at the end of Section 3 of my first reply to Angie that 'I suspect that a deontic view built to accommodate inequality and frustrated potential alongside harm will be the most congenial to my position.' That means there are multiple values at the foundations of my view: equality, flourishing, and harm-reduction. I have not committed here to a specific and perfectly worked-out moral theory; I do not have one and I'm not sure I ever will. (I don't think that is an obstacle to doing applied ethics, either, because it is possible to rely on moral intuitions rather than moral theory; or to put moral intuitions into a **reflective equilibrium** with moral theory—or with any number of different moral concepts, principles, and theories—in order to reach a view; or to look for coherence between a moral conclusion and other beliefs and commitments that we have. See discussion in List and Valentini 2016.) Still, I think I have said enough to accommodate the set of moral reasons that I gave for why it would be wrong for an individual man to buy sex. I also think this is enough to answer the question I posed in my first reply, which was whether Angie and I 'agree about what moral wrongness consists in but disagree about its implications for buying sex, or disagree about buying sex *because* we disagree about what moral wrongness consists in'. The answer is that we disagree about what moral wrongness consists in, and that explains why we disagree about the wrongness of buying sex. For her, it's all about autonomy. Sex workers' right to autonomy gives them a right to sex work, and that right trumps any consequentialist considerations about what might be good for women. That takes us to Angie's second challenge, which is how autonomy fits into my view.

Because I don't work within a rights framework, I don't think there's a trumping right to autonomy. I can capture what Angie understands as one kind of autonomy violation under the heading of harm-reduction. In fact, this translation helps to show that she rolls two very distinct kinds of things together as violations of autonomy. One is what some theorists call a *negative* right, to be free from certain types of treatment. Rape and sexual assault are violations of women's bodily integrity, they involve *doing something to her against her will*. Her sexual autonomy gave her the right to decide whether and when she wanted sexual contact; that autonomy is violated when sexual contact is inflicted without her consent. For me, that is a straightforward harm. Angie asks what happens on my view when this kind of harm comes up against good consequences. Because I haven't defended a simple consequentialist view on which all that matters is whatever creates the greatest utility, I am not vulnerable to these challenges. Harm is not made permissible because of the utility monster, or because a majority prefers it, or because it would lead to the greatest utility for the greatest number of people. Both of our views come to similar verdicts in the case of rape and sexual assault, and other violations of a woman's *negative* rights.

Where our views come to very different verdicts is on what some theorists call *positive* rights, in contrast to the negative rights just discussed. Angie treats these both together, taking a right to autonomy to include *both* the right to be free from sexual activity you haven't consented to, and the right to have sexual activity that you do consent to, including the right to have it as part of your occupation. Moral theorists who distinguish positive from negative rights have typically taken negative rights to be more morally weighty. It is *extremely* important that no one physically assault you; it is *quite* important that when you are in need, someone provide you with assistance. This tracks a more general distinction between 'doing' and 'allowing', or 'acting' and 'omitting' to act. I don't think in terms of rights, but if I did, I wouldn't think there was a *right* to have sexual activity that you do consent to, or a right to have such sexual activity as part of your occupation. I wouldn't think there was a right to a specific occupation in the first place. Freedom of occupation is surely important, but that only means not having someone else decide what your occupation is to be. It doesn't mean having a *specific* occupation—here sex work—as part of your option set. It may only mean having sufficiently many appealing occupations to choose between. Making one specific option unavailable isn't plausibly a harm, so if it's to be accommodated on my view, it must be in terms of equality, or flourishing. It's hard to see how either of these values could be made to justify keeping sex work on the table as an option for all women. Angie said 'individuals are equally worthy of moral concern and respect'. I agree with her about that. But, as Rae Langton has said in arguing that Ronald Dworkin—who Angie relies on for the claim that rights are trumps—should be anti-pornography on equality grounds (Langton 1990), equal respect does not mean equal treatment. Precisely because of a commitment to equality for women, we might refuse to countenance sex work (or pornography) as an option for any woman. That will mean *treating* sex workers differently by making it the case that there's something they'd like to do but can't in fact do. But that's not a failure of equal respect, and therefore not a problem for me (or for Dworkin).

4 The Role of Sexuality in Sex Inequality

Angie wrote at the end of her Section 2.4 that bad sex is a symptom of gender injustice (sex injustice), not a cause of it. She said:

> focusing on sex as the linchpin of sex inequality draws our atten-tion away from other more pressing matters of feminist concern such as securing women's basic rights and liberties, and their equal social status. For sure, sex is part of the story but arguably it is a relatively small cog in the ubiquitous patriarchal machine. For this reason, it is more likely that securing social justice for women will lead to women's equality and empowerment in the sexual domain, rather than the other way around.

The idea here is that there are *many* components to sex inequality, and those concerning women's sexuality are only small components rather than major components. Furthermore, in causal terms, we may not need to tackle them directly, because change to them will follow from tackling the bigger components. If we secure economic equality for women, for example, then women will not be depen-dent on men, and so will be able to demand more from men (rather than just taking what they can get). This will be true in the sexual domain as much as in other domains of social life. Strong, indepen-dent women will demand the kind of sex they want to be having, rather than accept the kind of sex men want to have.

There is something tempting about this view. It is highly con-ducive to Angie's position on sex work, because in putting the emphasis on 'bigger cogs' like economic equality, it becomes more important to let individual women make use of whatever oppor-tunities for making money there happen to be, and these include those opportunities connected to her sexuality, such as sex work and contract pregnancy (surrogacy). (Although to be fair, Angie did not name the bigger cogs, so she may have other things than economic equality in mind, and these in turn may be less obviously conducive to her position.) This view reintroduces my earlier worry, from Section 1, about propaganda. There is something off about the idea that women can achieve equality by leaning in to stereotypes about what they are for, rather than leaning way out of them. It also merely suggests, but does not establish, that components concerning women's sexuality are only small cogs in the patriarchal machine. On some theories of the origins and persistence of women's subordination, women's sexuality has been key: that women's loyalty to a conquering tribe could be ensured through rape and impregnation; that women could be used to provide labour for the agricultural revolution (by *reproducing* new labourers); that child-bearing and child-rearing kept women in a state of dependency on men (e.g. Lerner 1986; Firestone 1970). Over the last several thousand years, women's sexual activity has been tightly controlled, as well as women's reproductive capacities. She has long been confined to the 'private sphere', as a wife and mother. It is true that these roles involve more duties than *just* being pregnant and being fucked, but those two roles have nonetheless been integral to her situation. So what is the justification for seeing her sexuality as a 'small cog'?

Even if her economic and social inequality is more explanatory, right now, of her continuing subordination, it may be that economic sex inequalities, and social sex inequalities, are *themselves* best explained by issues relating to her sexuality (rather than, say, by competing non-sexual stereotypes about her lack of rationality or reason). There is ample evidence, for example, of women's workplace inequality in relation to motherhood. More women are in part-time work, or not in work at all, *because* more women than men choose to stay home with children when they have families, or to cut back their work hours (see e.g. Grimshaw and Rubery 2015). There are still strong sex-based stereotypes and expectations about what a good mother is like, and what women are for (in ways specifically relating to sex). Why not think these explain social and economic inequality, rather than the other way round? Why not think that knocking out these forms of sexual inequality would knock out social and economic inequality, by changing how men see women and what men expect from women (and how women see themselves and what women expect from themselves and other women), rather than the other way around?

Perhaps Angie is right that we could get equality in matters relating to sexuality from equality in social and economic matters. Suppose we're both right, and these are just two routes we might take. She could still argue that hers is preferable, because it involves matters that are squarely in the public domain, and that law and policy can be used to intervene on without much controversy. It's *better*, all things considered, to work for equality in the public domain, than to have to moralize at people (in the worst-case scenario) about the private domain. Would that be a reason to go her way? I concede that it might. But I am less optimistic, perhaps, than Angie is about what it would take to disrupt the social norms that make sex into sex-as-we-know-it. I am not sure that merely ensuring social and economic equality would be sufficient to this task, and I am not sure that attempting to secure social and economic equality *without* equality in sex-as-we-know-it could actually succeed.

Chapter 6

Finding Common Ground

Second Reply to Holly Lawford-Smith

Angie Pepper

This second reply is divided into two sections. First, I respond to Holly's objection that my view ignores problematic social structures and does not have the resources to bring about positive social change. In short, I argue that this is not true, and I detail some of the laws and policies that are compatible with my rights-based ethical framework. Second, I take a step back to reflect more generally on the disagreement between Holly and me. This second section aims to offer a clear summary of what Holly and I agree upon, as well as what we continue to disagree upon, and give you some advice on how to proceed when debating the ethics of buying sex.

I   Rights-Respecting Policy and Social Change

In her first reply to my argument, Holly suggests that one of the central differences between us is that her view is more concerned with the social structures within which we make choices. Indeed, Holly implies that because my rights-based position focuses on the autonomy of individuals 'choice *is* the end of the matter' (p. 119) for my view. This point of alleged disagreement between us also serves as an objection to my argument. Holly worries that my framework either ignores or cannot speak to the structural factors at play that shape and constrain our preferences, desires, and choices.

If it were true, Holly's complaint would have force: a position that left harmful social practices and institutions unquestioned would be inadequate. However, my position does not ignore the structural dimensions at play in the shaping of people's choices. At various points, I have explicitly said that we should be concerned about the structures and conditions within which women are choosing to sell

DOI: 10.4324/9781003169697-10

sexual services. For example, I have suggested that valid consent to the sale of sex is not possible in conditions of extreme economic duress, and I have suggested that women will not have maximal freedom of occupation unless they have a range of good employment options to choose from. I also agree with Holly that women's and men's sexual desires, preferences, and fantasies are influenced by the deeply entrenched systems of gender and sex inequality, and that this is something we should all be worried about.

More generally, I agree that anyone thinking about the ethics of buying and selling sex should be concerned about social structures including the patterns of norms, expectations, privileges, and disadvantages that constitute systems of gender. First, as Holly notes, the choice to undertake sex work, and the choice to buy sexual services are currently gendered: sex workers are mostly women, and sex buyers are mostly men. This is no accident, and the causes are complex. Yet we are where we are, and since sex workers rarely enjoy full protection under the law, and since sex workers are typically stigmatised because of their work, we should worry about the ways that disadvantage attaches to gender in commercial sex exchanges. Second, the value of sexual autonomy (and autonomy more generally) will be most fully realised when people are able to form, revise, and pursue a conception of the sexual good against just background conditions. Given that we currently live in unjust societies, injustice is likely to deform people's preferences and limit people's options so we should be worried about why most sex workers are women. Third, when societal pressures to take on disadvantageous options are very high, this threatens our ability to give valid consent to those options. So, we want to ensure that sex work is something that women genuinely choose to do as opposed to feeling like they have no other option, and we want to make sure that sex workers are able to leave sex industries.

With those thoughts in mind, the difference between Holly's view and mine is not that her view is concerned about social structures and mine is not. Rather, we both care about social structures but we disagree about what can and should be done about them. The solutions that Holly proposes involve legal prohibitions on commercial sex (Chapter 1, Section 3.4) and social prohibitions on hierarchical sex (Chapter 1, Section 3.5). The success of prohibitions depends on how fearful people are of the negative repercussions associated with doing what is prohibited. Accordingly, effective prohibitions carry costs for those who transgress them, which means that prohibitions tend to be punitive: if a person gets caught doing what is legally and socially prohibited, they may be liable to a variety of punishments. They may, for instance, be fined, get a criminal record, go to prison, be socially shamed, be publicly condemned, be shunned by friends and family, lose their job, find it difficult to secure accommodation, lose access to their children, and so on.

Whenever prohibitions are punitive, they require justification. This is because punishment deliberately harms people, and we need a very strong justification for deliberately harming people. Moreover, anyone looking to justify punishing people must show not just that punishment might bring about some good (e.g. social change), but that the subject of the punishment has no **moral right** not to be punished.

Throughout my contribution to this debate, I have defended the claim that the buying and selling of sexual services represent valuable options for many individuals. I have also argued that it is possible for a man to buy sex from a woman in a way that fully respects her rights and therefore does not involve wrongdoing. To my mind, people have a right to engage in commercial sex exchanges when doing so is compatible with the rights of those involved. That we have a moral right to buy and sell sex from one another is crucial. Recall, that in my view, rights are trumps, which means that we cannot justify overriding a person's rights by appealing to good consequences. This means that laws or policies that prohibit buying and selling sex go against the rights of everyone to buy and sell (not just those currently buying or selling sex, or those who get caught doing so). Furthermore, since people have a moral right to buy and sell sex, they have a moral right not to be punished for simply engaging in commercial sex exchanges.

Of course, none of our rights are absolute, and there may be circumstances in which it is permissible for the state to infringe on our rights. But all actions, laws, and policies that infringe on our rights stand in need of justification. Holly has sought to justify prohibitions on commercial and hierarchical sex but my arguments against Holly's moral position tell against such prohibitions: though we may have reason to wish the world were different, we must respect people's rights to sexual autonomy and freedom of occupation. We cannot trample over people's rights to prevent them from harming themselves or to change the social structures that inform their choices.

This last point is worth dwelling on for a moment. Over her two replies Holly argues that by the logic of my own argument, it is permissible to remove the option of selling sex and, moreover, that individual women have a duty not to sell sex. The basic idea is that since the autonomy interests of individual women are central to my argument, I should be committed to maximizing the autonomy of all women. Holly then suggests that allowing some individuals to perform sex work in the *here and now* diminishes their own autonomy and the autonomy of *all* women in the *future* (pp. 121–122). Moreover, Holly later contends that since (for her) sex work is incompatible with women's liberation it is legitimate to demand that women refrain from selling sex even when doing so comes at a significant cost to them. This is because actual and would-be women sex workers owe it to their fellow women to not act against the women's liberation movement (pp. 165–169).

It's important to see that these lines of argument rest on the questionable assumption that selling sex and women's liberation are incompatible. This is an assumption that I reject. (I also reject the implication that a woman cannot be a sex worker *and* a feminist.) Earlier I suggested that we should see bad sex as 'a *symptom* of systemic gender injustice as opposed to the *cause* of gender inequality' (p. 152). I think the same is true of bad sex work. Markets in sex are not inherently bad—a point Holly concedes (p. 8)—but existing markets do have bad elements such as the patterns of harm and disadvantage that are distinctively gendered. To my mind, the bad dimensions of existing sex markets are a *symptom* of gender injustice, not the *cause*. Individuals selling sex do not cause systemic gender oppression, their actions cannot plausibly be shown to produce the deeply entrenched inequality that marks the lives of women from birth to death. By selling sex Adele does not *cause* unequal access to education or educational attainment, Eva does not *cause* unequal opportunity, Maria does not *cause* unequal pay, Charlotte does not cause *unequal* access to medical resources, together they do not *cause* sexual harassment and domestic violence, nor do they *cause* inequality in family life and women's unequal political power. Whatever discrimination, disadvantage, and oppression women experience as a group they do not experience it *because* some individual women sell sex. Hence it is false to claim that the autonomy interests of sex workers are at odds with the autonomy interests of women as a group or the project of women's liberation.

If you are tempted to think that sex workers do, through the exercise of their rights to sexual autonomy and freedom of occupation, diminish the autonomy of all women (themselves included) ask yourself the following: what would happen if those individuals refrained from selling sex? How would their acts of self-sacrifice produce better options for themselves and everyone else? The simple answer is they will not. If Adele, Eva, Maria, and Charlotte give up sex work that will not make any difference to their options or the options of other women (and they will be worse off). That is because removing or forgoing the option of sex work will not magic into existence an increased range of employment options further down the line. Nor does sex work stand as an insurmountable barrier to the introduction of more and better options for women, or gender justice more generally. It is not the case that gender justice would already have been achieved but for some women performing sex work. Consequently, demanding that sex workers give up the jobs they prefer and value to promote women's autonomy is unwarranted: individual women sacrificing their own autonomy by refraining from selling sex will not enable or secure the autonomy of future women.

This does not mean that my view endorses the status quo or is silent on what might be done to maximise people's freedom and reduce harm. On the contrary, my position invites us to look for laws and policies that alleviate the worst effects of pernicious background conditions, while also promoting individual autonomy and protecting individual rights. Accordingly, my framework favours laws and policies that are autonomy-enabling and not autonomy-denying. Put simply, we should adopt laws and policies that give individuals more control over the shape of their lives and the power to make informed decisions for themselves. In what follows, I will discuss laws and policies that might be implemented to (i) make sex work safer and fairer, (ii) promote ethical sex buying, and (iii) reduce the occurrence and influence of hierarchical sex.

1.1   Sex Work: Harm Reduction, Meaningful Choice, and Workers' Rights

Throughout her contributions to this debate, Holly has emphasised the harm and risks of harm involved in sex work. It is these harms and risks of harm that lead Holly to argue that buying sex is morally wrong and that we can justify imposing legal prohibitions on commercial sex. I have suggested that sex work is not inherently dangerous work, and I have argued that harm and risks of harm are not sufficient to make buying sex morally wrong. However, this does not mean that I am unconcerned about the harms and risks currently associated with sex work. The rights of sex workers to live healthy lives, free from violence, stigma, discrimination, and exploitation must be protected and they are frequently not. However, unlike Holly, I do not think that prohibiting commercial sex exchanges is an appropriate or acceptable response to the harm experienced by sex workers. Rather, we should seek to strengthen the legal rights and protections of sex workers and ensure that they have meaningful options for work.

There are many laws and policies that might be introduced to ensure that sex workers are better protected against harm, that they have more control over the content and conditions of their work, and that their choice to take up sex work is meaningful. Here I give some examples. I should not be read as categorically endorsing the implementation of these policies. Context is everything and whether a particular policy or legal solution should be implemented will depend on careful consideration of the particularities of the sexual service, the features of the situation, and any potential negative consequences. However, what I aim to show is that there is much that might be done to reduce the harms and risks of harm associated with sex work that is compatible with the rights of sex workers and sex buyers.

The **criminalization** of sex work is the dominant regulatory approach globally (Sanders and Campbell 2014). However, there is 'strong research evidence that models of governance that seek to criminalize the organization, purchase or sale of sex puts sex workers (as well as their clients) in danger' (Sanders 2016, p. 102; see also Platt et al. 2018). Sex workers are especially disadvantaged under criminalization because sex work is regarded as immoral and illicit. This serves to stigmatise sex workers, alienate them, and leave them vulnerable to abuse, exploitation, and institutional discrimination (Vanwesenbeeck 2017). So, if one wants to reduce the harms and risks of harm associated with sex work, a good place to start is by changing the legal status of selling and buying sex.

There are two popular alternatives to the criminalization of sex work: **legalization** or **decriminalization**. Legalization removes criminal laws and penalties pertaining to sex work and mandates direct state regulation in the form of specific laws and policies that apply to sex industries but not to other forms of commerce. The kinds of regulations that might be put in place include licenses to sell sexual services, age restrictions, advertising restrictions, mandatory condom use, and mandatory sexual health screening for sex workers. Places that have legalized prostitution include Nevada (in the United States), the Netherlands, and Germany. Like legalization, decriminalization also removes criminal laws and penalties pertaining to the selling and buying of sex. However, unlike legalization, decriminalization does not involve unique government regulation: prostitution is treated just like any other occupation. In 2003, New Zealand became the first country to decriminalize prostitution with the passing of the Prostitution Reform Act.

Defenders of both legalization and decriminalization agree that sex work should not be criminalized but they disagree over whether, or to what extent, the state should regulate sex industries. Those who defend legalization (and therefore industry-specific regulation) argue that regulation is needed to manage and avoid the social problems associated with prostitution such as organized crime, and to protect the health and well-being of sex workers and their clients. Those who defend decriminalization (and are therefore against direct regulation) worry that regulation places unfair burdens on sex workers (see NSWP 2013; Mac 2016; Flanigan 2020, section 4.2.2). For example, the activist Juno Mac argues that

> Regulation sounds great on paper, but politicians deliberately make regulation around the sex industry expensive and difficult to comply with. It creates a two-tiered system: legal and illegal work. We sometimes call it 'backdoor criminalization.' Rich, well-connected brothel owners can comply with the regulations, but more marginalized people find those hoops impossible to jump through. And even if it's possible in principle, getting a license or proper venue takes time and costs money. It's not going to be an option for someone who's desperate and needs money tonight. They might be a refugee or fleeing domestic abuse. In this two-tiered system, the most vulnerable people are forced to work illegally, so they're still exposed to all the dangers of criminalization I mentioned earlier.
>
> (Mac 2016)

Moreover, others have pointed out that existing regulatory systems often fail to differentiate between sexual services and the needs of specific industries. For example, while mandatory condom use might be a desirable policy for sex workers in brothels, those who work in the pornography industry have challenged such requirements (Flanigan 2020, pp. 208–209).

Although regulation can be burdensome, discriminatory, and stigmatizing, unregulated decriminalization is also problematic (Weitzer 2013). Having no state regulation or monitoring in place would leave the rights and interests of sex workers, their clients, and the wider community unprotected. This suggests that we shouldn't abandon regulation entirely but develop regulatory frameworks that do not unfairly burden sex workers and are sensitive to differences in sexual services. Consequently, some argue that we should adopt a pragmatic approach to regulation which 'guarantees workers' rights and can enhance their health and safety; [...] imposes vital oversight over business owners; and [will] attract much more public support than a policy of simple, unrestricted decriminalization' (Weitzer 2013, p. 4; see also Shrage 2022).

In addition to removing the laws that criminalize sex work, various legal protections should be extended to sex workers to ensure that they are not exploited and that their status as equal citizens is fully recognised and protected. For example, as we saw in my opening statement (p. 90), the Global Network of Sex Work Projects defends eight sex workers' rights (NSWP 2013). If these rights were fully recognised, protected, and enabled, then many of the harms and vulnerabilities experienced by sex workers would cease to exist. To see why, let's consider each right in turn.

1   *Sex workers have a right to freedom of association.* This means that they have a right to come together with others to voice their opinions, campaign for their rights, engage in collective bargaining, and advocate for better working conditions. Securing this right is essential for enabling the political voice of sex workers and their inclusion in political discourse and decision-making. Moreover, by protecting this right, sex workers are able to advocate for and deliver community-based solutions that will reduce harm and increase well-being.

2   *Sex workers have the right to be protected by the law.* This right guarantees that sex workers receive equal treatment under the law and that they will not, for example, be unlawfully detained, have their testimony disregarded or be mistreated by law enforcement officers. Fully protecting and enabling this right reduces the harms and risks of harm associated with sex work by securing access to justice for sex workers when they are the victims of crime, including battery and sexual assault.

3 *Sex workers have a right to be free from violence.* This right demands not just that sex workers are protected against physical assault, coercive threats, forced labour, unlawful detention, and police brutality, but that there are appropriate mechanisms in place for sex workers to report crimes against them and have their reports taken seriously. Furthermore, insofar as criminalization is linked to increased violence against sex workers (Platt et al. 2018), criminal laws and penalties against sex work must be removed.

4 *Sex workers have the right to be free from discrimination.* This right demands an end to the institutional discrimination that sex workers suffer when they are denied access to important goods and services such as housing, healthcare, and the criminal justice system. Importantly, this right requires not just formal changes to law and policy but also a change in societal attitudes toward sex workers. In practice, this means that 'anti-discrimination legislation must be paired with broader educational and training initiatives to address stigma, prejudice, and hate against sex workers, and the people who associate with them' (NSWP 2013, p. 11). Stigma harms sex workers by making them victims of prejudice and discrimination, leaving them vulnerable to violence and exploitation, and inducing psychological stress (Vanwesenbeeck 2017, p. 1634). So, ending social stigma is essential to protecting the well-being of sex workers and minimizing the harms linked to their work.

5 *Sex workers have a right to privacy and freedom from arbitrary interference.* This right prevents sex workers from being victimized by police who routinely and arbitrarily detain them, healthcare workers who force them to undergo mandatory health testing and disclose confidential test results, governments that force them to register in databases, and other privacy violations.

6 *Sex workers have a right to health.* Sex workers are regularly harmed by being denied access to adequate healthcare and by coercive medical practices such as having their details shared without their consent, mandatory testing, biometric tracking and forced sterilization. The NSWP makes several recommendations in this area, including ensuring that sex workers have access to affordable healthcare, specialist and targeted health services, and requiring that health services should not be conditional on workers giving up their job (NSWP 2013, pp. 17–18).

7   *Sex workers have the right to move and migrate.* 'Travel restrictions faced by sex workers impede sex workers' civil and political engagement and right to organise, while disrupting their right to migrate and travel for family, work, and study purposes, or for tourism. They face refusal at border crossings, economic discrimination, and difficult visa/pre-travel clearance requirements—these barriers limit their access to intergovernmental and international civil society spaces and their meaningful involvement in policy discussions directly affecting their health and well-being' (NSWP 2019, p. 12). The negative effects of unfair travel restrictions represent another way in which stigma and institutional discrimination harm sex workers. Protecting sex workers' right to move and migrate does not entail securing special entitlements for sex workers to freedom of movement that are not enjoyed by everyone else. Rather, this right protects sex workers against the unfair discrimination that occurs when their freedom of movement is curtailed simply because of their occupation.

8   *Sex workers have the right to work and the freedom to choose their occupation.* Protecting this right entails, in the first instance, acknowledging that sex work *is* work. This right also demands that sex workers have the same legal protections as workers in other industries such as entitlements to annual leave, sick pay, parental leave, rest breaks, protection against unfair dismissal, accident compensation, pensions, and so on. By securing sex workers' labour rights many of the exploitative elements of employment in the sex industries will be eliminated and workers will have the power to improve their labour conditions.

Though all these measures are important, none of them addresses the structural issue of *why* women are disproportionately choosing sex work over men. Both Holly and I worry about the social influences and vulnerabilities that lead women to choose sex work. And I think we agree that one way of reducing the power of social influences and women's economic vulnerability would be to ensure that all women have meaningful employment opportunities that enable a decent standard of living. Moreover, I have argued that criminalizing commercial sex and prohibiting women from selling (and/or men from buying) is not an appropriate response to the problem of economic precarity and vulnerability. Removing options from women who already have few options does nothing to increase their autonomy and leaves them worse-off. Instead, we should make sure that women do not feel that sex work is their only option for survival. One way of achieving that would be to ensure that all citizens have an unconditional basic income as a right of residence (Van Parijs 2004).

1.2 Sex Buyers: Promoting Ethical Consumption

A further way to reduce the harms associated with sex work is to promote ethical sex buying. In my opening statement, I appealed to Teela Sanders's (2008) research on men who buy sex to show that men are not generally indifferent to the ethical dimensions of buying sex. Indeed, Sanders suggests that for many of the men she interviewed 'morals and ethics were a constant framework for their own behaviour and were always present in their decision-making' (ibid., p. 53). Accordingly, sex buyers are generally concerned about who they buy sex from, and they actively seek to avoid buying sex from people who are underage, have addiction issues, are coercively pimped, or are trafficked. However, as I noted, since existing ethical standards for sex buyers are determined by the buyers themselves and the community of buyers, they may not meet the demands of morality. This is because subjective and piecemeal standards may be self-serving, inconsistent, and inadequate.

With this last point in mind, I set out some ethical standards that sex buyers should adhere to when purchasing sex. Those standards aimed to secure morally decent commercial sex exchanges. To quickly recap, the principles included: (a) ensuring that one has free and informed consent; (b) respecting the sex worker's right to withdraw consent; (c) not attempting to purchase sexual services while under the influence of alcohol or drugs; (d) paying the full price for the services agreed to (you should not try to get 'extras' for free); (e) always practice safe sex; (f) attending regular sexual health screening; (f) reporting cases of suspected trafficking, sexual exploitation, and abusive pimping, to the relevant law enforcement authorities or charities.

Though some sex buyers may be guided by these principles most are probably not. Promoting an ethic of responsible sex buying is crucial to minimizing the risk of harm to workers and moral wrongdoing on the part of buyers. Accordingly, we need to find ways of cultivating an ethos of responsibility and ethical consumption among the community of sex buyers. The mechanisms for consumer education cannot be determined in isolation of the buying community because policies and services that are imposed from outside without consultation are less likely to be taken up. Instead, policymakers should work with consumer groups to devise effective educational strategies and campaigns.

Beyond trying to cultivate a more thoroughgoing, principled, and consistent sense of consumer responsibility among sex buyers, several other things might be done to help them fulfil their responsibilities. For example, buyers need education and information about how to identify exploitation and coercion, and there needs to be effective reporting mechanisms in place for buyers who do suspect that a sex seller is underage, trafficked, or coercively pimped. Additionally, the state must make sure that sexual health screening is accessible and free to all.

1.3 Towards Respect, Mutuality, and Women's Empowerment in Sex

In my first reply to Holly, I argued that while hierarchical sex may be bad, it does not always involve moral wrongdoing. Nonetheless, I suggested that we ought to be concerned about the limiting and harmful social norms and expectations of hierarchical sex. Hierarchical sex is bad for everyone, but it is especially bad for women because it can diminish a woman's sexual autonomy and reduce her opportunities for sexual fulfilment. Likewise, though some men may benefit from the privileging of male pleasure associated with hierarchical sex, the expectations can be similarly harmful to their ability to have meaningful and pleasurable sexual experiences.

Though I disagree with Holly's argument for a sex reset I am sympathetic to her thought that the world would be a better place without hierarchical sex. I also think that Holly is right to be concerned about the feedback loop between commercial and hierarchical sex. Commercial and non-commercial sex would be better if they were free of the problematic norms and expectations associated with hierarchical sex. So what can be done about hierarchical sex that is compatible with peoples' rights to sexual autonomy? Here I make some suggestions. Again, I am not saying that we should definitely implement these proposals, that they are the best solutions to the problem, or that this is an exhaustive list of possibilities. My central aim is to show that one can be committed to the kind of rights-based framework I endorse and also be committed to bringing about social and institutional change.

A good place to start is by thinking about human sexual development. Our sexual selves are not given but develop and emerge under the influence of a myriad of social and cultural factors. Consequently, we need to think seriously about how such influences might negatively affect the sexual development of children and adolescents and what kinds of measures might be introduced to promote healthy sexuality. Importantly, young children are not fully autonomous. This means that young children are not yet able to form, revise, and pursue a conception of the good and we do not hold them fully (if at all) accountable for their poor decision-making. Given that children are not yet fully autonomous, we do not act contrary to their autonomy interests when we interfere with their choices or control their options. Thus, we can permissibly introduce prohibitive policies to protect them against harmful influences without diminishing their agency.

Since it is permissible to act paternalistically toward children, it is permissible to prohibit the sexualisation of children and adolescents in marketing, advertising, and broadcasting. Similarly, it is permissible for the state to introduce regulation that prohibits the marketing of sexualised products to children or products that are either implicitly or explicitly associated with the sex industry. For example, the state could prohibit the marketing and sale of lacy padded bras for prepubescent girls, high-heeled shoes designed for girls from birth, and T-shirts with slogans such as 'future WAG' and 'porn star' (Coy 2009; Womack 2007).

Again, this is not about limiting the options and choices of adult women but rather limiting the effects of sexualised culture on the life prospects of girls and women. As Maddy Coy persuasively argues, the sexualisation of culture limits girls and women's autonomy by narrowing their horizons:

> When six-year olds are wearing jeans with 'princess' across the rear, having hair extensions, or singing about their lady lumps and growing up to want boobies displaying a sexualised identity is no longer a milestone of impending adulthood, but an integral part of identity development itself. This is how sexualisation limits girls' space for action—at the same time as it seems to offer opportunities for material gain, personal achievement and socio-cultural acceptance, and thus widen girls' choices, it fixes sexualisation as such a normal route that there is little space outside of it.
>
> (Coy 2009, p. 376)

If young girls' ambitions are sexualised such that they dream only of being beauty queens, glamour models, and footballers' wives, what they value and see themselves doing becomes very limited. Moreover, since sexualised ambitions rarely depend on a decent education, young girls with such ambitions are less likely to see the value in educational achievement and thereby further limit what is possible in the future. If we want to make sure that adult women who enter sex industries do so freely and have meaningful opportunities for alternative work and exit, then we need to ensure that young girls do not have their options narrowed by incessant messaging about their worth as sexual objects.

Both boys and girls are bombarded with messages about sex and sexuality that inform and shape their sexual development from a very young age. If we want to diminish hierarchical sex, then we need to think about how the sexualisation of children serves to perpetuate the norms and expectations of hierarchical sex. As we have seen, girls are subject to social messaging that locates their value in their sexuality and their status as sexual objects. By contrast, boys are subject to the messaging of **hegemonic masculinity**. Hegemonic masculinity captures the idea that though there are multiple forms of masculinity, there is one 'culturally exalted form of masculinity' (Carrigan et al. 1985, p. 592). Importantly, hegemonic masculinity entails a system of gendered norms and practices that embody and reinforce the dominance of men and the subordination of women. This dominant form of masculinity is not merely descriptive but normative: it tells boys and men what they *ought* to think, and how they *ought* to act, including how they *ought* to think about women, and how they *ought* to treat women.

Hierarchical sex, as Holly describes it, is sustained by the norms and practices of hegemonic masculinity that serve as the backdrop for boys' sexual development. In the sexual domain:

> hegemonic masculinity entails that 'real men' have (preferably large) penises, have sex with heterosexual, cisgender (non-transgender) women, do not form strong emotional ties (since this is associated with femininity), are entitled to women's bodies, are expected to be regularly sexually engaged and desiring sex, and are permitted to be aggressive and dominant to achieve their sexual goals.
>
> (Miller 2022, p. 165)

It is evident that something needs to be done to undermine the messaging of hegemonic masculinity to encourage the development of non-hierarchical heterosexual sexual identity in men. One potential route would be to elevate an alternative form of masculinity that promotes a standard of male heterosexual sexuality not premised on the dominance of men and the subordination of women (Miller 2022). We should therefore look to develop and promote positive visions of masculinity that involve cultivating attitudes of respect and mutuality in sex.

Beyond trying to limit the pressures imposed upon children, the state must equip children with the skills necessary for healthy sexual development (Cense 2019). These include the skills to identify personal desires and understand one's sexual identity; the skills to negotiate partnered sex including the process of giving and getting consent and speaking openly about sexual pleasure; and the skills required for sexual empowerment, including the ability to establish, adapt, and recognise boundaries, the ability to deal with the positive and negative outcomes of sexual experience, and the ability to make sense of the myriad of messages one may receive about sex and sexuality (see Arbeit 2014 for a full discussion of these skills and their importance).

These skills might be developed through a comprehensive sex education programme that includes a greater emphasis on the media literacy needed to critically engage with film, advertising, and pornography. To be clear, the purpose of media literacy education is not to condemn pornography use but rather to recognise its pedagogical and erotic value while also equipping young people with the skills needed to critically reflect on the images they consume (Goldstein 2020).

Pornography has a long history in human society and our desire to look at or create sexual images is here to stay, at least for the foreseeable future. However, that does not mean that pornography should not be regulated or that we shouldn't be worried about the messaging of mainstream **inegalitarian pornography**. As Holly rightly notes in her opening statement, much of the pornography currently produced and consumed is inegalitarian insofar as it privileges male pleasure and celebrates women's sexual subordination. More generally, we might say that inegalitarian pornography involves 'sexually explicit representations that as a whole eroticize relations (acts, scenarios, or postures) characterized by gender inequity' (Eaton 2007, p. 676). Consequently, there exists a 'widespread social practice of watching, for entertainment, men fuck women in dominating, degrading, painful, unequal ways' (p. 32, this volume). Even if you think (as I do) that such pornography should not be outlawed and people should not be punished for viewing it, we have good reason to be concerned about the effects this kind of pornography has in shaping our sexual selves and the ways that our sexual interactions play out.

Children and young people will inevitably access pornography (even with tighter regulations in place). Given this, and the potentially problematic influence of inegalitarian porn on our sexual development, the state arguably has a responsibility to foster greater diversity in pornography and fund pornography that promotes good sexual relations in terms of respect, mutuality, and diversity (with regard to actors, sexualities, and activities). This kind of pornography is sometimes referred to as **egalitarian pornography**, which 'is pornography that is premised on the full equality between sexual partners and hence does not eroticize any acts of violence, humiliation, or objectification or any of the gender stereotypes that help to sustain gender inequality' (Maes 2017, p. 211). The promotion of egalitarian pornography may help to combat the problematic messaging of inegalitarian pornography by promoting sexual ethics, norms and erotic tastes that we judge to be better or more virtuous. The extent that egalitarian porn can perform this role is yet to be seen, but as Mari Mikkola notes 'given how successful advertising is in shaping desire, it is not hugely implausible to hold that by making egalitarian, feminist pornography attractive, it would be possible to shape in beneficial ways what is commonly taken to be desirable' (2019, p. 228). Importantly, this proposal does not reduce options or rely on prohibition, but rather promotes greater diversity in available options including those that we think better capture the features of good sex and more virtuous erotic desires.

Lastly, it's worth reiterating the importance of achieving social distributive justice and substantive sex equality. Only when women's rights, freedoms, and opportunities are equal to men's will the forces that sustain hierarchical sex and diminish women's power in the sexual domain be diminished. This is simply because the power and control that many men enjoy in the sexual domain is a direct consequence of women's economic vulnerability and dependence. If women had more social power, then they would be able to exit relationships more freely and may feel less pressured to go along with sex that do not want.

SUMMARY

In this section, I have shown why feminists who prioritize individual rights in the ethics of sex should be concerned about the social structures that inform and shape our desires and preferences. And I have offered examples of the laws, policies, and regulations that are compatible with such a position. Before I move on, it's worth stressing that though I am against the legal and social prohibitions advanced by Holly, that does not mean that I think there are no grounds for extra legal protections in existing liberal democracies. For example, there should be laws protecting people against **intimate image abuse**, which involves intimate images being taken or shared without a person's consent. Such laws would make so-called revenge porn, upskirting, and downblousing criminal offences. This is just one example of where existing legal systems and social provisions fail people, mainly women, by allowing others to harm them and violate their rights to sexual autonomy. Though my approach argues against the state violating our rights to sexual autonomy to alter social structures, it also demands that the state protect our rights to sexual autonomy, privacy, and property against individuals who would violate those rights.

2 Propagandists and Ideologues: Finding Agreement in Disagreement

To close the debate, I want to say something about the nature of the disagreement between Holly and me and the two broad camps that we represent. Throughout the discussion, Holly has assumed a position that might be described as a **radical feminist** view, and I have taken up a position that might be described as a **liberal feminist** view. However, using these labels is not without complications. First, these labels have been applied to all manner of views, some with which we strongly disagree and would not want to be associated with. Second, specific feminist philosophical positions rarely fall neatly into one category or another. Moreover, the differences between positions are often overstated and rely on a very fixed understanding of what it is to hold a 'liberal' or 'radical' feminist position. As feminist philosopher Alison Stone notes, 'many individual feminist thinkers combine elements of several different positions—few thinkers endorse any single feminist position in its pure form' (Stone 2007, p. 16). I think this is true of both mine and Holly's views and therefore labelling our respective positions can be unhelpful insofar as it reinforces the differences between us and overlooks all that we share.

Lastly, the terms 'radical' and 'liberal' feminism have been used pejoratively by critics. Radical feminists are branded as dogmatic man-haters, who are anti-sex, anti-family, and pro-censorship. Liberal feminists, on the other hand, are accused of being 'so scared of offending men that they bend over backwards to maintain the status quo as opposed to seeking proper liberation for women' (Bindel 2020). Accordingly, to be a radical is to be unyielding, insensitive to difference, overly demanding and rights-denying. By contrast, to be a liberal is to be wishy-washy, toothless, insensitive to structural injustice, and a defender of the patriarchal status quo. Couched in these ways, neither position looks attractive! It is, then, understandable that many feminists are reluctant to nail their colours to either mast.

Regrettably, I think something of the popular caricature of the two positions—radical and liberal—can be found in the exchange between me and Holly. At various points in our debate, we take cheap shots at one another; shots that rely on oversimplifications of our respective views. On the one hand, Holly suggests that my liberal rights-based view leaves social structures intact and she implies that my position is a vehicle for patriarchal propaganda. On the other, I accuse Holly of denying the rights of individuals, and I come close to accusing Holly of being **unreasonable** in her attempt to impose her feminist ideology on others. And there we have it: Angie the propagandist and Holly the ideologue.

Fortunately, Holly and I are trained to identify and challenge this kind of rhetorical posturing. So, while we perhaps could have done better to tone down the more combative and uncharitable elements of the disagreement, we are able to see them for what they are and try to move beyond them. Indeed, we hope to have shown how fiercely felt disagreement between the two sides can be had in ways that are generally respectful and fruitful. Holly and I have both learnt from the exchange and our points of disagreement have been a catalyst for reflecting upon, altering, and rearticulating our respective views.

One thing to emerge from our debate is that it's not always easy to identify the precise points of disagreement. There is much that Holly and I agree on (more on that in a minute) but nonetheless the disagreement between us persists. Hopefully, you can see from how our debate has unfolded that the points of disagreement between us are reflected in our most deeply held theoretical and normative commitments. We have found ourselves talking past one another or misinterpreting one another's views (sometimes uncharitably!) because the foundational commitments of our respective positions were not laid bare from the start. This problem is not unique to us: people rarely lay bare their theoretical and normative commitments when they disagree about the ethics of selling and buying sex. But we hope to have shown what happens when you persist with the conversation and make a good-faith attempt to understand your opponent's position.

A second outcome is that Holly and I have learnt that appeal to empirical evidence has limited argumentative force. The social scientists, lawyers, and medical professionals who investigate sex work are often partisan: they typically have a preconceived view about the ethics of commercial sex, which means that their enquiries are often underpinned and motivated by a normative and political agenda. This means that researchers who begin with the view that sex work is work (as opposed to mere exploitation) are motivated to show that sex work is not inherently violent, that it is a valuable labour option for many, that sex workers are autonomous agents making meaningful choices and that not all people who buy sex act in morally reprehensible ways. Likewise, those researchers who start with the view that commercial sex is inherently exploitative are motivated to show that the majority of (if not all) prostituted people are the victims of violence, they are coerced into selling sex, commercial sex is disvaluable and denigrates prostituted people, and so on. As Michelle Dempsey notes, 'researchers offering empirical evidence regarding what prostitution is like seem to be trapped in a 'competing camps' mentality' (2019, p. 211).

Acknowledging the role of partisanship in the production of empirical evidence is important. Since the empirical evidence available to philosophers like me and Holly is shaped by the 'competing camps' mentality, both of us can cherry-pick from the numerous studies out there to support our respective arguments. Neither of us can do without empirical evidence. Our moral evaluation of sex buyers does depend, to some degree, on how commercial sex actually takes place in the world and the effects it has. But it's important to recognise that empirical evidence plays only a supporting role in the philosophical arguments that we have presented.

Though we will continue to disagree over the permissibility of buying sex, there is much that we agree on. We both agree that:

- All humans are equal in their moral status.
- All humans have equal basic rights.
- All humans have a right not to be harmed by others.
- All humans have a right not to be trafficked.
- All humans have a right to sexual autonomy.
- All humans have a right to freedom of occupation.
- No human has a right to do whatever they want.
- Social structures influence people's preferences, desires, and choices—and not always in ways that are good for individuals or collectives.
- Social structures can create patterns of disadvantage.

However, we continue to disagree over:

- The facts about harm and risk of harm.
- The factors that invalidate sexual consent.
- Whether hierarchical sex is always morally wrong.
- The bad consequences that might be invoked to infringe a right.
- The social and legal solutions that we ought to pursue to make the world a better place.

Throughout the numerous conversations we have had in writing this book we have learnt a lot about how *not* to argue about this topic. So, to conclude we want to finish by making some suggestions for how people ought to approach debates on the ethics of buying and selling sex. These are practical suggestions that should help you to avoid talking past your opponent, prevent you from making claims that cannot be substantiated, allow you to find common ground with one another, and move beyond the impasse that so commonly characterises this debate.

- Be clear about your normative ethical framework and your moral commitments.
- Approach all empirical evidence with caution and accept that the empirical evidence cannot settle the normative questions at stake.

- Think about what it would take to win the argument: what would it take for your opponent to convince you that their view is correct?
- Think about what you and your opponent agree upon: are there any policy recommendations that you can both endorse?

We hope that this advice helps to bring clarity to the debate as it is had in classrooms, pubs, between activists, and politicians, and in policy forums.

Further Reading

Holly Lawford Smith's Suggested Readings

The sources that I drew on in detail in my opening statement are those that I think are the most important for what we might call the radical feminist perspective on buying sex. These include Andrea Dworkin's *Intercourse* (1987), Kathleen Barry's *Female Sexual Slavery* (1979), Kate Millett's *Sexual Politics* (1970), and Catharine MacKinnon's *Toward a Feminist Theory of the State* (1989). As I mentioned earlier in this book, I think the second-wave feminists did a better job at taking sex seriously as a feminist issue, whether that was sex considered as the 'personal' (what I have been calling 'altruistic/hierarchical sex') or the 'political' (what I have been calling 'commercial sex' or 'the sex industry')—although of course they worked to challenge that very distinction between the personal and the political too. I am passionate about returning to second-wave texts as a way of course-correcting the inadequacies of today's mainstream feminism. There is an overview and many more references in my book *Gender-Critical Feminism* (2022) (gender-critical feminism, in my view, is a revival of radical feminism).

For those who enjoyed the debate format of this book, I can also recommend *Debating Sex Work* (2020), in which Lori Watson argues the radical feminist perspective on sex work against Jessica Flanigan, who takes the liberal feminist position.

There are serious epistemic obstacles to coming to have a well-informed view on prostitution, and the related issues (in my view) of pornography and 'ordinary' sex. Just think about it from the man's point of view: he doesn't know anything about the background of the woman he is buying for sexual use; he doesn't know her views about her work; he doesn't know what's going through her head as he fucks her. He watches porn, and she seems to like everything that is being done to her. He has casual sex, or even non-casual sex, and she lets him do what he wants to, and she seems to like it, or at least, she shows no signs of *not* liking it. Transparency is hard to achieve. There's no way to overcome it in all of these cases, especially not in pornography, but we can all work harder to try to understand *what it is like* for the women used in prostitution, pornography, and unequal, instrumentalizing, and/or dominating sex. To this end, film and literature are helpful. By far the best book I have ever read is Andrea Dworkin's *Mercy* (1990). It is an absolutely devastating portrayal of sexual use and abuse, from the woman's point of view. I'd also strongly recommend Phyllis Chesler's book *Requiem for a Female Serial Killer* (2020), which tells the story of the life of highway prostitute Aileen Wuornos, and the movie of Wuornos's life, *Monster* (2003). Kerryn Higgs's novel *All That False Instruction* (1975) also has some excellent observations of bad sex, as told from the perspective of a lesbian who has experienced good sex, but who is trying out life as a 'good heterosexual'.

Less obviously connected, but important for coming to have a view on a topic as politicized as sex buying, is work on propaganda. Kasja Ekis Ekman's book *Being and Being Bought* (2013) does a great job of explaining the way that the realities of sex work are obscured by the language we use to talk about it. There is a bigger question here, too, about why mainstream feminism is so committed to the dogma that 'sex work is work!'. One interesting perspective on this can be found in Jessica Joy Cameron's *Reconsidering Radical Feminism* (2018)—she talks about how different types of feminism make us feel about ourselves as subscribers to them.

One angle on sex-buying that I didn't take up in my contributions to this book is the hate speech (or vilification) angle. There has been plenty of discussion of pornography as hate speech, indeed it's one of most vibrant applications of the hate speech debate. There's also been some discussion of sexual objectification more generally, for example on billboards. But there's been less discussion of prostitution, probably because prostitution is much less obviously *speech*, and much more obviously *action*. But Jeremy Waldron, for example, in his book *The Harm in Hate Speech* (2012), talks about political aesthetics, specifically the politics of the appearance of a society or its visual landscape. His discussion is about hateful posters or billboards, but what about a visual landscape that includes massage parlours and brothels? Or to take an example from my own neighbourhood, what about the posters with tear-off tabs taped to lampposts, declaring 'Adventurous Women Wanted'? What does the visual reminder *that* women are wanted for sex work, and *that* women are being offered up as commodities behind closed doors, *express* about women in general, and might that count as a form of hate speech against women, or 'group defamation' of women in Waldron's terms?

Finally, Gail Dines's book *Pornland* (2010), and Gary Wilson's book *Your Brain on Porn* (2014), are important sociological contributions to this debate. Dines talks to young people on college campuses and reveals the negative impacts that porn is having on their sexualities and their relationships. Wilson reveals the impacts that men on internet forums are saying porn consumption is having on their lives, including their sexual lives. Causal questions remain about the links between pornography and sex-buying, and either/both and bad sex more generally.

Angie Pepper's Suggested Readings

In defence of the claim that it can be morally permissible for men (or anyone else) to buy sex from women (or anyone else), I have referenced many excellent works that I encourage the reader to look up. Here I highlight some books and papers that may be especially useful for someone new to the debate. I also take the opportunity to list a few other readings that are useful introductions to topics that I did not have the space to explore in full.

Reading on consent and sexual consent. Philosophers have puzzled over the nature and value of consent, as well as the question of what gives consent its normative power, and they have explored the idea of consent in many practical contexts such as in medicine, sport, and politics. For more detailed explorations of both conceptual and normative issues pertaining to consent, see Franklin Miller and Alan Wertheimer's edited volume *The Ethics of Consent: Theory and Practice* (2010) and Andreas Müller and Peter Schaber's edited volume *The Routledge Handbook of the Ethics of Consent* (2018).

Though the idea of sexual consent has been central to my argument, my treatment of the topic has been brief. If you want a more in-depth look at sexual consent, read David Archard's *Sexual Consent* (1998) and Alan Wertheimer's *Consent to Sexual Relations* (2003). Comparing these two works may be particularly insightful for the reader who is interested in questions of coercion and sexual consent.

Reading on exploitation. I regret not having had the space to attend more thoroughly to the question of whether buying sex constitutes an impermissible form of exploitation. If you're interested in an introduction to what counts as exploitation and when exploitation is morally wrong, I recommend Matt Zwolinski, Benjamin Ferguson, and Alan Wertheimer's excellent introduction to 'Exploitation' in *The Stanford Encyclopedia of Philosophy* (https://plato. stanford.edu/archives/win2022/entries/exploitation/). The bibliography is extensive and is a good starting point for someone looking to learn more about the nature of exploitation and the ethics of exploitative markets.

Reading on the decriminalization and legalization of sex work. If you are interested in defences of decriminalization and legalization, and arguments about which is to be preferred, then I recommend the following three readings. Jessica Flanigan offers a compelling defence of decriminalization in her and Lori Watson's *Debating Sex Work* (2020). Laurie Shrage has a helpful discussion of the difference between decriminalization and legalization in 'Contract Sex: Decriminalization Versus Legalization' published in the journal *Sexuality, Gender and Policy* (2022). Writing from a sociological perspective, Ronald Weitzer shows how regulation represents a practicable and desirable alternative to criminalization in *Legalizing Prostitution: From Illicit Vice to Lawful Business* (2012).

Reading on the philosophy of sex. Our debate over the ethics of buying sex raises general questions in the philosophy of sex. For example, what is sex? What is the value of sex? What is good sex? Does having sex with someone always mean that we treat them as an object? What might a feminist heterosexuality look like? And so on. For a brief yet excellent introduction to the philosophy of sex, I recommend Raja Halwani's 'Sex and Sexuality' in *The Stanford Encyclopedia of Philosophy* (https://plato.stanford.edu/archives/sum2023/entries/sex-sexuality/). See also Patricia Marino's 'Philosophy of Sex' published in the journal *Philosophy Compass* (2014). For more detailed answers to these questions and many others, take a look at *The Routledge Handbook of Philosophy of Sex and Sexuality* edited by Brian D. Earp, Clare Chambers and Lori Watson (2022).

Glossary

A fortiori A technical term philosophers use, meaning 'from the stronger argument'. For example, 'all humans sleep, so *a fortiori*, Angie sleeps'.

All things considered judgement When someone makes an all things considered judgement that A is better than B, they have considered all the relevant factors in the determination of that judgement.

Altruistic sex Holly's term for the sex women have with men under current conditions (see also the corresponding hierarchical sex).

Androcentrism Society being centred on men. First used by Charlotte Perkins Gilman in the title of her 1911 book *Our Androcentric Culture, or The Man Made World*. She wrote 'To the man, the whole world was his world; his because he was male; and the whole world of woman was the home; because she was female. She had her prescribed sphere, strictly limited to her feminine occupations and interests; he had all the rest of life; and not only so, but, having it, insisted on calling it male.' Then a few sentences later: 'That one sex should have monopolized all human activities, called them "man's work," and managed them as such, is what is meant by the phrase "Androcentric Culture."'

Aristotelians Those who are committed to the ideas of the Ancient Greek philosopher Aristotle. (Sometimes 'neo-Aristotelians', if they have substantially revised or updated Aristotle's own views).

Asymmetric criminalization A specific version of the criminalization approach to the sex industry which involves criminalizing only the johns, pimps, and third parties directly involved in the selling of sex, and *not* the sex worker herself. This approach generally seeks support for sex workers to exit the sex industry.

Camming Camming involves cam performers engaging in interactive online sex shows with paying clients. Performers typically set tipping goals and the more clients tip by pledging tokens, the more happens on screen. Clients can also request the performance of certain sexual acts and chat more generally with the performers.

Conception of the good A person's conception of the good life is comprised of a coherent ordering of values, rooted in a view of what gives life and its pursuits their meaning.

Conception of the sexual good A person's conception of the sexual good life.

Consequentialism A moral theory that identifies the right action as whichever would have the best consequences, as measured by our preferred metric (e.g. happiness, well-being, preference-satisfaction). In its narrower form, utilitarianism (associated with the philosopher Jeremy Bentham), the metric is happiness.

Criminalization The enactment of legislation and criminal penalties that make sex work illegal.

Decriminalization The removal of legislation and criminal penalties that make sex work illegal.

Deontology A moral theory that identifies right action with that conforming to a set of categorical rules or imperatives. Most closely associated with the philosopher Immanuel Kant.

Directed duties Duties that an agent owes *to* some party. If Angie has a directed duty *to* Holly, then Holly would be wronged if Angie failed to fulfil that duty.

Egalitarian pornography Egalitarian pornography depicts all sexual partners as equal and eschews the eroticization of violence, humiliation, and gender stereotypes.

Existentialists A school of French philosophy concerned with questions about existence and meaning. Famous proponents include Jean-Paul Sartre, Maurice Mearleau-Ponty, and Simone de Beauvoir. On one recent definition, existentialism is 'a categorical moral imperative of authenticity' (Webber 2018, p. 19).

Experiments in living This phrase comes from the pragmatist tradition. In application to large-scale moral experiments, see discussion in (Anderson 2014).

Freedom of occupation The freedom to choose and take up one's career.

Gynocide Female (gyn-) + genocide. This term appears to have been first used by Andrea Dworkin in *Our Blood* (1976), then included in Mary Daly's feminist dictionary, defined as 'planned, institutionalized spiritual and bodily destruction of women; the use of deliberate systematic measures (such as killing, bodily or mental injury, unliveable conditions, prevention of births), which are calculated to bring about the destruction of women as a political and cultural force, the eradication of Female/Bio-logical religion and language' (Daly 1987, p. 77).

Hegemonic masculinity The culturally dominant ideal of masculinity that forms the basis of patriarchal social orders.

Hierarchical sex Holly's term for the sex men have with women under current conditions (see also the corresponding **altruistic sex**).

Inegalitarian pornography Inegalitarian pornography eroticizes women's subordination and men's dominance.

Interest theory of rights According to the interest theory of rights the function of rights is to protect fundamental interests—interests sufficiently weighty to ground duties on the part of others (Raz 1986).

Intimate image abuse The non-consensual taking and sharing of intimate images.

Legalization The removal of legislation and criminal penalties that criminalize sex work and the implementation of regulation that determines the conditions under which sex is lawful.

Lexical priority This is the idea of putting principles in a priority ordering so that if they clash, we know which one to give priority to. It was introduced as 'lexical order' in John Rawls's 1971 book *A Theory of Justice*. He wrote 'This is an order which requires us to satisfy the first principle in the ordering before we can move on to the second, the second before we consider the third, and so on. A principle does not come into play until those previous to it are either fully met or do not apply' (p. 38).

Liberal feminism Central to the liberal feminist agenda is the goal of securing women's equality with men and promoting women's autonomy. Furthermore, the liberal feminist project is concerned with the formal and informal barriers to women's equality and the direct and indirect pressures that diminish women's autonomy. However, in cases where liberal values conflict, liberal feminists typically prioritize the rights and liberties of individual women which means that, for example, they generally reject legal restrictions on pornography and the criminalization of prostitution.

Maid A receptionist in a brothel or massage parlour who is charged with vetting clients, ensuring that clients abide by the house rules, and monitoring clients during their visits.

Male gaze Sexual or beauty objectification of women, conducted through the gaze (staring/leering) of men. Originally a concept in feminist film theory (see e.g. Loreck 2016).

Moral agents Moral agents are those agents with the ability to reflect on their reasons for action, apprehend moral principles, determine what morality requires in any given situation, and choose to act (or not) in accordance with the demands of morality. Cognitively unimpaired adult humans are the paradigm example of a moral agent. By contrast, human babies and nonhuman animals are typically regarded as lacking the capacities required for moral agency.

Moral duty When we have a moral duty to do (or not do) something, then we are morally required to do (or not do) that thing. For example, if you were under a duty to give money to charity, that would mean that you are morally required to give money to charity. That is, giving money to charity is not optional.

Moral right If you have a moral right to something, you are morally entitled to act in a certain way and/or have others act in a certain way. For example, if you have a moral right to follow your religion, then you are morally entitled to do so and others are under a duty not to interfere with your religious practice.

Moral wrong When something is morally wrong, we are morally required not to do it and/or to prevent it from happening.

Morally impermissible When something is morally impermissible it is morally wrong, and we are morally required not to do it and/or to prevent it from happening. For example, it is morally impermissible to torture puppies, so we are morally required not to torture puppies and to prevent others from torturing puppies (if we are in a position to stop them, and when stopping them does not involve unreasonable costs to ourselves).

Morally permissible When something is morally permissible, we are morally permitted, but not morally required, to do that thing. For instance, I may be morally permitted to play football on Saturdays, but I am not morally required to do so.

Negative representation The absence of representations of a particular subject, usually a member of a social group of interest to contemporary identity politics (e.g. race, sex, sexual orientation). Contrasts with positive representation, which is to portray a particular subject in a flattering light.

Normative   Normative claims tell us how things *should be* (i.e. how our social world *ought* to be organised, how we *ought* to act, what we *ought* to think, and so on).

Normative ethical framework   A framework of rules or principles that determines what we ought to do and provides us with the tools to morally evaluate our actions, institutions, ways of life, and so on.

Normative individualism   Normative individualism maintains that individual human beings are equally worthy of moral concern and respect, irrespective of sex, gender, race, ethnicity, sexuality, nationality, and so on. It also requires that every human being be regarded as an end in themselves, which means that every person should be valued for their own sake and never used as a *mere* means to some other person's ends. Lastly, normative individualism requires that we *should* prioritise the interests of individuals over those of other collective entities such as families, religious groups, communities, or the state.

Normative power   A normative power is a power to alter rights and duties directly through the exercise of our will. Common examples of normative powers are promising and consenting. When we make a promise, we create a duty to do the thing we've promised, and when we consent, we give someone permission to do something that they typically are under a duty not to do.

Paternalism   A state or individual acts paternalistically when they interfere with a person's liberty and are motivated by the claim that the person interfered with will be better off or protected from harm.

Pimp   An individual who manages the activities and income of one or more sex workers, for financial gain.

Presumptive reason   A presumptive reason grounds an expectation that one must either comply with whatever action the reason calls for or show why one can act contrary to what the reason demands.

Radical feminism   Radical feminists generally maintain that all sex work is violence against women, and that all women sex workers are victims. Indeed, radical feminists reject the term 'sex work' because it assumes that selling sex is a legitimate form of labour as opposed to violent exploitation, preferring instead to use the term 'prostituted women'.

Reasonable   A conception of the good/sexual good is reasonable when it is compatible with the demands of justice. Reasonable persons accept that there is a plurality of reasonable yet conflicting conceptions of the good/sexual good, which given rise to reasonable disagreement about what the good (sexual) life looks like.

Republican freedom   Secure protection from arbitrary interference by another person or persons. Originally theorised in the context of protection of the individual against arbitrary interference by the state. Contrasted with negative freedom, which may not be secure. (The difference is whether someone *can* interfere with your liberty, as opposed to their *in fact* not doing so).

Reset   To start again. In Holly's usage, a reset for pornography means starting again with the most basic content.

Right to buy sex   A moral right to buy sexual services from those who wish to sell them. The right to buy sex is neither a right to sex nor a right to have sexual services sold.

Right to sell sex   A moral right to sell sexual services to those who wish to buy them.

Romance tourism   People who travel to exotic locations in search of sex and romance typically in exchange for meals, hotel rooms, and gifts such as clothes.

Separateness of persons   The basic fact that persons are metaphysically distinct, which means that we are discrete entities with minds and bodies that are our own and not shared with anyone else.

Sex hierarchy   A social hierarchy in which male/man is considered superior to female/woman. Evidenced by sex ratios in positions of power and authority, wage gaps, social stereotypes, and the cultural centring of men and men's needs/interests, among other things.

Sex strike   A period of time in which there is no sex, generally for moral or political reasons.

Sexual autonomy   We have sexual autonomy when we have control over with whom we have sex and under what circumstances, and when we are free to form, revise, and pursue our conception of the sexual good.

Sexual exclusion   People experience sexual exclusion when they are unable to access meaningful sexual experiences.

Street workers   Street or outdoor sex work typically involves individual workers soliciting to sell sex in outdoor locations such as streets, residential neighbourhoods, industrial areas, train stations, car parks, and recreational parks. Typically, the sex act takes place outdoors but may sometimes happen indoors in a nearby location such as a hotel.

Symmetry Argument   When a person is morally permitted to sell something, then it is morally permissible for another person to buy that thing.

Token of consent   The words or deeds that communicate consent. For example, saying 'yes', giving a thumbs-up, or nodding.

Unreasonable   A conception of the good/sexual good is unreasonable when it is incompatible with the demands of justice. For example, an unreasonable conception of the good might entail violating the basic rights of others. Unreasonable persons are those who seek—through use of coercive political power and/or social and moral pressure—to impose their conception of the good/sexual good on others and repress other reasonable conceptions of the good/sexual good.

Utility monster   Robert Nozick's famous example of an individual "who get[s] enormously greater gains in utility from any sacrifice of others than these others lose" (1974, p. 41).

Virtue theory   A moral theory that identifies the right action with whatever a virtuous agent would in fact do. The virtues are traits such as courage, benevolence, and wisdom. Historically associated with the Ancient Greek philosopher Aristotle.

Bibliography

ABS. 2021. 'Sexual Violence—Victimisation', 24 August, www.abs.gov.au/articles/sexual-violence-victimisation

AIHW. 2020. 'Sexual Assault in Australian', August, www.aihw.gov.au/getmedia/0375553f-0395-46cc-9574-d54c74fa601a/aihw-fdv-5.pdf.aspx?inline=true

Anderson, Elizabeth. 2014. 'Social Movements, Experiments in Living, and Moral Progress: Case Studies from Britain's Abolition of Slavery', The Lindley Lecture, The University of Kansas, 11 February.

Appel, Jacob M. 2010. 'Sex Rights for the Disabled?', *Journal of Medical Ethics* 36(3): 152–154.

Arbeit, Miriam R. 2014. 'What Does Healthy Sex Look like among Youth? Towards a Skills-Based Model for Promoting Adolescent Sexuality Development', *Human Development* 57(5): 259–286.

Archard, David. 1998. *Sexual Consent* (Boulder, CO: Westview Press).

Atchison, Chris, Laura Fraser, and John Lowman. 1998. 'Men Who Buy Sex: Preliminary Findings of an Exploratory Study', in James E. Elias, Vern L. Bullough, Veronica Elias and Gwen Brewer (eds), *Prostitution: On Whores, Hustlers and Johns* (Amherst, NY: Prometheus Books): pp. 172–203.

Atkinson, Ti-Grace. 1970. 'The Institution of Sexual Intercourse', in *Notes from the Second Year: Major Writings of the Radical Feminists* (New York: Radical Feminism).

Atkinson, Ti-Grace. 1974. 'Vaginal Orgasm as a Mass Hysterical Survival Response', in Ti-Grace Atkinson, *Amazon Odyssey* (New York: Links Books).

Baker, Trevor. 2015. 'Can Fois Gras Ever Be Ethical?', *The Guardian*, 14 January, www.theguardian.com/lifeandstyle/2015/jan/14/can-foie-gras-ever-be-ethical.

Baldwin, Margaret. 1992. 'Split at the Root: Prostitution and Feminist Discourses of Law Reform', *Yale Journal of Law and Feminism* 5(47): 47–120.

Bareket, Orly, Kahalon Rotem, Shnabel Nurit, and Peter Glick. 2018. 'The Madonna–Whore Dichotomy: Men Who Perceive Women's Nurturance and Sexuality as Mutually Exclusive Endorse Patriarchy and Show Lower Relationship Satisfaction', *Sex Roles: A Journal of Research* 79(9–10): 519–532.

Barry, Kathleen. 1979. *Female Sexual Slavery* (New York: New York University Press).

Barwulor, C., A. McDonald, E. Hargittai, and E. M. Redmiles. 2021. '"Disadvantaged in the American-Dominated Internet": Sex, Work, and Technology', *Proceedings of the 2021 CHI Conference on Human Factors in Computing Systems*: 1–16.

Bates, Laura. 2020. *Men Who Hate Women* (London: Simon & Schuster).

BBC. 2019. 'What Is India's Caste System?', 19 June, www.bbc.com/news/world-asia-india-35650616.

Beasley, Chris. 2008. 'The Challenge of Pleasure: Re-imagining Sexuality and Sexual Health' *Health Sociology Review* 17 (2): 151–163.

Bennett, Jessica. 2020. 'What if Instead of Calling People Out, We Called Them In?' *The New York Times*, 19 November, www.nytimes.com/2020/11/19/style/loretta-ross-smith-college-cancel-culture.html.

Benoit, Cecilia, Michaela Smith, Mikael Jansson, Priscilla Healey, and Douglas Magnuson. 2021. 'The Relative Quality of Sex Work', *Work, Employment and Society* 35 (2): 239–255.

Bernstein, Elizabeth. 2007. 'Sex Work for the Middle Classes', *Sexualities* 10 (4): 473–488.

Bilardi, Jade E., Amanda Miller, Jane S. Hocking, Louise Keogh, Rosey Cummings, Marcus Y. Chen, Catriona S. Bradshaw, and Christopher K. Fairley. 2011. 'The Job Satisfaction of Female Sex Workers Working in Licensed Brothels in Victoria, Australia', *The Journal of Sexual Medicine* 8 (1): 116–122.

Bindel, Julie. 2020. 'Liberal Feminism Has Failed Women', www.aljazeera.com/opinions/2020/11/16/feminisms-second-wave-has-failed-women (accessed 2 August 2022).

Brennan, Jason, and Peter M. Jaworski. 2015. 'Markets Without Symbolic Limits', *Ethics* 125(4): 1053–1077.

Brennan, Jason, and Peter M. Jaworski. 2016. *Markets Without Limits: Moral Virtues and Commercial Interests* (London: Routledge).

Brownmiller, Susan. 1975. *Against Our Will: Men, Women and Rape* (New York: Bantam).

Caldwell, Hilary, and John de Wit. 2019. The Characteristics and Motivations of Women Who Buy Sex in Australia', in Susan Dewey, Isabel Crowhurst, and Chimaraoke Izugbara (eds), *The Routledge International Handbook of Sex Industry Research* (London: Routledge).

Caldwell, Hilary, and John de Wit. 2021. 'Women's Experiences Buying Sex in Australia—Egalitarian Powermoves', *Sexualities* 24 (4): 549–573.

Cameron, Jessica Joy. 2018. *Reconsidering Radical Feminism* (Vancouver: UBC Press).

Carrigan, Tim, Bob Connell, and John Lee. 1985. 'Toward a New Sociology of Masculinity', *Theory and Society*, 14 (5): 551–604.

Casal, Paula. 2016. 'Mill, Rawls and Cohen on Incentives and Occupational Freedom', *Utilitas* 29(4): 375–397.

Cense, Marianne. 2019. 'Navigating a Bumpy Road: Developing Sexuality Education that Supports Young People's Sexual Agency', *Sex Education* 19(3): 263–276.

Chadwick, Sara B., Miriam Francisco, and Sari M. van Anders. 2019. 'When Orgasms Do Not Equal Pleasure: Accounts of "Bad" Orgasm Experiences During Consensual Sexual Encounters', *Archives of Sexual Behavior* 48(8): 2435–2459.

Chesler, Phyllis. 2020. *Requiem for a Female Serial Killer* (New York: New English Review Press).

Clack, Beverley (ed.). 1999. *Misogyny in the Western Philosophical Tradition* (Basingstoke: Palgrave Macmillan).

Cook, Beverley. 2018. 'Six Things You Should Know about the Suffragette Hunger Strikes', 5 October, www.museumoflondon.org.uk/discover/six-things-you-didnt-know-about-suffragette-hunger-strikes.

Coy, Maddy. 2009. 'Milkshakes, Lady Lumps and Growing up to Want Boobies: How the Sexualisation of Popular Culture Limits Girls' Horizons', *Child Abuse Review: Journal of the British Association for the Study and Prevention of Child Abuse and Neglect* 18(6): 372–383.

Cunningham, Scott, and Todd D. Kendall. 2011. 'Prostitution 2.0: The Changing Face of Sex Work', *Journal of Urban Economics* 69(3): 273–287.

Daly, Mary, and Jane Caputi. 1987. *Webster's First New Intergalactic Wickedary of the English Language* (Boston, MA: Beacon Press).

Danaher, John. 2020. 'A Defence of Sexual Inclusion', *Social Theory and Practice* 46(3): 467–496.

Danaher, John. 2022. 'Is There a Right to Sex?' in Brian D. Earp, Clare Chambers and Lori Watson (eds) *The Routledge Handbook of Philosophy of Sex and Sexuality* (London: Routledge): 50–64.

Davidson, Pete. 2020. *Alive From New York* (Netflix).

Day, Elizabeth. 2013. 'Mary Beard: I Almost Didn't Feel Such Generic, Violent Misogyny Was about Me', *The Guardian*, 26 January.

De Boer, Tracy. 2015. 'Disability and Sexual Inclusion' *Hypatia* 30(1): 66–81.

Dempsey, Michelle Madden. 2010. 'Sex Trafficking and Criminalization: In Defense of Feminist Abolitionism', *University of Pennsylvania Law Review* 158: 1729–1778.

Dempsey, Michelle Madden. 2012. 'How to Argue About Prostitution', *Criminal Law and Philosophy* 6 (1): 65–80.

Dempsey, Michelle Madden. 2019. 'Prostitution' in Alexander, Larry, and Kimberly Kessler Ferzan, eds. *The Palgrave Handbook of Applied Ethics and the Criminal Law* (Basingstoke: Palgrave Macmillan).

Dines, Gail. 2010. *Pornland: How Porn Has Hijacked Our Sexuality* (Melbourne: Spinifex Press).

Duffy, Bobby. 2018. 'Other People Are Having Way, Way Less Sex than You Think They Are', *The Conversation*, 9 August, https://theconversation.com/other-people-are-having-way-way-less-sex-than-you-think-they-are-101153.

Dunham, Jeremy, and Holly Lawford-Smith. 2017. 'Offsetting Race Privilege', *Journal of Ethics and Social Philosophy* 11(2): 1–23.

Dworkin, Andrea. 1987. *Intercourse* (New York: Basic Books).

Dworkin, Andrea. 1990. *Mercy* (New York: Four Walls Eight Windows).

Dworkin, Andrea. 1993. 'Prostitution and Male Supremacy' *Michigan Journal of Gender and Law*, 1(1): 1–12.

Dworkin, Andrea. 2000. *Scapegoat* (New York: The Free Press).

Dworkin, Andrea. [1974] 2019. 'Renouncing Sexual "Equality", 1974', in *Last Days at Hot Slit*, Johanna Fateman and Amy Scholder (eds) (Cambridge, MA: MIT Press).

Dworkin, Ronald. 1984. 'Rights as Trumps' in Jeremy Waldron (ed.) *Theories of Rights* (Oxford: Oxford University Press): 153–167.

Dworkin, Ronald. 1994. 'A New Map of Censorship', *Index on Censorship* 1(2).

Dworkin, Ronald. 1991. 'Two Concepts of Liberty', in Edna Ullmann-Margalit and Avishai Margalit (eds) *Isaiah Berlin: A Celebration* (London: Hogarth Press).

Earp, Brian D., Clare Chambers, and Lori Watson (eds). 2022. *The Routledge Handbook of Philosophy of Sex and Sexuality* (Abingdon: Routledge).

Eaton, Anne W. 2007. 'A Sensible Antiporn Feminism', *Ethics* 117 (4): 674–715.

Ekman, Kasja Ekis. 2013. *Being and Being Bought* (Melbourne: Spinifex).

Evershed, Nick. 2021. 'The "Rule of Law": How the Australian Justice System Treats Sexual Assault Survivors', *The Guardian*, 17 March.

Fabre, Cecile. 2006. *Whose Body Is it Anyway?: Justice and the Integrity of the Person* (Oxford: Oxford University Press.

Firestone, Shulamith. 1970. *The Dialectic of Sex* (New York: William Morrow).

Firestone, Shulamith. 1968. 'When Women Rap about Sex', in New York Radical Women (eds), *Notes from the First Year* (New York: Radical Feminism).

Flanigan, Jessica. 2020. 'In Defense of Decriminalization' in Lori Watson and Jessica Flanigan, *Debating Sex Work* (New York: Oxford University Press).

Ford, Jessie V., Esther Corona Vargas, Itor Finotelli Jr, J. Dennis Fortenberry, Eszter Kismödi, Anne Philpott, Eusebio Rubio-Aurioles, and Eli Coleman. 2019. 'Why Pleasure Matters: Its Global Relevance for Sexual Health, Sexual Rights and Wellbeing', *International Journal of Sexual Health* 31(3): 217–230.

Frank, Katherine. 2002. *G-Strings and Sympathy: Strip Club Regulars and Male Desire* (Durham, NC: Duke University Press).

Frye, Marilyn. 1983. *The Politics of Reality* (New York: Crossing Press).

Gilman, Charlotte Perkins. [1915] 1979. *Herland* (New York: Pantheon).

Giobbe, Evelina. 1990. 'Confronting the Liberal Lies About Prostitution', in *The Sexual Liberals and The Attack on Feminism*, Dorchen Leidholt and Janice Raymond (eds), (Oxford: Pergamon Press).

Goldman, Emma. [1910] 2002. 'The Traffic in Women', *Anarchism and Other Essays* 177. Reprinted in *Hastings Women's Law Journal* 13: 9–19.

Goldstein, Alanna. 2020. Beyond Porn Literacy: Drawing on Young People's Pornography Narratives to Expand Sex Education Pedagogies, *Sex Education* 20(1): 59–74.

Greer, Germaine. 2018. *On Rape* (Melbourne: Melbourne University Press).

Grimshaw, Damian, and Jill Rubery. 2015. 'The Motherhood Pay Gap: A Review of the Issues, Theory and International Evidence', Conditions of Work and Employment Series No. 57, www.ilo.org/global/publications/working-papers/WCMS_348041/lang--en/index.htm

Halwani, Raja. 2023. 'Sex and Sexuality', in Edward N. Zalta and Uri Nodelman (eds), *The Stanford Encyclopedia of Philosophy*, https://plato.stanford.edu/archives/sum2023/entries/sex-sexuality.

Ham, Julie, and Fairleigh Gilmour. 2017. '"We All Have One": Exit Plans as a Professional Strategy in Sex Work', *Work, employment and society* 31 (5): 748–763.

Haworth, Abigail. 2013. 'Why Have Young People in Japan Stopped Having Sex?' *The Guardian*, 20 October.

Herold, Edward, Rafael Garcia, and Tony DeMoya. 2001. 'Female Tourists and Beach Boys: Romance or Sex Tourism?', *Annals of Tourism Research* 28(4): 978–997.

Hester, M., M. Natasha, A. Matolcsi, A. Lana Sanchez, and S. J. Walker. 2019. 'The Nature and Prevalence of Prostitution and Sex Work in England and Wales Today', Home Office and the Office of the South Wales Police and Crime Commissioner.

Higgs, Kerryn. 1975. *All That False Instruction* (Sydney: Angus & Robertson).

Hoagland, Sarah Lucia. 1988. *Lesbian Ethics* (Palo Alto, CA: Institute of Lesbian Studies).

Jackson, Robert Max. Undated. 'Analyzing the Persistence of Gender Inequality: How to Think about Origins', draft manuscript, https://pages.nyu.edu/jackson/future.of.gender/Readings/DownSoLong--Persistence&Origins.pdf

Jackson, Sarah. 2015. 'The Suffragettes Weren't Just White, Middle-Class Women Throwing Stones', *The Guardian*, 12 October.

Jary, Marta. 2021. 'Married At First Sight Fans Lust Over Groom Jason Engler after His Bride Alana Lister Reveals What He ALWAYS Does for Her in Bed', 7 March, www.dailymail.co.uk/tvshowbiz/article-9335161/Married-Sight-fans-lust-groom-Jason-Engler-Alana-Listers-sex-confession.html.

Jeffreys, Sheila. 2009. *The Industrial Vagina* (Abingdon: Routledge).

Jeffreys, Sheila. 1997. *The Idea of Prostitution* (Melbourne: Spinifex Press).

Jones, Angela. 2020. *Camming: Money, Power, and Pleasure in the Sex Work Industry* (New York: New York University Press).

Jones, Kyle G., Anne M. Johnson, Kaye Wellings, Pam Sonnenberg, Nigel Field, Clare Tanton, Bob Erens et al. 2015. 'The Prevalence of, and Factors Associated With, Paying for Sex Among Men Resident in Britain: Findings from the Third National Survey of Sexual Attitudes and Lifestyles (Natsal-3)', *Sexually Transmitted Infections* 91(2): 116–123.

Kantor, Leslie M., John S. Santelli, Julien Teitler, and Randall Balmer. 2008. 'Abstinence-Only Policies and Programs: An Overview', *Sexuality Research and Social Policy* 5(3): 6–17.

Kingston, Sarah, Natalie Hammond, and Scarlett Redman. 2020. *Women Who Buy Sex: Converging Sexualities?* (Abingdon: Routledge).

Kingston, Sarah, Natalie Hammond, and Scarlett Redman. 2021. 'Transformational Sexualities: Motivations of Women Who Pay for Sexual Services', *Sexualities* 24(4): 527–548.

Kinnell, Hilary. 2006. 'Murder Made Easy: The Final Solution to Prostitution?' in Rosie Campbell and Maggie O'Neill (eds), *Sex Work Now*, pp. 141–168 (Uffculme: Willan Publishers).

Koedt, Anne. 1968. 'The Myth of the Vaginal Orgasm', in New York Radical Women (eds), *Notes from The First Year* (New York: Radical Feminism).

Langton, Rae. 1990. 'Whose Right? Ronald Dworkin, Women, and Pornographers', *Philosophy and Public Affairs* 19(4): 311–359.

Langton, Rae, and Caroline West. 1999. 'Scorekeeping in a Pornographic Language Game', https://web.mit.edu/langton/www/pubs/Scorekeeping.pdf

Lawford-Smith, Holly. 2016. 'Offsetting Class Privilege', *Journal of Practical Ethics* 4(1): 23–51.

Lawford-Smith, Holly. 2018. 'What's Wrong with Collective Punishment?', *Proceedings of the Aristotelian Society* 118(3): 327–345.

Lawford-Smith, Holly. 2022a. *Gender-Critical Feminism* (Oxford: Oxford University Press).

Lawford-Smith, Holly. 2022b. 'Was Lockdown Life Worth Living?' *Monash Bioethics Review* 40: 40–61.

Leeds Revolutionary Feminist Group. 1981. *Love Your Enemy? The Debate Between Heterosexual Feminism and Political Lesbianism* (London: Onlywomen Press).

Lerner, Gerda. 1986. *The Creation of Patriarchy* (Oxford: Oxford University Press).

List, Christian, and Laura Valentini. 2016. 'The Methodology of Political Theory', Herman Cappelen, Tamar Gendler, and John Hawthorne (eds), *The Oxford Handbook of Philosophical Methodology* (Oxford: Oxford University Press).

Loreck, Janice. 2016. 'Explainer: What Does the "Male Gaze" Mean, and What about a Female Gaze?' *The Conversation*, 6 January.

Lovelace, Linda. 1980. *Ordeal* (New York: Kensington Publishing Corporation).

Lowman, John and Chris Atchison. 2006. 'Men Who Buy Sex: A Survey in the Greater Vancouver Regional District', *Canadian Review of Sociology/Revue canadienne de sociologie*, 43: 281–296.

Mac, Juno. 2016. 'The Laws that Sex Workers Really Want', www.ted.com/talks/juno_mac_the_laws_that_sex_workers_really_want/transcript?language=en (accessed 20 August 2022).

Mac, Juno, and Molly Smith. 2018. *Revolting Prostitutes* (London: Verso).

MacKinnon, Catharine. 1985. 'Pornography, Civil Rights, and Speech', *Harvard Civil Rights-Civil Liberties Law Review* 20: 2–70.

MacKinnon, Catharine. 1989. *Toward a Feminist Theory of the State* (Cambridge, MA: Harvard University Press).

MacKinnon, Catharine. 1995. 'Pornography Left and Right', *Harvard Civil Rights-Civil Liberties Law Review* 30: 143–168.

MacKinnon, Catherine. 2011. 'Trafficking, Prostitution, and Inequality', *Harvard Civil Rights Civil Liberties Law Review* 46: 271–309.

Maes, Hans. 2017. 'Falling in Lust: Sexiness, Feminism, and Pornography', in Mari Mikkola (ed.), *Beyond Speech: Pornography and Analytic Feminist Philosophy* (New York: Oxford University Press).

Marino, Patricia. 2014. 'Philosophy of Sex', *Philosophy Compass* 9(1): 22–32.

May, Simon Căbulea. 2015. 'Directed Duties', *Philosophy Compass* 10(8): 523–532.

McGlynn, Aidan. 2016. 'Porn as Propaganda', 12 September, https://blogs.lse.ac.uk/theforum/porn-as-propaganda/

McGregor, Joan. 2013. 'Sexual Consent', in Hugh LaFollette (ed.), *International Encyclopedia of Ethics* (Malden: Blackwell).

McKeganey, N., and M. Barnard. 1996. *Sex Work on the Streets* (Buckingham: Open University Press).

Mgbako, Chi Adanna. 2020. 'The Mainstreaming of Sex Workers' Rights as Human Rights', *Harvard Journal of Law and Gender* 43(1): 91–136.

Mikkola, Mari. 2022. 'Pornography and the "Sex Wars"', in Brian D. Earp, Clare Chambers, and Lori Watson (eds) *The Routledge Handbook of Philosophy of Sex and Sexuality*, pp. 513–526 (London: Routledge).

Mikkola, Mari. 2019. *Pornography: A Philosophical Introduction* (Oxford: Oxford University Press).

Mill, John Stuart. [1859] 1978. *On Liberty*, ed. Elizabeth Rapaport (Indianapolis, IN: Hackett Publishing Company).

Millan-Alanis, Juan Manuel, et al. 2021. 'Prevalence of Suicidality, Depression, Post-traumatic Stress Disorder, and Anxiety among Female Sex-Workers: A Systematic Review and Meta-analysis', *Archives of Women's Mental Health* 24: 867–879.

Miller, Franklin, and Alan Wertheimer (eds). 2010. *The Ethics of Consent: Theory and Practice* (New York: Oxford University Press).

Miller, Shaun. 2022. 'Heterosexual Male Sexuality: A Positive Vision', in Brian D. Earp, Clare Chambers, and Lori Watson (eds), *The Routledge Handbook of Philosophy of Sex and Sexuality* (New York: Routledge).

Millett, Kate. [1970] 2000. *Sexual Politics* (Champaign, IL: University of Illinois Press).

Mukherjee, Neel. 2014. *The Lives of Others* (London: Chatto & Windus).

Murray, Pete. 2014. 'Conception of the Good' in Jon Mandle and David Reidy (eds), *The Cambridge Rawls Lexicon*, pp. 130–132 (Cambridge: Cambridge University Press).

National Archives. Undated a. 'The Suffragette Newspaper', www.nationalarchives.gov.uk/education/resources/suffragettes-on-file/the-suffragette-newspaper/

National Archives. Undated b. 'The Suffragettes: Deeds Not Words', https://cdn.nationalarchives.gov.uk/documents/education/suffragettes.pdf

Nolsoe, Eir, and Matthew Smith. 2022. 'The Orgasm Gap: 61% of Men, but Only 30% of Women, Say They Orgasm Every Time They Have Sex', 10 February, https://yougov.co.uk/topics/lifestyle/articles-reports/2022/02/10/orgasm-gap-61-men-only-30-women-say-they-orgasm-ev

Nozick, Robert. 1974. *Anarchy, State and Utopia* (New York: Basic Books).

NSWP. 2013. 'Consensus Statement on Sex Work, Human Rights, and the Law', https://nswp.org/sites/default/files/ConStat%20PDF%20EngFull.pdf (accessed 6 June 2022).

NSWP. 2019. 'Policy Brief: Sex Workers and Travel Restrictions', www.nswp.org/sites/default/files/sex_workers_and_travel_restrictions_-_nswp_2019_0.pdf (accessed 31 August 2022).

Nussbaum, Martha C. 1998. '"Whether from Reason or Prejudice": Taking Money for Bodily Services', *The Journal of Legal Studies* 27 (S2): 693–723.

Onlywomen Press. 1981. *Love Your Enemy? The Debate between Heterosexual Feminism and Political Lesbianism* (London: Onlywomen Press).

ONS. 2016. 'Women Shoulder the Responsibility of "Unpaid Work"', 10 November, www.ons.gov.uk/employmentandlabourmarket/peopleinwork/earningsandworkinghours/articles/womenshouldertheresponsibilityofunpaidwork/2016-11-10

O'Shea, Tom. 2021. 'Sexual Desire and Structural Injustice', *Journal of Social Philosophy* 52: 587–600.

Overall, Christine. 1992. 'What's Wrong with Prostitution? Evaluating Sex Work', *Signs: Journal of Women in Culture and Society* 17(4): 705–724.

Park, Ju Nyeong, Michele Decker, Judith Bass, Noya Galai, Kriti Jain, Katherine Footer, and Susan Sherman. 2021. 'Cumulative Violence and PTSD Symptom Severity Among Urban Street-Based Female Sex Workers', *Journal of Interpersonal Violence* 36(21–22): 10,383–10,404.

Pateman, Carole. 1988. *The Sexual Contract* (Cambridge: Polity Press).

Perkins Gilman, Charlotte. [1911] 2009. *Our Androcentric Culture, or The Man Made World*, archived at Project Gutenberg, www.gutenberg.org/files/3015/3015-h/3015-h.htm

Pew Research Center. 2019. 'About Nine-in-Ten Partnered Bisexuals Are in Opposite-Sex Relationships', 18 June, www.pewresearch.org/fact-tank/2019/06/18/bisexual-adults-are-far-less-likely-than-gay-men-and-lesbians-to-be-out-to-the-people-in-their-lives/ft_19-06-18_bisexuals_about-nine-in-ten-partnered-bisexuals-in-opposite-sex-relationships/

Pinkham, Sophie. 2014. 'Sofiya Tolstoy's Defense', *The New Yorker*, 21 October, www.newyorker.com/books/page-turner/sofiya-tolstoys-defense.

Pitcher, Jane. 2019. 'Intimate Labour and the State: Contrasting Policy Discourses with the Working Experiences of Indoor Sex Workers' *Sexuality Research and Social Policy* 16(2) 138–150.

Platt, Lucy, and Teela Sanders. 2017. 'Is Sex Work Still the Most Dangerous Profession? The Data Suggests So', *London School of Hygiene and Tropical Medicine*, 16 August, www.lshtm.ac.uk/newsevents/expert-opinion/sex-work-still-most-dangerous-profession-data-suggests-so.

Platt, Lucy, Pippa Grenfell, Rebecca Meiksin, Jocelyn Elmes, Susan G. Sherman, Teela Sanders, Peninah Mwangi, and Anna-Louise Crago. 2018. 'Associations Between Sex Work Laws and Sex Workers' Health: A Systematic Review and Meta-Analysis of Quantitative and Qualitative Studies', *PLoS Medicine* 15(12): e1002680.

Potterat, John, Devon Brewer, Stephen Muth, Richard Rothenberg, Donald Woodhouse, John Muth, Heather Stites, and Stuart Brody. 2004. 'Mortality in a Long-Term Open Cohort of Prostitute Women', *American Journal of Epidemiology* 159(8): 778–785.

Precel, Nicole, Rachael Dexter, and Eleanor Marsh. 2019. 'Are We Failing Victims of Sexual Violence?', *The Age* and *The Sydney Morning Herald*, 13 September.

Primoratz, Igor. 2001. 'Sexual Morality: Is Consent Enough?' *Ethical Theory and Moral Practice* 4(3): 201–218.

Pruitt, Deborah, and Suzanne LaFont. 1995. 'For Love and Money: Romance Tourism in Jamaica', *Annals of Tourism Research* 22(2): 422–440.

Radcliffe-Richards, Janet. [1980] 1994. *The Sceptical Feminist* (Harmondsworth: Penguin Books).

Radin, Margaret. 1987 'Market-Inalienability', *Harvard Law Review* 100(8): 1849–1973.

Rawls, John. [1971] 1999. *A Theory of Justice* (Oxford: Oxford University Press).

Rawls, John. 2001. *Justice as Fairness: A Restatement* (Cambridge, MA: Harvard University Press).

Rawls, John. 2005. *Political Liberalism*, expanded edition (New York: Columbia University Press).

Raz, Joseph. 1986. *The Morality of Freedom* (Oxford: Clarendon Press).

Reeson, Oliver. 2022. 'Notness: Review: Oliver Reeson on Yves Rees', *Sydney Review of Books*, 9 May, https://sydneyreviewofbooks.com/review/rees-all-about-yves-notes-from-transition.

Rich, Mokoto. 2019. 'Going Solo: The Japanese Women Rejecting Marriage for the Freedom of Living Single', *The Independent*, 9 August, www.independent.co.uk/life-style/love-sex/marriage/japan-women-marriage-relationship-independence-happy-life-a9042636.html.

Riddell, Fern. 2018. 'Suffragettes, Violence and Militancy', 6 February, www.bl.uk/votes-for-women/articles/suffragettes-violence-and-militancy.

Rorty, Richard. 1991. 'Feminism and Pragmatism', *Radical Philosophy* 59: 3–14.

Russ, Joanna. [1975] 2010. *The Female Man* (London: Gollancz).

Sanders, Teela. 2005a. *Sex Work—A Risky Business* (Uffculme: Willan Publishing).

Sanders, Teela. 2005b. 'Blinded by Morality? Prostitution Policy in the UK', *Capital and Class*, 29 (2): 9–15.

Sanders, Teela. 2007. 'The Politics of Sexual Citizenship: Commercial Sex and Disability', *Disability and Society* 22(5): 439–455.

Sanders, Teela. 2008. *Paying for Pleasure: Men Who Buy Sex* (Uffculme: Willan Publishing).

Sanders, Teela. 2016. 'Inevitably Violent? Dynamics of Space, Governance and Stigma in Understanding Violence Against Sex Workers', *Law, Politics and Society*, 71: 93–114.

Sanders, Teela, and Rosie Campbell. 2014. 'Criminalization, Protection and Rights: Global Tensions in the Governance of Commercial Sex', *Criminology and Criminal Justice* 14(5): 535–548.

Sanders, Teela, Maggie O'Neill, and Jane Pitcher. 2017. *Prostitution: Sex Work, Policy and Politics* (Oxford: Sage).

Sanders, Teela, Jane Scoular, Rosie Campbell, Jane Pitcher, and Stewart Cunningham. 2018. *Internet Sex Work: Beyond the Gaze* (Basingstoke: Palgrave Macmillan).

Satcher, David. 2001. 'The Surgeon General's Call to Action to Promote Sexual Health and Responsible Sexual Behavior', *American Journal of Health Education* 32(6): 356–368.

Satz, Debra. 1995. 'Markets in Women's Sexual Labor', *Ethics* 106(1): 63–85.

Satz, Debra. 2010. *Why Some Things Should Not Be for Sale: The Moral Limits of Markets* (Oxford: Oxford University Press).

Schaber, P., and A. Müller. (eds). 2018. *The Routledge Handbook of the Ethics of Consent* (Boca Raton, FL: Routledge).

Schulhofer, Stephen J. 1998. *Unwanted Sex: The Culture of Intimidation and the Failure of Law* (Cambridge, MA: Harvard University Press).

Schulze, Erika, Sandra Isabel Novo Canto, Peter Mason, and Maria Skalin. 2014. 'Sexual Exploitation and Prostitution in Its Impact on Gender Equality', European Parliament, Directorate-General for Internal Policies, Citizens' Rights and Constitutional Affairs.

Shrage, Laurie. 2022. 'Contract Sex: Decriminalization Versus Legalization', *Sexuality, Gender and Policy* 5(1): 8–25.

Soft White Underbelly. 2022. 'Ex Transgender Woman Interview—Jake', 30 April, www.youtube.com/watch?v=Vj-aGNMEiNU

Soothill, Keith. 2004. 'Parlour Games: The Value of an Internet Site Providing Punters' Views of Massage Parlours', *The Police Journal* 77(1): 43–53.

Spencer, Andrew, and Dalea Bean. 2017. 'Female Sex Tourism in Jamaica: An Assessment of Perceptions', *Journal of Destination Marketing and Management* 6(1): 13–21.

Srinivasan, Amia. 2021. *The Right to Sex* (London: Bloomsbury).

Stone, Alison. 2007. *An Introduction To Feminist Philosophy* (Cambridge: Polity).

Tadros, Victor. 2016. *Wrongs and Crimes* (Oxford: Oxford University Press).

Thompson, Dennis. 2016. 'Anatomy May Be Key to Female Orgasm', 21 April, https://medicalxpress.com/news/2016-04-anatomy-key-female-orgasm.html.

Tickell, John. 2003. *Laughter, Sex, Vegetables and Fish* (New York: Crown Content).

Ting, Inga, Nathanael Scott, and Alex Palmer. 2020. 'Rough Justice: How Police Are Failing Survivors of Sexual Assault', *ABC News*, 27 January.

Tolstoy, Sophie. 1929. *The Countess Tolstoy's Later Diary: 1891–1897*, trans. Alexander Werth (New York: Payson and Clarke).

UNODC. 2009. 'Global Report on Trafficking in Persons: Executive Summary', February.

UNODC. 2022. 'Global Report on Trafficking in Persons 2022'. United Nations publication E.23.IV.1.

Van Parijs, Philippe. 2004. 'Basic Income: A Simple and Powerful Idea for the Twenty-First Century', *Politics and Society* 32(1): 7–39.

Vanwesenbeeck, Ine. 2017. 'Sex Work Criminalization Is Barking Up the Wrong Tree', *Archive of Sex Behavior* 46: 1631–1640.

Wagoner, Bryce (dir.). 2012. *After Porn Ends* (Netflix).

Waldron, Jeremy. 2012. *The Harm in Hate Speech* (Cambridge, MA: Harvard University Press).

Ward, H., Cindy Mercer, K. Wellings, K. Fenton, B. Erens, A. Copas, and A. Johnson. 2005. 'Who Pays for Sex? An Analysis of the Increasing Prevalence of Female Commercial Sex Contracts among Men in Britain', *Journal of Sexually Transmitted Infections* 81(6): 467–471.

Watson, Lori. 2020. 'Sex Equality Approach to Prostitution', in Lori Watson and Jessica Flanigan, *Debating Sex Work* (New York: Oxford University Press).

Webb, Carolyn. 2017. '"A Ripping Yarn": New Book Tells How Famous Kiwi Shoe Polish Was Made in Oz', *The Age*, 25 May, www.theage.com.au/national/victoria/a-ripping-yarn-new-book-tells-how-famous-kiwi-shoe-polish-was-made-in-oz-20170523-gwbjoc.html.

Webb, Simon. 2011. *Dynamite, Treason and Plot: Terrorism in Victorian and Edwardian London* (History Press).

Webber, Jonathan. 2018. *Rethinking Existentialism* (Oxford: Oxford University Press).

Weitzer, Ronald. 2007. 'Prostitution: Facts and Fictions', *Contexts* 6(4) 28–33.

Weitzer, Ronald. 2012. *Legalizing Prostitution: From Illicit Vice to Lawful Business* (New York: NYU Press).

Weitzer, Ronald. 2013. 'Prostitution as a Legal Institution', www.cato-unbound.org/2013/12/04/ronald-weitzer/prostitution-legal-institution.

Wertheimer, Alan. 2003. *Consent to Sexual Relations* (Cambridge: Cambridge University Press).

Willis, Ellen. 1993. 'Feminism, Moralism, and Pornography', *New York Law School Law Review* 38(1): 351–358.

Wilson, Gary. 2014. *Your Brain on Porn* (Margate: Commonwealth Publishing).

Wingfield-Hayes, Rupert. 2013. 'Japan: The Worst Developed Country for Working Mothers?', *BBC News*, 22 March, www.bbc.com/news/magazine-21880124.

Womack, Sarah. 2007. 'The Generation of 'Damaged' Girls', *Telegraph*, February 2, www.telegraph.co.uk/news/uknews/3347564/The-generation-of-damaged-girls.html (accessed August 2002).

Young, Iris Marion. 2004. 'Responsibility and Global Labor Justice', *The Journal of Political Philosophy* 12(4): 365–388.

Zwolinski, Matt, Benjamin Ferguson, and Alan Wertheimer. 2022. 'Exploitation', in Edward N. Zalta and Uri Nodelman (eds), *The Stanford Encyclopedia of Philosophy*, https://plato.stanford.edu/archives/win2022/entries/exploitation/.

Index

all things considered judgement 142,
157, 203
altruistic sex 16–23, 27, 135,
146, 199; beliefs about 59;
commercial elements of 10; as
culture 62; definition of 9, 21,
203; elimination of 38, 40, 45,
152, 170; improvement of 31;
moral prohibition of 136, 148–50;
as oppression 23, 167; reset of
40, 44, 48, 60; social movement
against 33, 45–6, 171; tools to
intervene on 34, 44, 149; *see also*
hierarchical sex
androcentrism 122, 203
Aristotelians 133, 203
asymmetric criminalization 30,
33, 203
autonomy: of children 190; right to
165–6; individual 182; of women
119–23, 164–9, 181, 188; *see also*
sexual autonomy

buying sex: arguments against xiii,
53–62, 67, 105–11, 131, 153,
158–9; from children 64–5, 94; as
complicity in violence 54, 66–7;
criminalization of xiv, 52, 183–4,
202; ethics of 1–4, 178–9, 196–7;
impermissibility of 8, 102, 157,
202; irresponsibly 159; as moral
gamble 51, 53; moral right to 71,
84, 95–8, 98, 208; permissibility
of 64, 98, 102, 110, 125, 134, 136,

140, 197; prohibition of xiv, 64,
99, 105, 115, 180; reasons for xi,
14–15, 70, 96–8, 154; responsibly
xvii, 67, 84, 134, 98–101, 106,
109, 113, 149, 155, 159, 188; and
sexual exclusion 95–6; as unethical
consumption 49, 51–3, 136, 154

camming 68, 92–3, 121, 125, 204
celibacy 40, 73, 152
celibacy syndrome 46
child bride 29
conception of the good 42, 72–4, 137
conception of the sexual good 82, 97,
153, 208
consequentialism 2, 127, 129, 136,
139, 204
consent 24–7, 64, 75–80, 111–15,
145, 174; capacity to xvii, 99,
125; concept of 45; conditions
of 77–9; inability to 126;
invalidation of 111; obligation to
149; philosophical account of xix;
reading on 201; sex filmed without
16; and sexual autonomy 76; and
sex work 92–5, 157; valid xvi,
xviii, 65, 77, 80, 112, 143, 155,
158, 179; withdrawal of 100, 188;
see also token of consent

Dempsey, M. 52, 105–15, 196
deontology 2, 127, 130, 133, 136–7,
139, 143, 204; *see also* moral
philosophy

directed duties 136, 142–3, 204
Dworkin, A. 10, 16–18, 22–6, 28, 42, 121, 128, 199, 200
Dworkin, R. xii–xiii, 57, 175

East London Suffragettes 164
erotic dancer 68–9, 88, 121
existentialists 133, 204
experiments in living 60, 204

feminism: cause of 146; as democratic project 170; goal of 30; language of 169; liberal xii, xiv, 119, 168–9, 194–5, 199, 205; mainstream 199–200; radical xii–xiii, 22, 67, 119, 147–8, 168, 194–5, 199, 207; second-wave 171; sex positive 31, 147, 152
feminist utopia see sex equality utopia
freedom of occupation, 85–7, 89, 91, 155, 179–80; importance of 174; right to 160, 164, 197

gender inequality see sex inequality
gynocide 18, 205

hegemonic masculinity 191–2, 205
hierarchical sex: abstaining from 45; and bought sex xix, 53, 124, 139–40, 149; continuation of 172; definition of 27, 205; disvaluable elements of 135; elimination of 38–40, 48, 152, 170–1; expectations associated with 189; forces that sustain 193; immorality of 55, 61, 132; influence of 182; moral prohibition of 136, 142–4, 148–50, 179–80; norms of 152, 191; as ordinary sex xiii, 146; and pornography 31; reset of 60; social movement against 33–4, 171; societies 58, 167; tools to intervene on 34, 44; and vulnerability 51, 61; see also altruistic sex
homosexuality 139; criminalization of 74, 81; and pornography 15; representation of 46; see also lesbian

human trafficking 50, 65, 154; see also sex trafficking

interest theory of rights xiii, 74–5, 143, 205
intersectional identities xiv, 3
intimate image abuse 16, 194, 205

Leeds Revolutionary Feminist Group 23, 171
lesbian 32; feminist women 171; perspective 200; political 73, 171; as porn category 26; sex 15, 20–1, 46; see also homosexuality
liberal individualism xii, xiv–xv, 166, 169; see also normative individualism
liberalism see liberal individualism

MacKinnon, C. xiv, 20, 24–8, 30, 119, 120–3, 199
male gaze 46, 207
marriage 10, 17, 20, 62, 128; celibacy before 73; institution of 9; intimacy of 97; rape within 3, 28–9, 44, 58; traditional conception of 57
moral agent 136
moral duty 2, 75, 136, 157, 204; to refrain from buying sex 106, 156, 159
moralism 170–2
moral right 86–7, 156–7; to be punished 180; to buy sex 64, 71, 84, 96, 98, 160, 180; definition of 204; to not be tortured 75; to sell sex 64, 84, 89, 158, 180; to sexual autonomy 74; to sexual pleasure 143–4
moral philosophy 44, 72, 126–34, 136–7, 139
moral wrong 68, 107, 126–30, 146, 172–3, 204; of buying and selling sex 70, 96, 104, 113; holistic theory of 127; of non-consensual sex 114

negative freedom 28, 53, 208
negative representation 48, 206

negative right 174
normative claim 76, 128, 207
normative ethical framework 2, 136, 139, 197, 207
normative individualism 135, 137–8, 207; *see also* liberal individualism; separateness of persons
normative power 76, 111, 201, 207

ordinary sex 8–9, 15, 21, 199; as harmful 132–3; *see also* altruistic sex; hierarchical sex
orgasm 4, 20–1, 22, 41–2, 140–4; gap 16–17; and pornography 57; statistics on 141

Pankhurst C. 153–4, 166
philosophy of sex 202
political philosophy 44, 72
pornography 4, 147, 193, 200–1: abstaining from watching 150; addiction 37; amateur 11, 33–4; and capitalism 16, 44; demand for novelty in 36–7; depiction of pleasure 21; disapproval of 15; egalitarian 103, 204; industry 184; inegalitarian 145, 192–3; issues of 199; as propaganda for sexual subordination 15, 30, 57; as prostitution 11, 33; regulation of 37; reset of 33–4, 37–40, 60; as sex education 41; women coerced into 121
positive rights 174
prostitutes *see* sex workers
prostitution *see* sex work

rape 94, 122, 176: all sex as 24–7; and diamond industry 49; failure to prosecute 18; legality of 3, 44; in marriage 28–30, 44, 58; risk of 121, 131; and sex industry 50, 53–4; survivors of 55; as tool of war 60; without prostitution 60; as wrong 174; *see also* sexual assault
Raz, J. xiii, 74
reflective equilibrium 173

representations of sex 46–8; *see also* pornography
revenge pornography *see* intimate image abuse
rights as trumps xiii, 135, 138–9, 159, 175, 180
romance tourism 67, 208

same-sex sexual relations *see* homosexuality
Satz, D. 30–1, 45, 57–8
separateness of persons 135, 137–8, 208
sex equality utopia 32–3, 150–1, 169–70
sex hierarchy xiv, 29, 50, 124; background of 126, 167; definition of 208; end of 59; propaganda for 62; sex-hierarchical societies 58; world without 8, 27, 31–3; *see also* hierarchical sex; sex inequality
sex inequality 8, 27, 32, 115, 130, 179; and altruistic sex 21–2; bad sex as symptom of 152, 175; conditions of 67, 78, 139; facts about 30; and gender stereotypes 193; inequality of pleasure 21, 28, 144; role of sexuality in 168, 175–7; social structures that perpetuate 166–7; *see also* sex hierarchy
sex industry 8, 29, 44, 66, 112, 134, 184, 199: abolition of xix, 60; appeal of 96; aspects of 14; cultural meaning of 10; entering 94; leaving 121; nature of 97; and pornography 33–4; products associated with 49, 190; pull of 97; safety of 108; and sexual health 151–2; working in 37; *see also* sex work
sex reset 38–9, 42–5, 60, 135–6, 150–3, 169–71, 189; *see also* sex strike; altruistic sex
sex strike 40–1, 152, 208
sex trafficking 11–13, 50, 65, 94, 125; across boarders 29; demand for 62; and international law 44; preventing 115; and prostitution 13; reporting of xviii, 188; reports

on 12; victims of 100, 105–6, 109, 112; *see also* human trafficking
sexual assault 36, 122, 174, 185; childhood sexual abuse 19, 22, 44, 54–5, 122, 191; laws prohibiting 44, 185; and negative rights 174; prevalence of 19, 146; prosecution of 19; statistics on 19; survivors of 130; *see also* rape
sexual autonomy: and consent 75–6; definition of 71–2; diminishing of 113, 189; and freedom of occupation 86; as fundamental human good 84, 153; importance of 82; interest in 74–5, 81, 115, 155; practices limiting 72; right to 74–5, 80–6, 95–6, 98, 104, 116, 136, 138–9, 144–5, 172–4, 180; and sexual experimentation 79; of sex workers 113–14, 168; threats to 151; undermining of 92; value of 157, 179; and women's rights 86
sexual exclusion 81–2, 95–6, 153, 208
sexual health 141, 151; clinic 66, 82; screening xvii–xviii, 100–1, 183, 188–9; and sexual education 72; and wellbeing 100
sexual inclusion 80–2
sexual instrumentalization 18, 28–9
sexual pleasure 20, 38, 41–2, 85, 140–4, 192; depiction of 21; experience of 22; and human wellbeing 154; inequality of 21–2, 28, 144; moral right to 143–4; and mutual pleasure-giving 26; and orgasm 141; self-administered 40; and sexual autonomy 72; women as instruments for 123, 134, 140
sexual slavery *see* sex trafficking
sex work: abolition of 33, 38, 48, 67, 87, 164, 171, 175, 182; as choice 121, 124, 160, 179, 183; and coercion 111, 121; conditions of 103; criminalization of 33, 99, 184–5, 187, 205; decriminalization of 171, 183–5, 204; ethics of 3; harm of 30–1; and hierarchical sex 53, 61; inseparability of sex

worker from 38–9; language of 89; legalization of 183–4, 205; legal regulation of 36, 44–5, 179–80, 184–5; and male dominance 102–3, 167; as occupation 89, 91–2, 174; perspective on 199; and pornography 9, 11, 16, 33–4; realities of 200; representations of 11; reset of 40; right to undertake 155, 173; risks associated with 86; and sex trafficking 13, 50, 54, 154; violence in 125; as work 196; *see also* sex industry; sex workers
sex workers 13, 70, 99, 106, 121, 149, 154–5; autonomy of 168, 181; buyers responsibility to 100–1; cheating with 60; coercion of 66; depression among 13; employment options of 160; Global Network of Sex Worker Projects 90; harm to 110; high-end 11; indoor 94; job satisfaction of 88; legal rights of 183; male 15; as means 134; minimising risk of 115; mistreatment of 50–1; murder of 18–19; not using 150; PTSD among 13; rights of 183, 185–8; rights movement 89–90; sexual autonomy of 113–14; and suicide ideation 13; unknown background of 56; violence against 66, 99, 196; vulnerability of 55; *see also* sex industry; sex work; street workers
slavery 3, 39, 122–3, 132
slut-shaming 151
social hierarchy: of biological sexes 124; and buying sex 57–8; how to change 167; injustice of 123; privileges of 62, 127, 132; world without 8, 27; *see also* sex hierarchy
social movement for women's equality *see* women's rights movement
street workers 11, 13, 19, 61, 65, 125, 208; consent of 94; and destitution 55–6, 61
stripper *see* erotic dancer
suffragettes 163–5, 167–8
symmetry argument 156, 209

theory of rights xii–xiii, 74–5, 143
token of consent 78, 80, 113, 209;
    see also consent

utility monster 138–9, 173–4, 209

virtue theory 2, 127, 130, 136,
    139, 209

women's agency *see* autonomy of
    women
Women's Freedom League 164
women's liberation xv, 8, 23, 39, 164,
    181; ends of 86; project of 169
women's rights movement 132, 139,
    173, 181
Women's Social and Political Union
    163–4

Taylor & Francis Group
an **informa** business

Taylor & Francis eBooks

www.taylorfrancis.com

A single destination for eBooks from Taylor & Francis
with increased functionality and an improved user
experience to meet the needs of our customers.

90,000+ eBooks of award-winning academic content in
Humanities, Social Science, Science, Technology, Engineering,
and Medical written by a global network of editors and authors.

TAYLOR & FRANCIS EBOOKS OFFERS:

A streamlined
experience for
our library
customers

A single point
of discovery
for all of our
eBook content

Improved
search and
discovery of
content at both
book and
chapter level

REQUEST A FREE TRIAL
support@taylorfrancis.com

Routledge
Taylor & Francis Group

CRC Press
Taylor & Francis Group

Printed in the United States
by Baker & Taylor Publisher Services